ARMS & ARMOUR OF THE Samurai

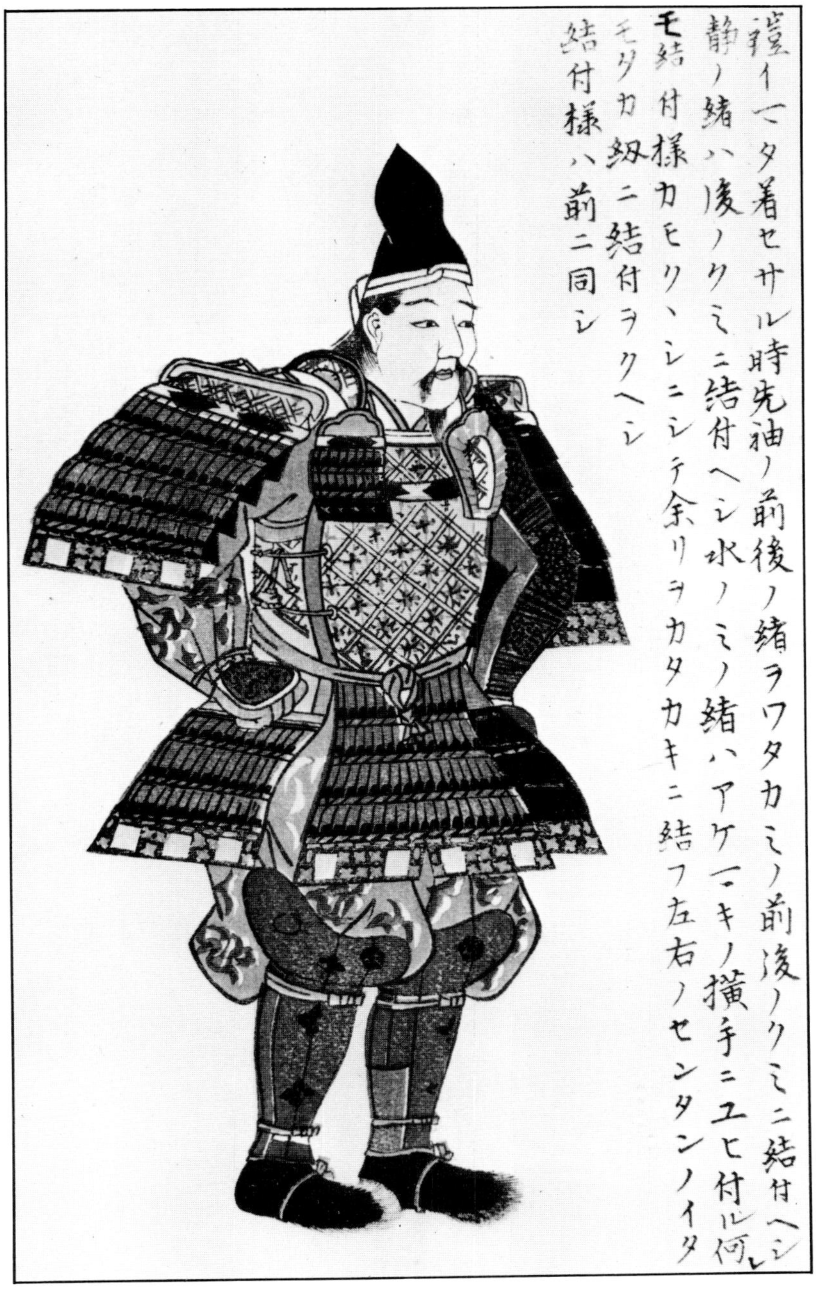

ARMS & ARMOUR OF THE Samurai

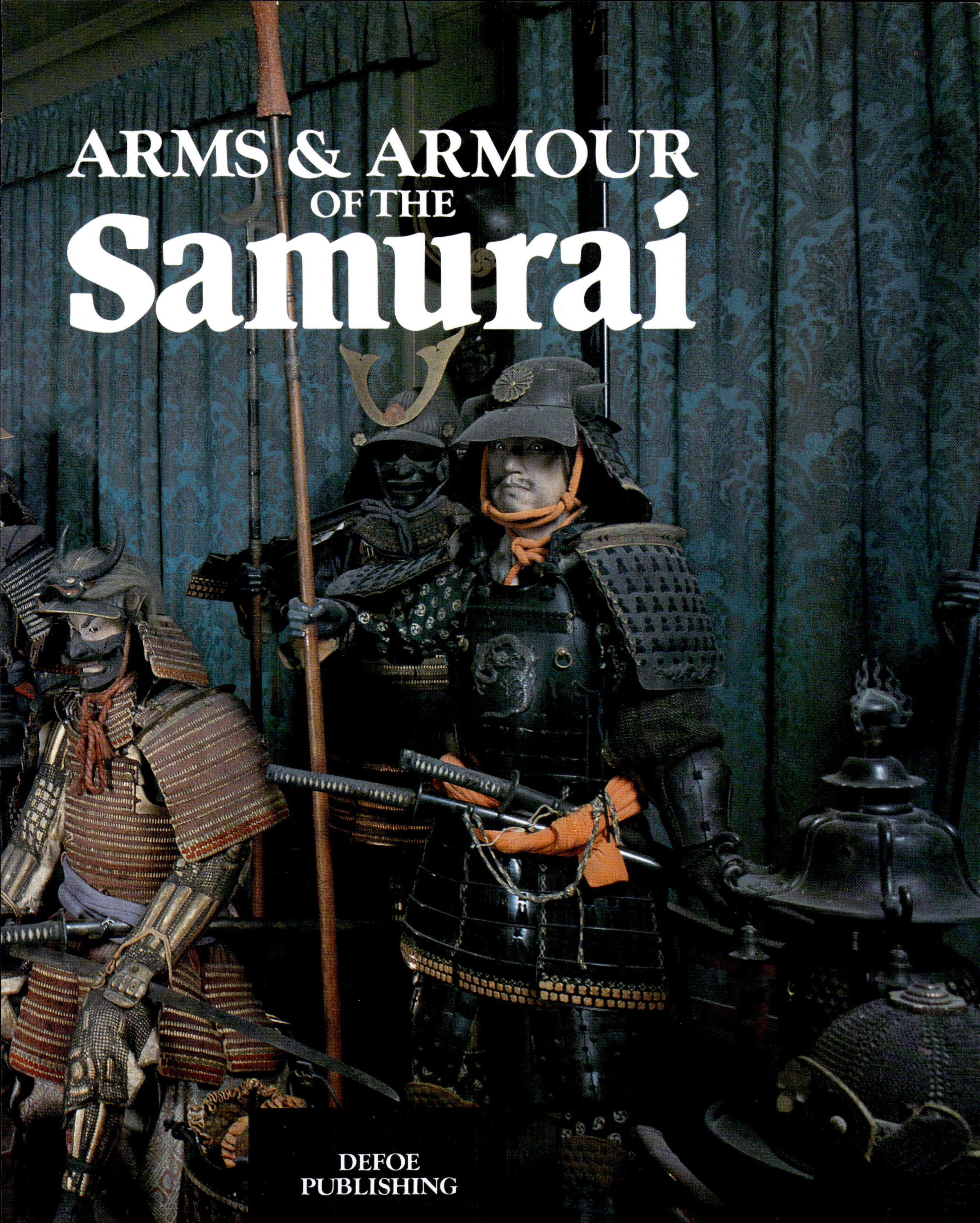

DEFOE PUBLISHING

Published by Defoe Publishing
53 Defoe House
Barbican Center
London EC2Y 8DN

Produced by Bison Books Ltd
176 Old Brompton Road
London SW5 0BA
England

ISBN 1 870 98105 7

Printed in Hong Kong

Lettor, se truovi cosa che t'offenda in questo modestissimo librino non te maravigliar. Perche DIVINO, et non humano, e quel ch'e senza Menda.

(Reader, if you find something that offends you in this modest little book, do not be surprised. For divine, not human, is that which is without fault.)

From an Italian book of the 17th C.

Page 1: Samurai of the Nambokucho period wearing an o yoroi.

Pages 2-3: Two hundred years and half a world away: a collection of Japanese armour assembled in the 1930s and 1940s displayed in an English country house.

Pages 4-5: Samurai in action as depicted in the thirteenth century scroll, the Heiji Monogatari Emaki.

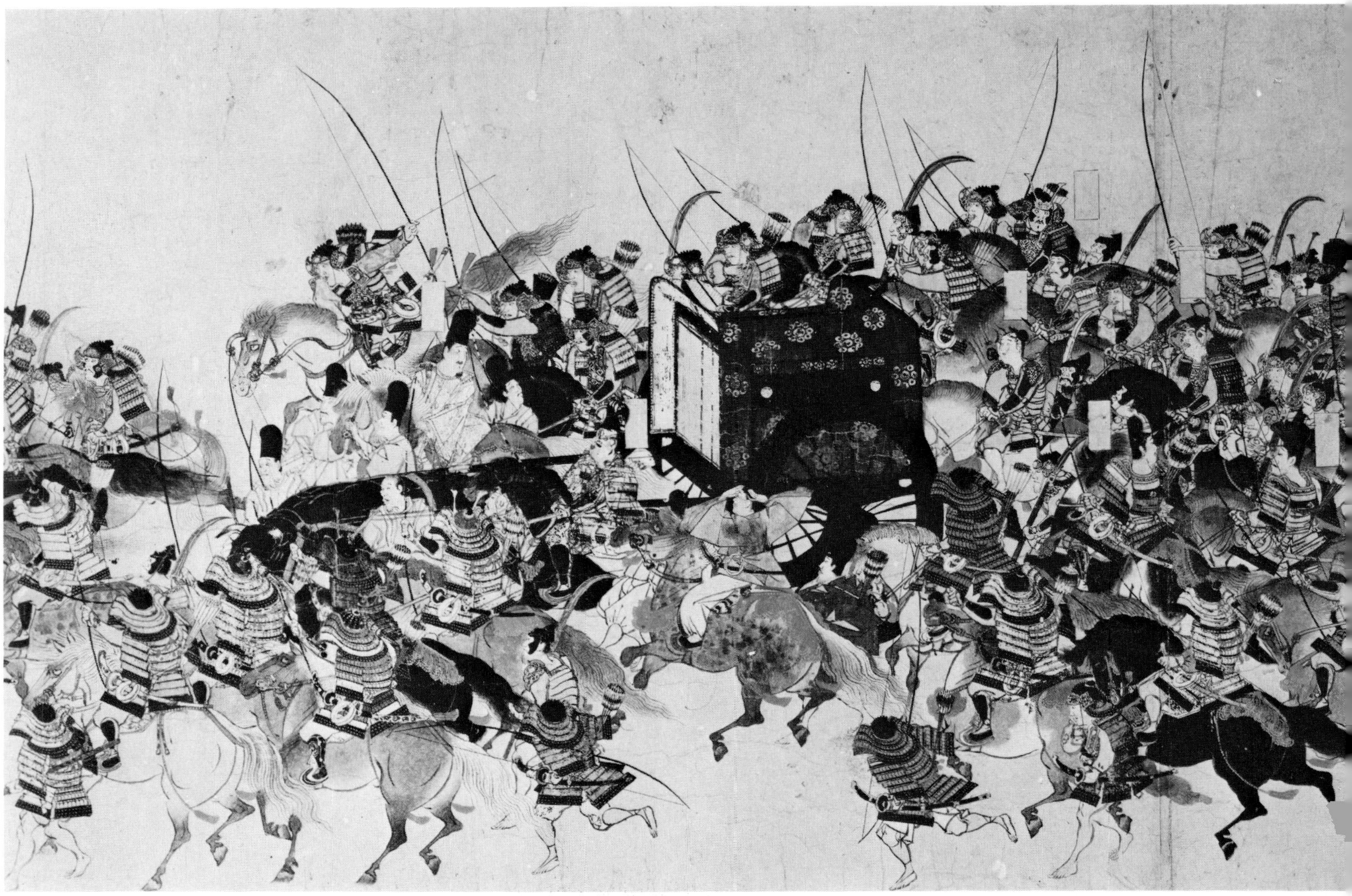

Contents

Foreword

by Dr Y Sasama President of the Japan Armour and Militaria Research Association

Although not formulated until some time during the seventeenth century, the code of Bushido is as old as the samurai class itself. The philosophies of Buddha, Chu-Tsu, Confucius and the ancient Gods of the Shinto faith were tempered by the spirit and thought of the Japanese people to produce an ethical system which the samurai strove to follow. The true spirit of Bushido requires a sincere observance of the following eight points:

Jin – to develop a sympathetic understanding of people
Gi – to preserve the correct ethics
Chu – to show loyalty to one's master
Ko – to respect and to care for one's parents
Rei – to show respect for others
Chi – to enhance wisdom by broadening one's knowledge
Shin – to be truthful at all times
Tei – to care for the aged and those of a humble station.

At the very heart of this discipline, formed by generations of samurai, was the realization that there was a need for such an ethical base as well as the need to learn the techniques of survival on the battlefield.

The study of Bushido is a difficult path, and one which the authors have striven to follow. Indeed, through long years of studying Kendo and Iai do, they have come to understand the fundamentals of Bushido. In the true spirit of the sixth tenet, they have broadened their knowledge by making an extensive study of the weapons, equipment, armour and defences of the samurai.

The current upsurge of interest in the West has led to the authors, regarded as experts in the field, being asked to fill the need for an introductory volume on the subject. As a Japanese, I am extremely happy if the results of their lengthy studies lead to a better understanding of Japan, its history and its people. For this reason I can recommend this work.

Periods of Japanese History and Art

The dates used in this book are those published by Suwa Tokutaro in his *Nihonshi no Yoryo*, Obunsha, Tokyo, 1957.

Jomon	– 8
Yayoi	8 – 300
Yamato	300 – 710
Nara	710 – 794
Early Heian	794 – 898
Late Heian	898 – 1185
Kamakura	1185 – 1333
Nambokucho	1336 – 1392
Muromachi	1333 – 1573
Sengoku	1482 – 1558
Momoyama	1573 – 1603
Edo	1603 – 1868

Notes on the Japanese used in the text

Many of the characters used in the study of arms and armour are of some antiquity they will not be found in a modern character dictionary and substitutes are used for others. Furthermore, even characters that are in general use are on occasions read in a way that is peculiar to the subject. To avoid errors, the authors have made every effort to check all of the terms used in this book against readings, often written phonetically, by modern Japanese authorities. The Hepburn system of Romanization has been used throughout with the exception of the indication of long vowel sounds. In many cases, compound terms have been split, without hyphenation, to ease pronounciation.

The reader should be aware of the frequent modification that is made to the initial sound of the second component in compound words. Typical changes are:

hoshi + hachi = hoshi bachi
uchi + katana = uchi gatana
hineno + shikoro = hineno jikoro

Names used in the text are those by which the person is most widely known and are written in the traditional way with the family name first. Equally, the traditional names of provinces have been used.

Left: A superb ni mai do gusoku of the Edo period complete with all its accessories.

CHAPTER ONE
The Origins of the Warrior Class

Right: Haniwa of fired clay from a tomb of the Yamato period representing the style of armour now called tanko (lit short armour).

Japan is unique among the world's major powers in being a country which, until recent times and with but two minor exceptions, fought all its battles on its own soil. No other nation has seen such long civil strife in which group after group struggled to gain power, only to be toppled in turn. These groups sought not the throne, which continued in an unbroken line, but the power to manipulate through it, while maintaining all the while the semblance of royal control.

In such a climate it is hardly surprising that the study of military matters was held in high esteem. This, and the fierce family pride of the Japanese, has resulted in the preservation of ancestral and votive arms and armours from the eighth century down to the middle of the last century, when they were finally laid aside in favour of the uniforms and weapons styled on those worn in the West.

Mythology has it that the sun goddess Amaterasu sent her grandson from heaven to Japan to bring the sacred symbols of power – the sword, the comma-shaped jewel and the mirror – and to bring order to the people. Archaeology suggests that the people we now know as the Japanese are the descendants of successive waves of invaders from the Chinese and Korean mainlands and from the islands of Southeast Asia. Establishing themselves at first on the southern island of Kyushu, they set about consolidating their position and driving northwards the original inhabitants of Caucasian type, who are now represented by the few Ainu who survive on Hokkaido.

The invading peoples brought with them a knowledge of working bronze, and produced spear and arrow heads that differ little from those found from the Bronze Age cultures of Europe. During the period from the

Right: Yamato period tanko having the plates laced together with leather thongs.

second century BC to the second century AD, further groups brought with them two important innovations: the working of iron and the practice of dolmen burial. It is from these sometimes enormous burial mounds that the remains of armours, swords and spear heads have been excavated which allow us to reconstruct in almost every detail the military equipment in use at the time.

Iron plates of considerable size and intricate shape demonstrate the skill with which these early armourers could handle their intractable raw material, and show that a long tradition of iron working must have existed in their homelands. There remains, however, one curious anomaly. In the earliest finds, the plates of the armours were fastened together with leather thongs, a feature which suggests that they were copies in iron of earlier versions made entirely from leather or perhaps bark. Evidence that this was probably the case is given by the use until recent times of remarkably similar hide armours in the Szechuan region of China. It was not long, however, before both rivets and rudimentary hinges were incorporated in these constructions, showing that even at this remote period the Japanese were quick to adapt new technologies to their needs. These early armours, now called *tanko*, were designed for fighting on foot with sword, spear and bow, and closely resemble the tonlet armours developed at the beginning of the sixteenth century in Europe for foot combat tournaments – a remarkable example of parallel development, albeit centuries apart.

Tanko were provided with a *kabuto* (helmet), which was characterized by a prominent beaked front which jutted out over the brow to protect the wearer's face; a feature that gives rise to their modern Japanese name of *shokaku tsuki kabuto* (battering-ram helmet). Their main constructional element was an oval plate, the *shokaku bo*, slightly domed for the head with a narrow prolongation in front that curved forwards and downwards where it developed a pronounced central fold. Two horizontal strips encircling the head were riveted to this frontal strip: the lower one, the *koshimaki* (hip wrap), formed the lower edge of the helmet bowl; the other, the *do maki* (body wrap), was set at about the level of the temples. Filling the gaps between these strips and the shokaku bo were small plates, sometimes triangular but more commonly rectangular in shape. Because the front projected so far from the head, the triangular gap beneath was filled by a small plate, the *shoshaku tei ita*, whose rear edge bent downwards into a flange that rested against the forehead.

Fastened through holes in the koshimaki at the sides and back, were a series of broad leather thongs onto which were laced about five horizontal U-shaped strips of iron forming a defence for the neck, called the *shikoro* on all later helmets. Each strip was hung in such a way that it overlapped the one above to leave no gaps, and yet allowed either side or the back to move independently upwards with the wearer's movements.

Worn with these rather curious but no doubt effective helmets was a body armour, *do*, similarly constructed from plates riveted to a framework of strips. Almost all the surviving examples fitted closely to the body, and had a pronounced waist so that they sat firmly on the hips.

The do excavated from the earliest tombs are provided with an opening down the front which was fastened by ties of cloth. This style must have involved considerable gymnastics and needed several assistants to put on the do, since the strips of iron from which it was made are continuous around the body and the whole affair had to be sprung open to admit the wearer. This defect was recognized and rectified in later models which, from the heavily corroded remains, appear to have been fitted with a hinged section on the right

Below: Shokaku tsuki bachi from the Yamato period.

Opposite page left: Saddle of lacquered wood. Momoyama period.

Opposite page right: Umabari, a type of lancet carried in a pocket in the face of a sword scabbard for bleeding horses.

Right: Yamato period tanko of riveted plates.

front or, occasionally, on both sides. The deep cut-outs for the arms left a standing extension at the front, reaching to the upper chest, and a similar, rather higher, section at the back. To these extensions were fastened a pair of cloth shoulder straps called *watagami* (over the shoulders), which transferred some of the not inconsiderable weight from the hips to the shoulders.

Protecting the lower body and tying over the flanged lower edge of the do was a flared skirt, called rather appropriately the *kusazuri* (grass rubbing), since it reached to just above the knee. Like the shikoro, it was made of 10 or more horizontal lames, laced to internal leather thongs, and split down either side to allow some movement when walking. No protection was provided for the lower legs at this date, but rock carvings show that long baggy trousers were worn, tied with a drawstring just below the knee.

The shoulders and upper arms were covered by an arrangement of curved plates, the *kata yoroi* (shoulder armour), running from front to back and extending as far as the elbow, which were permanently fastened to a plate defence for the neck and upper chest called *akabe yoroi* (neck armour); the combination is almost identical to the 'Almain collar' worn in Europe during the sixteenth century with munition armours. Unlike the European version, which was worn under the shoulder straps of the cuirass to help distribute the weight, the Japanese wore it above the watagami, overlapping the top edges of the do at the front and back. Completing the outfit were long, tubular, tapering cuffs of plate fitted with a small panel of leather-laced scales which formed a defensive cover for the back of the hand.

As was normal on all later armours, the metal surface was given a coating of natural lacquer as a protection against the humidity of the Japanese climate. Some slight decoration to what must have been very sombre-looking armours was afforded by a border of leather thonging, sewn through holes along the sharp edges of all the major elements, and by a bunch of pheasant-tail feathers tied to iron prongs provided for that purpose on top of the helmet.

Found with these armours were the remains of simple self bows (made from a single piece of wood), arrowheads, socketed spear heads and long swords with straight single-edged iron blades. The swords were carried in scabbards covered in sheet copper and decorated with punched designs. Some had a hilt ending in a bulbous, slanting pommel of copper, *kazuchi no tsurugi* (mallet-headed sword), while others, *koma no tsurugi* (Korean sword) had ring-shaped pommels, occasionally enclosing silhouettes of animalistic design. The lengths of these weapons vary between just under two feet (0.6m) to four feet (1.2m) with three feet (0.9m) being the average. Two of these swords were excavated in Higo and Musashi provinces; they

Below: Horse muzzles of russet iron.

have inlays of silver representing horses and flowers on their blades and were probably imported from China. In most cases, some form of *tsuba* (flat hand guard) was fitted and this was pierced, generally with a trapezoidal opening. However, some have been found with comma-shaped holes representing the sacred jewels, which must surely point to native manufacture.

Thus equipped, the Yamato people, as they called themselves, lived a frontier life that was already beginning to show something of the social structure of historic Japan. A contemporary Chinese document, the *We-jen Chuan* notes that the peoples of the outlying islands of Tsushima and Iki sailed to the markets of both the Northern and Southern Dynasties of China. Of the southern region of Japan it records that 'in the various kingdoms there are markets where necessary items are traded. The Yamato Court oversees them.' This is a clear indication that the colonized territory was already divided into provinces responsible to a central court.

Naturally, this young, vigorous nation was awed by the sophisticated culture of its powerful neighbour, China. Religion, technology, government and the arts of China were assiduously studied and slavishly copied whenever possible. The system of Chinese writing was adopted and adapted to the spoken language of the Japanese, to become the bane of Japanese and non-Japanese students ever since. Artists and craftsmen were persuaded to come to Japan to train Japanese pupils in their styles and methods. In short, what occurred was almost a wholesale importation of one culture and its superimposition on another. However, Buddhism, the imported religion, did not entirely supplant the indigenous Shinto religion; the two co-existed peacefully and still do today.

Among the imports were a considerable number of horses or, to be more accurate, ponies, of the type used by the Mongols on their periodic expansions from the steppes of Central Asia. They were sturdy, shaggy-

Right: Stirrups of russet iron decorated with chrysanthemums and clover in silver overlay. Edo period.

coated beasts which later commentators describe as having wild dispositions and, particularly true of stallions, a tendency to bite the knees of their riders. Uncouth animals they may have been, but they were invaluable to the Japanese because they could cover considerable distances over rough terrain. Initially the Japanese used the same harness as their Chinese counterparts, a wooden saddle reinforced and decorated with metal, and plain, open stirrups suspended by chains. By the early Heian period, the stirrup had acquired an enclosed toecap and a rearward extension of the tread; this was quickly modified, by the loss of the sides of the toecap, into the characteristic open-platform stirrup, which the Japanese continued to use until the nineteenth century. Not only horses were imported, lamellar armour was also adopted from the Asiatic mainland, and modified to suit Japanese taste.

Below: Tsuki mabisashi bachi, a type of helmet introduced from the Asiatic mainland together with armour of scale construction and horses.

Armour of lamellar construction is of great antiquity, having originated somewhere in the Middle East. It was used by the Egyptians and, later, the Romans, spreading eastwards into Central Asia and northwards into Eastern Europe, reaching as far as Scandinavia. Although differing in minor details, lamellar armour was always constructed from more-or-less rectangular, overlapping scales of metal or leather, laced together into rows which were then laced vertically, each row overlapping the one above so that the tops of the scale heads were visible. The result was a flexible defence whose efficiency lay in its ability to absorb the energy of a blow in the lacing sandwiched between the rows of scales before penetration could begin. It was in fact an early version of the laminated armour that modern military technology has only recently rediscovered.

Although the tanko continued to be made, the new style of construction was developed into a complementary armour for mounted use. Called *keiko* or *kake yoroi* (hanging armour) and made entirely from iron scales laced together with leather thongs, these armours were similar in form to the armour made and worn in Tibet as late as the nineteenth century and to the few surviving armours made by the Ainu peoples in northern Japan. The do of a keiko resembled a sleeveless coat, opening down the front and provided with a flared skirt extending to mid-thigh. At the waist was a row of elongated incurved scales, which rested on the hips, with sometimes a similar row along the lower edge of the skirt, whose purpose is obscure. Over this was worn a collar and upper-arm guards combination comparable with that worn with the tanko, but made entirely of scales. The tubular defence for the forearms was no longer of plates, but of narrow vertical splints, this time without any protection for the hand. The legs are always a vulnerable target of a horseman, so leg armour was provided in the form of sections of scales; a tapered section tied above and below the knee, another wrapped around the lower leg with ties at the back.

With the keiko came a new style of helmet, called *mabisashi tsuki kabuto* because of the prominent pierced horizontal peak riveted to the front lower edge. More or less circular in plan, and fitting close to the head, it was constructed in a similar way to the earlier helmets; the koshimaki and do maki were still used, but now took the form of complete rings held together by the infilling of rectangular plates. Closing the top was a circular iron plate, the *fuse ita*, onto which was riveted an ornamental arrangement of two iron cups connected by an iron rod through their bases. It has been suggested that the lower of these cups was to accommodate the wearer's hair, but the fuse ita was solid at this point, making it more likely that the whole arrangement was to carry a plume, which would have been tied to the holes in the rim of the upper cup. The shikoro fitted to these helmets was made of metal strips arranged exactly like those on the shokaku tsuki kabuto.

The distinctive feature of these helmets was the peak. It was lobed in outline and fretted with either a geometric design or one of stylized tendrils. One of these helmets, made of gilded copper and hence unsuited to real use, is decorated with a punched design of fishes and birds which extends onto the plates of the bowl. Since shoes, also of gilded copper, have been found in a tomb, they, like the helmet, were probably made as grave goods for a person of considerable rank.

Left: A haniwa representing a warrior wearing a scale armour called keiko. The neck guard is divided so that the front portions can be fastened under the chin to give greater protection to the face.

Apart from the actual remains of armours and other weapons found as burial deposits, our knowledge of the military equipment is considerably extended by finds of *haniwa*, fired-clay models of figures, animals and inanimate objects, which were placed in the superstructure of the tombs. These do not seem to have been substitutes for people buried with the dead as was common in China, since no evidence of this practice has been found in Japan, but rather served as markers, which were erected upon posts around the mound of the grave. Whatever their real purpose, a large proportion of these charming figures represent warriors, and from them it is possible to see the way in which the two styles of armour evolved and combined as all possible combinations of plate and scales were tried out. This experimentation is hardly surprising since the armourers themselves were a mixture of native Japanese, Koreans and Chinese. Since few actual armours have been excavated, and most of these are fragmentary, haniwa provide invaluable secondary evidence about styles of armour and helmets. A group of warrior figures show keiko being worn with a simple bowl-shaped helmet of vertical plates, some of which are provided with exaggerated rivets, and surmounted by an inverted iron cup – these helmets are almost identical to those worn in contemporary China. These models differ from surviving helmets in having the shikoro made of scales, split vertically just behind the ears, with the front sections tying under the chin to guard the face. Why no examples have been unearthed of what seems to have been a common type of helmet, while numbers of the rarely depicted mabisashi tsuki kabuto have been found remains a mystery. Possibly peaked helmets were in fact the exception, worn perhaps by nobles as an indication of their rank, while the haniwa represent warriors of lower status, wearing common armour in their role as tomb guardians.

Right: Haniwa clearly showing the fabric shoulder straps supporting the tanko.

As the Yamato people pushed the frontier and the 'barbarians' further from the court, Emperor Kotoku, backed by the powerful aristocratic Fujiwara clan, gathered together the nobles and announced a new system of government based on that of T'ang China. It was in effect a declaration of absolute monarchy; all lands belonged to the throne and those who worked it would pay for its use in taxes. A series of royal decrees was issued in 646 to this effect, called the Taika Reform. Also included was legislation aimed at establishing internal peace by banning the wearing of swords by all except those guarding the capital and territorial borders. The lack of success of this particular enactment can be judged by the fact that a watered-down version had to be passed again in 696.

By the middle of the eighth century, the court was firmly established in Nara, a city based on those of T'ang China. Prosperity in the country was increasing so rapidly that there was an increasing demand for luxury goods. The famous Sho so in at Nara, established by the widow of the Emperor Shomu in 756 to house his personal belongings as a shrine to his memory, contains among its treasures items from distant parts of the world imported through China. Stored there originally were 90 keiko and 10 tanko; sadly,

Above: An eighteenth century reproduction of a sword mounting used at court since the Heian period.

however, these were later borrowed to arm Imperial troops during a rebellion and were never replaced. All that now survive are a few fragments of a keiko laced in purple doeskin; this represents the oldest non-excavated armour in Japan.

Fortunately, the Sho so in collection still contains a considerable number of spears, swords and other weapons. Among the former are socketed spear heads about 10 inches (25cm) long, with elegant diamond-sectioned blades, some of which have a down-curving hook just above the socket. All were referred to in inventories by the generic name of *hoko*, although others with curious crank-shaped sword-like blades mounted on short, cord-bound shafts, are distinguished by being described as *te boko* (hand spears).

Many of the swords preserved at the shrine are undoubtedly of Chinese manufacture but a few at least of the short swords and knives are thought to be indigenous. These, when polished by modern methods, show that the swordsmiths were beginning to experiment with techniques that were to create the most perfect hand-to-hand weapon the world has seen.

Swordsmiths throughout the world have been hindered by the mutually exclusive properties of toughness and hardness of steel. Having only an empirical understanding of the complex metallurgy involved, they adopted a variety of techniques in an attempt to make a blade that was hard enough to take and keep a cutting edge, yet tough enough not to break easily. The interaction between iron and carbon, and the effect of temperature changes on the combination is enormously complex. Put very simply, iron reacts with an excess of carbon at high temperatures to produce a compound which on slow cooling becomes tough and soft. On the other hand, if the compound is cooled rapidly, the transformation does not have time to occur and the high temperature form is retained, leaving the steel very hard but as brittle as glass. Lowering the level of carbon below a critical limit reduces this capacity to harden until, with almost-pure iron, it ceases altogether. A further factor that has a considerable bearing on sword technology is the fact that all metals are made up from a mass of interlocking crystals whose size influences the mechanical properties of the metal. Deformation causes the crystals to fragment, hardening the metal, but also introduces dislocations that, if taken to excess, cause the structure to collapse. This is exactly the principle we all use to break a piece of wire by bending it back and forth. During this process the metal can be felt to harden as the crystals are progressively broken down, reaching a maximum just before the metal begins to crack. In sword making, therefore, it is important to know just how far the forging process should be taken; too little and the metal is not as hard as it could be, while overworking causes it to become weak and more liable to fracture.

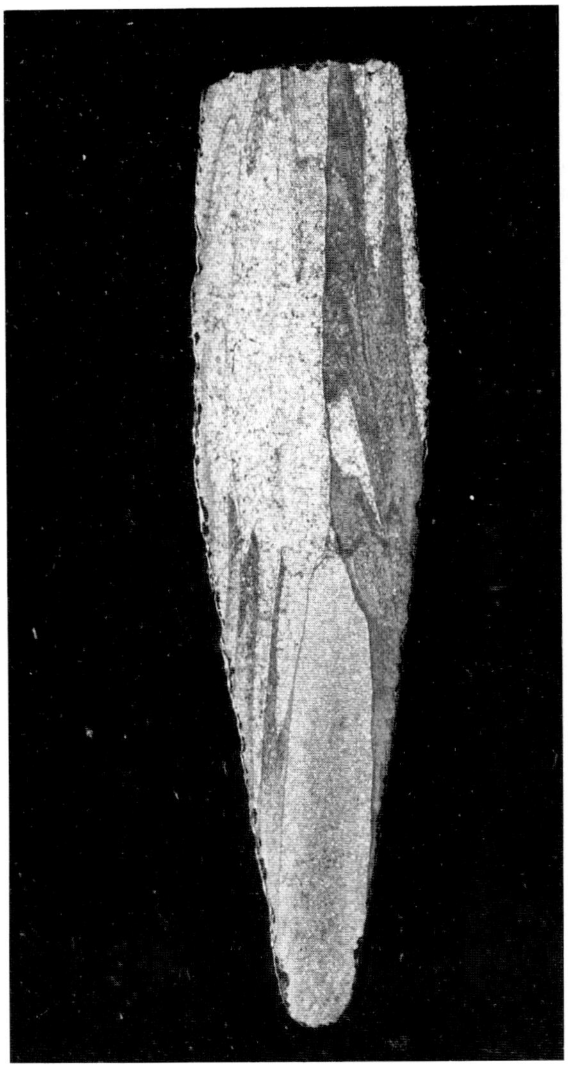

Right: Cross-section of a sword blade made in variation of the wari ha kitae technique in which the steel forming the cutting edge is sandwiched between pieces of only partially mixed softer metal.

In Europe swordsmiths compromised by making blades that were tempered, that is, they were first made fully hard, but very brittle, then reheated to a lower temperature, allowing some of the hardness to dissipate. This process produced blades that were at once moderately hard and reasonably tough. In India and the Middle East, an alternative compromise was reached; a mixture of high-carbon steel and almost-pure iron, which cannot be hardened, was forged together. This formed a mixture which, when heated and quenched, produced a blade with an edge that had both hard and soft parts, the one sharing its properties with the other and, incidentally, producing the 'watered steel' effect so admired in their blades.

Japan's answer to this problem was sometimes to produce a blade like the Middle Eastern blades, but more often they made a high-carbon-steel cutting edge and welded it to a low-carbon-steel body. This was then heat treated in such a way that only the edge was hardened; although brittle, this was supported and prevented from breaking by the soft, malleable body of the blade. This is exactly the same principle that is now used for tungsten-carbide-tipped machine tools. Over the centuries, many different techniques were evolved that achieved this aim, but all involved the smith in careful preparation of the materials, which he then assembled into a composite billet from which the sword itself was made.

No one now knows when this method of construction was perfected, but by the tenth century blades were being made which had all the characteristics expected of true Japanese swords. Nothing has come down to us of the working methods of smiths from the tenth century, but we know from historic writings and from modern smiths using traditional methods that parts of the process were regarded as religious ceremonies. At these times the forge would be decorated with straw rope and cut-paper, symbols of the Shinto faith, while the smith himself would dress in court robes, after symbolic washing. Some smiths are said to have taken religious observation even further and abstained from alcohol, women and eating certain foods during the forging of a blade. Inevitably there were others who did not carry things quite so far. Noda Hankei, whose work was renowned and much sought-after during the early Edo period, seems to have spent much of his life sleeping off the effects of drink in the more dubious quarters of the capital – his body was found in the gutter one morning cut in two by one of his own blades.

Recent research suggests that in historic times, the manufacture of a blade began with the careful selection of small pieces of steel from the impure mass of slag and metal formed in the blast furnace. These were stacked onto a previously prepared iron plate which was welded to a long iron rod which acted as a handle, and wrapped with paper and string to make a compact block which held the whole precarious pile together. A thin slurry of clay and straw ash in water was poured over everything, both to protect the bundle until it was positioned in the fire, and to act as a flux, easing fusion. The hearth used by the swordsmith took the form of a long, narrow pit lined with clay. Air was supplied by bellows operated by the smith himself and the hearth was fuelled with carefully selected pieces of charcoal. As soon as the correct temperature was reached, the partially fused block was transferred to the anvil and welded solid by the smith's assistants, who struck with sledge hammers at the spot indicated by the smith. By carefully controlling the intensity and position of the blows, the block was drawn out to twice its length and half its thickness while maintaining the width and keeping the edges square. After reheating, the underside of the block was cleaned by pouring water over the anvil then hammering the block on it; this caused an explosive release of steam which carried with it the surface coating of scale and dirt from the fire.

Now followed the part of the forging operation on which so much depended; to cut the block almost in two with a chisel, bending it back on itself and then welding the joint together so that no scale or unwelded gaps were included that would cause weaknesses in the final blade. Great care was taken to ensure that the surface of the anvil, and hence the welding surface it produced, was perfectly smooth and that there were no pockets that would trap scale or slag. That this folding operation was done not once, but sometimes as many as 15 times, to produce metal with fewer inclusions of slag than many modern steel samples, is little short of miraculous and a testimony to the skill and dedication of these master craftsmen. During the long process of folding, heating and welding, impurities in the metal were eliminated and some of the carbon was probably burnt out but, more importantly, the metal was made homogeneous and the grain structure was refined, with a corresponding increase in hardness.

To form steels of intermediate hardness, a compound block would be made by welding soft iron and steel together, and then folding and welding this until the two metals were mixed to the required degree. Repeating the folding process many times produced a virtually homogeneous metal. Fewer foldings however left the two grades of metal in layers which, when the finished blade was polished, were visible as the beautifully patterned surface effects, *hada*, on the finished sword. Sakakibara Kozan, writing in his book *Chukokatchu Seisakuben* on the manufacture of steel for armour, warns that the foldings should not exceed 15 otherwise the 'hardness' would be lost and the steel will become *kuzureru* (decayed). He also warns that if high-carbon steel is used initially, more than

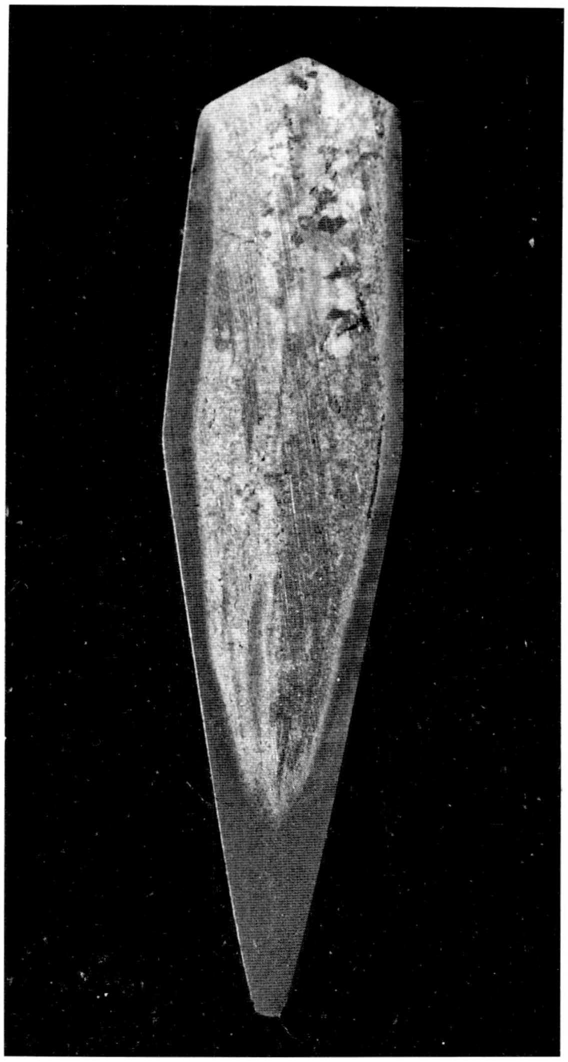

Left: Cross-section of a sword blade made by the kobushi kitae process in which a soft core is wrapped in high carbon steel. In this case the core shows a coarse crystalline structure towards the back and there is a welding defect, visible as a dark line, on the right.

five foldings will ruin it by burning out too much of the carbon. On the other hand, Suishinshi Kawabe Gihachiro Masahide, a swordsmith working in the early nineteenth century who devoted much of his life to rediscovering the secrets of the old swordsmiths, describes in detail how the bed of the hearth could be soaked with water the night before to prevent carbon being lost.

Using these methods, the smith could produce the various grades of steel that he needed for a blade, and by simple tests such as the examination of the colour and texture of a fractured surface, could judge very closely the properties each possessed. His next task was to assemble the different pieces, each carefully shaped, into a billet from which the final blade could be made. It was in the manner by which this was done that most variations occur. Sometimes a block was notched along its length and a strip of high-carbon steel welded in, *wari ha kitae* (split-edge forging). A variant was to wrap the high-carbon metal around a low-carbon core, *kobushi kitae*

(fist forging). A more complex construction using five grades of steel, arranged to form the edge, back, cores and sides, gave what was called rather confusingly *san mai zukuri* (three-plate style), considered to be the best method by an old swordsmith, Horii Taneyoshi, at the end of the last century.

By careful orientation of those pieces of metal that had only received a few folding operations, the smith could regulate the type of surface effects visible on the sides of the finished blade. If the surface was parallel to the folds, small irregularities would reveal a beautiful burl-wood grain when ground flat; if at right angles or beaten on an angle, a striated effect was produced. Some even went as far as corrugating the metal so that when polished it showed regular undulating striations, along the length of the blade.

Once the composite billet had been prepared, it was drawn out into a strip of the approximate size and shape of the blade using a wooden gauge, to determine the proportions and curve. Using a smaller hammer, the smith then carefully shaped the *shinogi* (ridge) and single edge that was characteristic of most blades, leaving the final shaping and cleaning to be carried out with a draw shave and files while the blade was clamped to a wooden block. If after careful examination no defects were revealed and the smith was satisfied with his work, he would then punch a hole called a *mekugi no ana*, through the *nakago* (tang), which was used to hold the blade into its mounts, before passing the blade for hardening.

Giving the blade a hard, tempered edge while leaving the remainder soft was

Left: Scene from the Heiji Monogatari Emaki *showing samurai searching a courtier's bullock cart.*

achieved by coating the blade with a layer of clay which, when dry, was thinned by scraping away all but a thin film from the edge, in a pattern that was characteristic of the smith's working tradition. Masahide maintained that any clay was suitable, if sticky, and that he obtained his from the province of Dewa; he mixed it with powdered whetstone and charcoal before use. He also mentions that his experiments led him to believe that some of the old smiths used borax in addition to the clay, but he was attempting to reproduce by any means that he could find, features of old blades that in the past had arisen from the materials and methods used.

When dry, the clay-coated blade was heated in the specially darkened smithy so that the temperature of the hot metal could be judged by its colour. For a delicate narrow *yakiba* (cutting edge), the blade could only be heated to dull red, to localize the hardening, but for more robust patterns, bright red or orange was permissible. When at precisely the right temperature, the heat-softened blade was plunged edge down into water, which was also at a critical temperature. The layer of clay surrounding the blade delayed the chilling of the body sufficiently to prevent it being hardened while allowing the full rapid cooling to take place along the edge. It was during this stage that the blade assumed most of its graceful curve; the differential quenching caused the back to contract more than the edge. If the smith had misjudged things, this difference in contraction caused undue stressing that could, in extreme cases, cause cracking of the hardened edge with the total loss of the time and labour expended.

Little wonder that this was regarded as the most sacred part of the whole process, and that prayers were offered to a shrine set up in the forge before it was undertaken.

The smith would then chisel his name on the tang, if he had not done so before, perhaps including other details such as the province in which he worked and the date. Traditionally, spring water was considered to be at the correct temperature during the second and eighth months, and most dated swords indicate these months, irrespective of when they were actually made. Any decoration on the blade, such as carvings or grooves, would also be cut into the soft metal body of the blade before it could be finally finished.

In all probability the earlier swordsmiths would then themselves grind the blade into its final shape and keen edge but in later times this was a separate craft. The sword polisher used a dozen or more stones of increasing fineness that not only smoothed and polished the metal, but also revealed the complex structures introduced into the metal by the forging and hardening processes it had undergone. It is from a close study of these details, together with the subtle shape of a blade, that sword appraisors are able to assign a blade to a given maker even when, as is often the case, the swordsmith had chosen not to sign it.

By the middle of the eighth century Nara had become a capital of considerable sophistication, with palaces, mansions and Buddhist temples housing priceless libraries and art treasures from China. The government, however, had grown weak and the Imperial armies were suffering all too many defeats from the Ainu on the northern borders. Ambitious nobles and the clergy were constantly plotting to place their favourites in positions of power at court. By 784 Emperor Kammu could tolerate the situation no longer and, aided by the ever-scheming Fujiwara clan, decided to move the capital to a more auspicious location. After some initial difficulties the site of modern Kyoto was chosen, which although only 25 miles from Nara, was considered sufficiently distant to escape from the influence of the monks. On this gently sloping plain with mountains guarding the northeast (which as everyone knew was the direction chosen by demons to launch their attacks) a new Chinese-style city called Heian-Kyo (the Capital of Peace and Tranquillity) was built. Initially the move was a great success but on Kammu's death in 806, the power struggle to influence affairs of state began once again. Ultimately it was the Fujiwara who gained the ascendance and by using titles such as 'Chancellor' and 'Regent', gained control of the throne by providing a seemingly inexhaustible supply of beautiful daughters as brides for the Emperor.

Entrenched in their magnificent capital and turning inward from the rest of the world, the courtiers and nobles of Heian society developed a refined culture which emphasized poetry, music, art and fashion while much of the remainder of the country, populated mainly by farmers, struggled to exist. Minor members of the Imperial Family and the younger sons of the aristocracy were dispatched to act as stewards of provincial estates and as local representatives of the government. They became in fact a class of landed gentry, *ji zamurai*, the backbone of the armed forces; putting on their armour and rallying with their retainers to suppress rebellion and continue the process of expansion ever northwards. These minor aristocrats formed two major groups; adopting the names of Taira and Minamoto they were based in the western and eastern regions of Japan respectively.

Following the almost wholesale adoption of Buddhism and the resultant cessation of dolmen burials and their associated haniwa, actual examples of arms and armour of the period are reduced to occasional archaeological finds. What evidence there is suggests that armours of plate had finally been abandoned in favour of a version of the keiko, modified into a poncho-like garment with openings under each arm filled by separate pieces fastened to the body. The shape and construction of the helmet was also changing and was now distinctly conical; it was made of vertical tapering plates riveted to a koshimaki at the bottom and surmounted by an inverted iron cup that housed the wearer's hair. Horses were now reasonably plentiful and almost all fighting was between groups of mounted men.

With the Fujiwara firmly in control of the country by manipulation of what were virtually puppet emperors, the Taira and the Minamoto began of gain prestige by acting as the armed forces of the regency in what were mainly policing roles; the Ainu were now an issue only in the extreme north. One particularly troublesome problem was the result of a

Above: A certificate of authenticity issued in 1667. It assigns the authorship of a blade to Muneyasu and values it at 6 gold mai and 5 momme of silver.

quirk of legislation incorporated in the Taika Reform which exempted some of the nobility and temples from paying taxes on their land holdings. Playing on this, many of the Fujiwara, minor members of the Imperial Family and particularly the monastic orders situated in the mountains to the north of the capital, set up lucrative business schemes whereby they accepted nominal ownership of land in exchange for a small percentage of the annual yield. Looking after these interests, as well as more legitimate affairs of state, became the prerogative of the Taira and Minamoto.

Farther from the capital the situation grew steadily worse throughout the eleventh century as local magnates, virtually ignored by a court totally engrossed in itself, refused to pay taxes, and banded together for self-protection. They formed what amounted to private armies which were fully capable of dealing with such forces as the government could muster. This same blatant disregard for the law was also shown by the monastic orders, which employed their own armies of mercenaries, only slightly legitimized as *sohei* (novices). On several occasions these armies of monks, wearing armour under their clerical robes and wielding their favourite weapon, the *naginata*, marched on the capital, carrying with them sacred palanquins to force the somewhat superstitious courtiers to accede to their demands.

From this time weapons and armour were deposited in temples as votive offerings, indicating the importance and prestige that was beginning to be attached to them – and also perhaps the growing prestige of the military. Some of these deposits have survived almost intact to the present day, but it is impossible to say how many more would have survived had not the temples, in particular, suffered systematic burning because of their involvement in politics during Japan's long civil wars. We must, however, be grateful that at least some of this unique legacy is available for study – unmatched by anything elsewhere in the world.

During this period of growing chaos there were glimmers of light as the occasional Emperor broke free from the grasp of the Fujiwara and either ruled directly or, more commonly, abdicated in favour of a weak son and ruled from retirement. This very Japanese institution of the 'Cloistered Emperors' was insufficient to halt the decline of the brilliant social life that Heian-Kyo had enjoyed for so long. Much of the city was already in ruins and bandits roamed the derelict areas, raiding mansions and palaces alike. In the rest of the country, the 'teeth and claws of the Fujiwara', the Minamoto, together with the Taira, were becoming more self-assertive as they realized the potential power they could wield and the growing weakness of the court.

CHAPTER TWO
The Samurai during the Gempei Wars

Far right: Red-laced maru do yoroi traditionally associated with Minamoto Yoshitsune, a commander of the Minamoto during the Gempei wars whose career was later idealized by artists. Heian period.

As Heian culture gained confidence during the ninth century it looked less often to China for its inspiration, becoming more inward looking and relying more on native sources of talent. The official link was broken in 894 when, exactly 100 years after the capital's founding, the diplomatic mission planned for that year was cancelled. The adoption of Chinese military philosophy declined even earlier and a school for *samurai* (one who serves), the *Butokukan*, had been set up in the capital. Here the martial arts were cultivated by officer cadets of high family.

During the tenth and early eleventh centuries the increased availability of horses led to the evolution of a style of fighting that depended to a large degree on the ability of the combatants to discharge arrows from horseback while charging their opponent at full gallop – wheeling away at the last moment to re-form. This ability to use a bow, *yumi*, was deemed so important, that the term *kyusen no ie* came to mean 'samurai family', although its literal meaning is 'bows and arrow family'. Indeed, all contemporary accounts of battles record the strength of each side solely in terms of the numbers of bows present. As the eleventh century advanced, these tactics acquired some of the ritualistic qualities of the duel. Battles degenerated into a mêlée, with individual warriors shouting challenges, declaring their pedigree and past achievements before launching into an attack on whichever opponent they had singled out. Ceremonies were devised such as that of presenting the heads of the slain to the victorious

Right: Scene from the Heiji Monogatari Emaki *showing samurai and their retainers attacking the imperial palace. Kamakura period.*

commanders after the battle; honour and, more importantly, rewards, were bestowed on those who had killed the highest ranking opponents. With each warrior bent on glory, commanders could do little to control the impetuosity of their forces and any attempt at using them tactically was futile.

Foot soldiers played little part in the military strategy of the day, being relegated to a supporting role. Each noble would be accompanied by a number of lightly armed retainers on foot, who carried their lord's helmet and other equipment to the scene of the battle, but who played no part in the initial stages of the fighting itself; their duty was to rush in between the horses, arrows and flailing swords, to give assistance when their lord or his opponent was unhorsed.

In 1156, the first year of the period of Hogen, a dispute arose over succession to the throne that resulted in calls for support going out from both the current Emperor, Go-Shirakawa, and the 'Cloistered Emperor' Sotoku. Their loyalties divided, both the samurai and the armed monks of Nara took sides. Each group contained a mixture of both Taira and Minamoto, with the result that, as in many civil wars, fathers faced sons from the opposing lines. This division of the family between the two opposing forces did not always arise from a sense of conviction; the Japanese, being pragmatists, frequently adopted such a strategy to ensure that at least a part of the family would survive, whatever the outcome. The inevitable battle was fought during a July night, with all the formality and style expected of perfect samurai: challenges and counter-challenges were issued, charges were made and arrows shot. The only deviation from good form was the burning of Sotoku's headquarters when it became evident that it would take too long to capture it in any other way, leaving the defenders little choice but to flee.

In itself the whole affair was little more than an incident in which a few were killed and Sotoku was banished, but its legacy was to plunge the country into further civil war. One of the commanders, Taira Kiyomori, was rewarded, much to the chagrin of the Minamoto, by a powerful position at court. Discontent increased when Kiyomori, as skilled in politics as he was in arms, rose rapidly through the ranks, inevitably, perhaps, making enemies among both the Fujiwara and the Minamoto in the process.

Right: Scene from the Heiji Monogatari Emaki. *Armed retainers carry trophy heads on their naginata (pole arms). Kamakura period.*

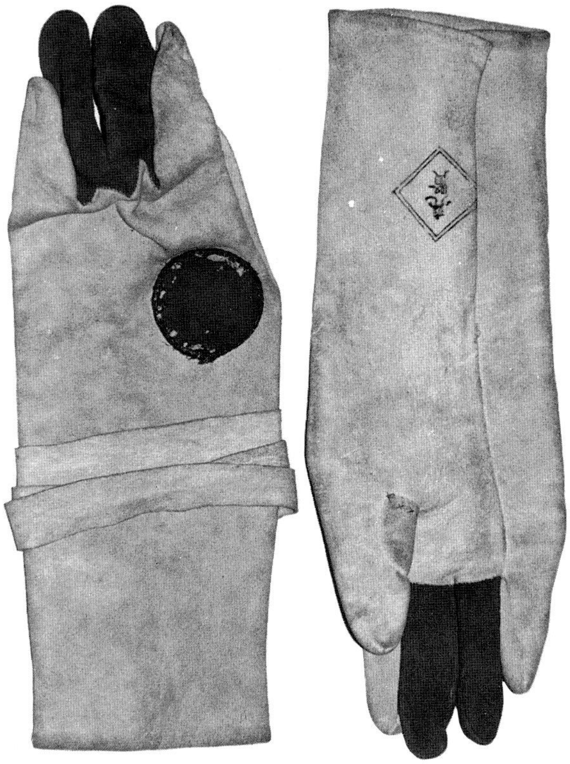

Left: Yugake (archer's gloves) for wearing with armour. Made of white leather, the two centre fingers in brown. Momoyama period.

Resentment grew with each promotion until 1160 when a force of 500 Minamoto attacked the palace itself, kidnapping Go-Shirakawa, who was now 'cloistered', and imprisoning Emperor Nijo in an attempt to regain some of their former power. There followed a month of fighting in and around the capital, until the Taira finally regained control of the situation and embarked on a programme of executions and retribution of unparalleled savagery. Every adult Minamoto they could find was put to the sword, with the exception of one old man who had refused to take part in the attack. Only the Minamoto children were spared; they were exiled to various monasteries or adopted into Taira households on the assumption that they no longer posed a threat.

Every written character used by the Japanese has at least two pronunciations – the native Japanese sound for the idea it expresses and the way the Chinese pronounced the character during the Nara period or, more accurately, how the Japanese thought they did. Using the Chinese pronunciation, which was always favoured by scholars of the classics, the names Minamoto and Taira become Gen and Hei which, when compounded, gives the name to the wars between these two great houses – The Gempei Wars.

Historically important as these opening battles of the Gempei Wars were, they illustrate vividly how parochial Heian society was when a force of just 500 could capture and hold the throne against the Imperial forces for the best part of a month. Even allowing for poor communications, events in the capital meant little to most of the population, to whom the courtiers and their world seemed as remote as the gods themselves.

Although not unknown in Japan, the recurved composite bows of the Asiatic horseman played no part in these battles and were never adopted by the Japanese. The horn and sinew needed for these bows came from cattle, but few were kept because most Japanese were Buddhists, and eating meat or handling anything derived from dead animals was abhorrent to them. In later periods, tasks such as executions or the slaughter of animals and the preparation of leather were carried out by the *eta*, a class of people considered subhuman and totally outside society because of their occupation. That leather figures largely in military equipment supposes that, once prepared, it somehow became transformed and lost its defiling

Left: Glove for archery practice of dark blue leather covering the thumb and first two fingers only. Edo period.

Above: Box of lacquered leather for storing archers' gloves. Momoyama period.

Right: Arrows displayed in an open quiver. Muromachi period.

Below: Various arrow heads, including pierced flat arrow heads with a cherry blossom design.

properties; an attitude of mind similar to that assumed by those who ate venison and assuaged their consciences by calling it 'mountain whale.' The Japanese bowyers, however, turned to the materials they had in abundance: wood and, especially, bamboo.

To obtain the power needed in a war bow while retaining a cross-section of reasonable proportions, it was necessary to adopt a laminated structure. During the early Heian this was achieved by making the bow of deciduous wood and backing it with bamboo; that is the body of the bow was of wood with a thick facing of bamboo fastened onto the side farthest from the archer when drawing the bow. By the middle of the Heian, performance was further improved by adding an additional facing of bamboo on the opposite, or belly side of the bow. Although glued carefully with hide glue, the most powerful adhesive available, joints involving bamboo are notoriously unreliable and they had to be augmented by bindings of rattan which differ considerably in number and position. Additional pieces of wood were spliced in at each end, then glued and bound in position to reinforce the nocks for the string. Bindings of rattan and leather marked the grip. Almost all traditional bows were lacquered to prevent damp weakening the glued joints; the most popular colour scheme was black with the bindings picked out in red. When being carried to and from the battlefield, or when in storage, bows were further protected by tubular bags of cloth which tied at the ends.

Poor glue adhesion imposed a severe limit on the stressing the bow could withstand. To limit the stress, the bow had to be long; an average bow was about 6½ feet (2m) in length, but some were much longer. One bow, said to have been the property of Yuasa Matashichiro, is 8 feet 9 inches (2.7m) long, and is still preserved in the temple at Itsukushima. This temple also houses an 8-foot 6-inch (2.5m) long bow which belonged to Ihara Koshiro. Even bows of less heroic lengths than these would have been hopelessly impractical on horseback had the bowyers not arrived at the simple expedient of moving the grip downwards from the centre and, by careful shaping, making the upper limb do much of the work. This left a short lower limb that could be easily manipulated over the horse's neck.

Tsuru (bowstrings) were of plant fibre, usually hemp or ramie, coated with wax to

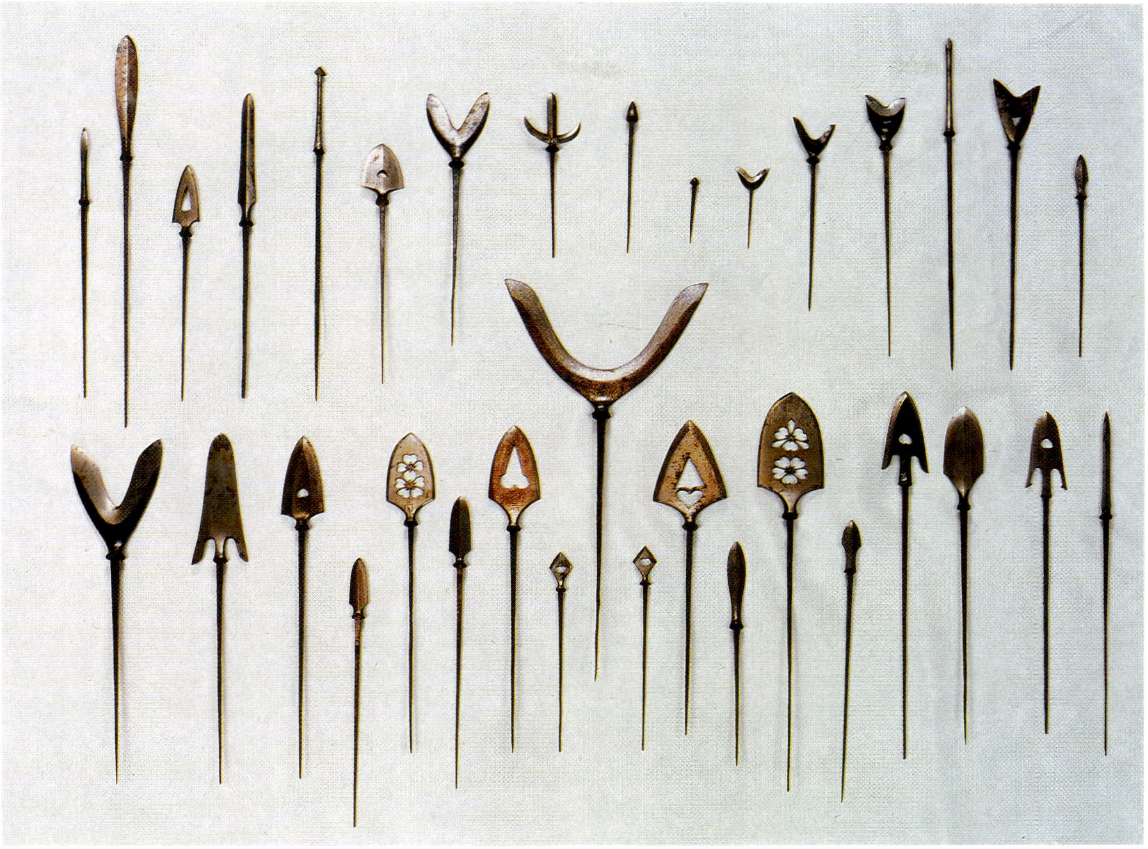

Left: The wide range of sizes and shapes of arrow heads is evident in this selection. The large arrow head in the centre could not be shot; it was probably a votive offering or presentation piece.

give a hard, smooth surface. The upper end was bound with red silk ribbon, the bottom end with white. Loops were formed by means of a timber hitch rather than being part of the string's construction, or formed by separate cords as in China. The upper loop was also provided with an extra tab of silk so that the string could be held in the teeth, leaving both hands free to brace the bow. In some cases this was too much for one person to manage – one way of gauging the strength of a bow was to count the number of men needed to string it.

Like most Asiatics, the Japanese drew the string with the right thumb hooked under the arrow and locked by the first two fingers resting on the thumbnail. This requires that the arrow be positioned on the right of the bow as viewed by the archer, not on the left as when the string is drawn with the fingers. Unlike the Chinese, the Japanese apparently did not use thumb rings of stones or ivory to protect the ball of the thumb from the pressure of the string, wearing instead a leather glove, *yugake*. Those worn while practicing often only covered the first two fingers and had an enlarged thumb reinforced with horn or leather at the point of contact with the string. In war, where such a glove would have hindered the handling of a sword or even the arrows, a pair of more ordinary gloves were worn, again reinforced, but only with a small double layer of leather on the inside of the right thumb. Made of coloured or patterned leather, the two centre fingers are for some reason frequently of a different colour from the rest.

To draw the bow the archer held the bow above the head, to clear the horse, and then moved his the hands apart as the bow was brought down, to end with the left arm

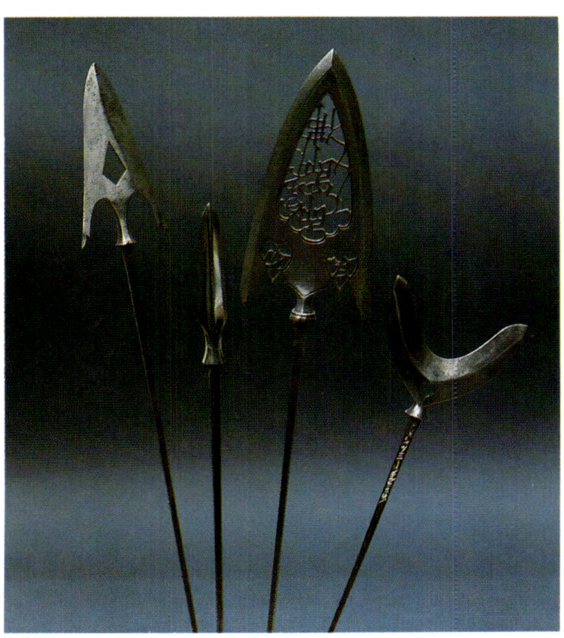

Left: Arrow heads were made in hundreds of styles. The large flat arrow head of the broadhead type (second from right) has an inscription in positive silhouette and is intended as a votive offering or for presentation.

Right: A quiver that has survived from the Heian period preserved in the storehouse of a temple. These ebira were worn on the right hip, the shafts of the arrows being secured to the upright frame by a cord.

Far right: An Edo period reproduction of an ebira of cane, rawhide and leather. The deer skin suggests that it was made as part of a hunting outfit.

straight and the right hand near the right ear. This style of drawing the bow was formalized by the Ogasawara family. The alternative style, *heiki ryu*, practised by foot soldiers, resembled that used in Europe – the draw was begun with the bow held horizontally, level with the waist. Drawing these asymmetric bows requires a very loose hold by the bow hand since the upper limb moves forward in an arc, ending with the grip at a considerable angle from the vertical. To release, the fingers supporting the thumb were relaxed, allowing the string to slip off the glove and, as it returned to its resting position, allowing the bow to rotate in the hand so that it ended with the string touching the outside of the bow arm. This permitted the Japanese to dispense with a bracer for the protection of the inside of the left wrist, although occasionally a *yugote* (loose sleeve) was worn on the left arm to protect the clothing underneath.

The *ya* (arrows) had bamboo shafts. These were cut in November and December, when they were in the best condition, and prepared by shaving off the nodes and outer skin. The nock for the bowstring was cut immediately above a node, for strength, in the end farthest from the root in the growing plant so that the taper was towards the nock. Each shaft was softened in hot sand and then carefully straightened, using a notched stick for leverage. On better sets of arrows from the Edo period, shafts were sorted to ensure that the positions of the nodes matched and looked even when carried in a quiver. They were finished by bindings of lacquered fibre below the nock and above the head, to prevent splitting at these vulnerable points, and in many cases the signature of the maker was added on the nock binding in red lacquer.

There were normally three fletchings, although arrows fitted with a particularly large head had four. Because of the problem of adhesion, fletchings were glued in place and then bound to the shaft by the ends of their quills. All manner of feathers were pressed into use, but various eagle, hawk, crane and pheasant tail feathers are by far the most common. On most arrows the fletchings were left either untrimmed or cut parallel to the shaft, using the natural slope of the barbs at each end. For the very best sets, the area of the shaft between and around the fletchings was lacquered gold or decorated in some other way.

Ya no ne (arrowheads) were made by specialist smiths. They sometimes signed their work, either on the blade or in minute characters on the tang. They were produced in a multiplicity of shapes and sizes. Many were highly decorative and enormous; these were never meant to be shot, but were intended for presentation and votive purposes. Fanciful names exist, or have been invented, for the hundreds of varieties, but all can be assigned into one of three major groups.

Narrow four-sided heads These are often almost square in section and are named after the leaf they resemble, for example *yanagi* (willow-leaf shape) or *sasa no ha* (bamboo-leaf shape). Like the bodkin heads of Europe, their purpose was to pierce deep and, if needed, to punch holes through armour. Most war arrows were fitted with heads of this type. Related to these are various acutely pointed heads (*togari ya*), and the less common chisel pointed heads, which both served a similar function.

Barbed broadhead types (hira ne) These are shaped like the base of a flat-iron and are flat in section with a narrow sharpened edge. These exhibit most variation and were often pierced with heraldic or flower designs in negative silhouette, their shape lending themselves to this form of decoration. Less common are specimens with poems or other characters in positive silhouette, in which almost the entire area of the blade is occupied by the decoration, leaving only a narrow band as the cutting edge. Some complete sets have two arrows, one fitted with a decorated hira ne; the other with a forked head. Some historians claim these would have been used against a high-ranking opponent, and others that it would have been shot to signal defeat – both highly improbable reasons.

Forked arrow heads Named *karimata* after their resemblance to a flock of geese in flight, forked arrow heads range in size from a fraction of an inch to as much as several inches across the points. Most were probably for hunting, but several do appear in picture scrolls of battles. In the past it has been suggested that they were used to cut the fastening cords of armour, or to damage the rigging of ships. Despite having four fletchings to prevent the arrow spinning it would have taken a remarkable archer to ensure the arrow struck the cords or rigging with its head at right angles to them, not to mention the difficulty of doing so from a moving horse in battle. The purpose of forked arrow heads was to increase the chance of hitting something by increasing the width of the head. One type of arrow that was regularly fitted with a forked arrow head had a bulbous whistle of horn or wood immediately below the head and was used for signalling in war, an idea copied from the Chinese.

Whatever the type, all arrowheads were fitted firmly into the shaft of the arrow solely by a long, slender tang forged in one piece with the head; a concave neck separated the tang and head and formed a shoulder to butt against the end of the shaft. They were carried, slung on the right hip, in a quiver called an *ebira*. This had a box-like lower section fitted with a grid of bamboo or hide strips, which gripped the heads, and an openwork frame rising from the back edge to which the shafts were loosely tied by a cord. Drawing an arrow from such a quiver involved grasping it just above the head, lifting it clear of the grid, then pulling it forwards until the shaft was clear of the cords.

The gorgeous panoply these warrior nobles wore was quite different from the crude armours of the earlier periods, and reflects in colours and mountings the refined tastes developed by Heian society. In comparison with later armours they were somewhat angular and had a rather ungainly appearance, but they were admirably suited to the warfare of the time. Made of scales in a similar way to the keiko, these armours incorporated new methods of construction and lacing, and new materials were used in their decoration.

Heian-period scales were large and made either from rawhide or iron. The great weight of armours made entirely of iron prohibited their general use. The two materials were either alternated along each row to give a construction called *ichimai maze*, or the iron scales would be concentrated in those areas needing the greatest protection, giving a con-

Left: Types of scales (l-r): kozane, the most usual pattern; shikime zane, a rare type of scale assembled with a double overlap resulting in rows of triple thickness; iyozane, a type of scale designed to avoid a large overlap, lightening the armour and reducing the number of scales needed.

Right: Patterns of armour lacing reflected personal taste. There were many styles, just a few of which are illustrated. (Top row from left to right) shikime odoshi, susogoi odoshi, omodaka odoshi, tsumadori odoshi. (Bottom row from left to right) mongara odoshi (the owner's crest forms the basis of this pattern) hadasusogoi odoshi, tatewake odoshi, katatsumadori odoshi.

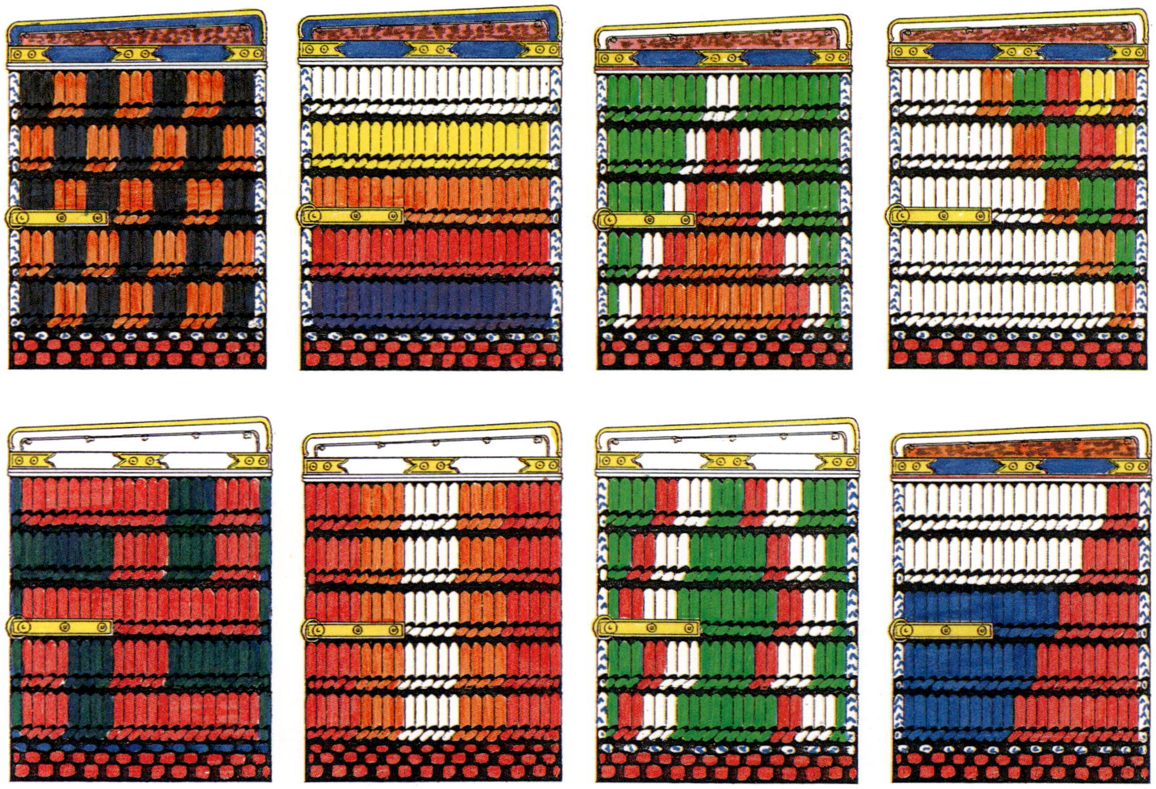

struction called *kane maze*. The hide came from the skins of both cattle and horses and was simply prepared by soaking in water to induce bacterial fermentation which loosened the hair and fatty tissues. After scraping and cleaning, the skins were stretched and dried to give a tough, translucent material whose only real defect was that it absorbed moisture and softened. One famous armour of the Minamoto is said to have been made exclusively from the leather of cows' knees, on the principle that this must be the toughest part of the hide, owing to their habit of kneeling.

Each *sane* (scale), measured about 2 inches (5cm) by 1½ inches (4cm), and was punched with 13 holes in two groups. The lower group of eight holes was called the *shita toji no ana*, and the upper group of five holes the *kedate no ana*. To protect them against damp, they were lacquered before being assembled into rows by leather thongs laced through the lower holes so that each scale overlapped by half the one to its right, giving a double thickness throughout – a special half scale being added at each end of the row to maintain the thickness. Because the rows constructed in this way had a tendency to sag as the lacing stretched with age, a few armours were made from scales which had three columns of holes, *shikime zane*, which extended the overlap and prevented this, but added considerably to the weight. The leather lacing, called *shita toji*, which fastened

Below right: Individual kozane were fastened together into rows by the shita toji, leather thongs laced through the lower holes in the scales.

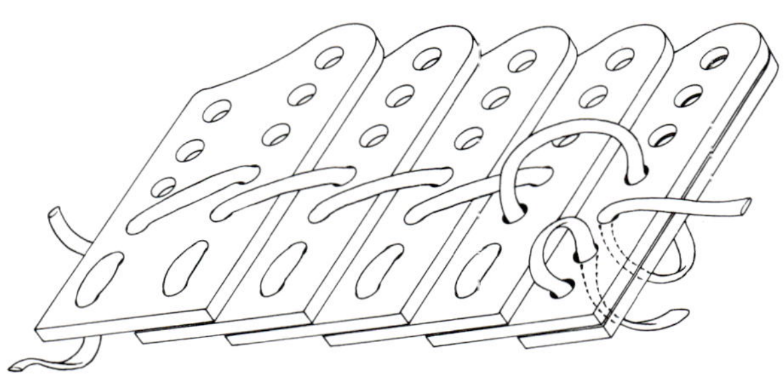

Far right: Rows of kozane were assembled into armour by the lacing, odoshi ge (yellow). A thicker braid, the mimi ito, bordered each section while the bottom row of scales had the shita toji laced as decorative cross-knots (red) called hishinui.

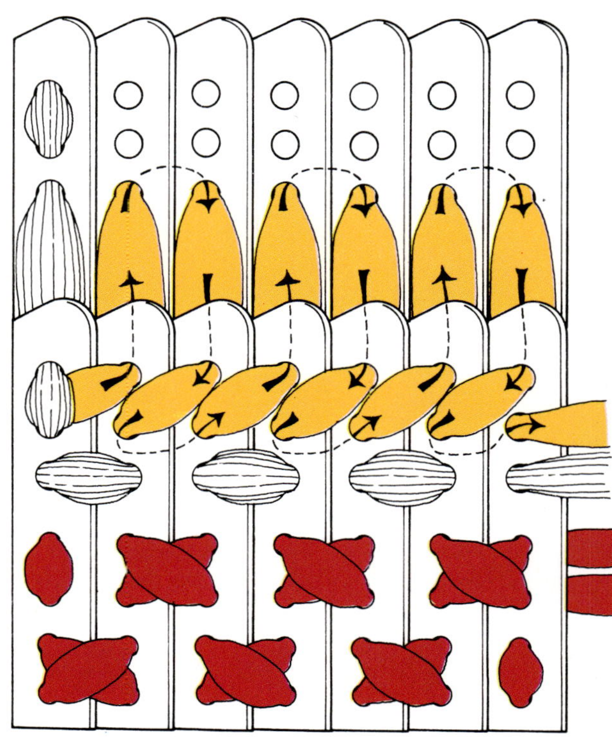

the scales into rows, remained visible on the lowest row of each section and, to make it more decorative, it was laced as a series of cross knots, *hishinui* (lozenge sewing), and picked out in red lacquer. Because of this, the lowest row of scales on a piece of scale armour with this knotting visible is called the *hishinui no ita.*

Once the rows of scales had been prepared, they were fastened to each other vertically by the lacing, called *odoshi ge*. During the early Heian period the odoshi ge was frequently of leather, either plain or dyed with a simple repeat pattern of flowers or geometric ornament. It is the colour, material and pattern of this lacing, together with the style of do, that the Japanese use to describe an armour.

While leather was never totally abandoned as a lacing material, it was only available in a limited range of colours and in relatively short lengths, which made the process of lacing an armour difficult. As a consequence it was soon superseded by a flat silk braid, produced in lengths of about 10 feet (3m). The number of strands of silk dictated the width. These braids were prepared on a special loom or frame in which the worker knelt. The predyed threads, wound on lead-filled bobbins to regulate the tension, were passed over and under pairs of other threads to produce a characteristically ribbed braid. Occasionally an alternative material, made by wrapping strips of twill silk cloth around a tough fabric core, was used in such a way that the overlap was concealed underneath; the same strategy was occasionally employed later, using cheaper fabrics, for munitions armours.

A wide range of colours were used for lacing. By far the most common colour chosen in later periods was dark blue, because the

Above: The top plate, kanmuri ita, of this Momoyama period shoulder guard is covered with shoehei gawa – printed leather decorated with the date 1352.

O yoroi

indigo dye used acted as an ultraviolet filter and protected the silk from damage by light. Many of the other colours, particularly the reds (dyed with madder), and the purple (dyed with soya), had just the opposite effect tendering the silk and accelerating its decomposition. For this reason it is uncommon to find armours laced in these colours that have survived with their lacing intact.

Multi-coloured combinations that were not of one of the recognized standard patterns were called *iro iro odoshi* (varied colour lacing); those that used shades of one colour fading to white at the bottom are called *nioi* and if reversed, with white at the top, *susogoi*.

There seems to be no evidence that the colours chosen for an armour represented any family or clan allegiance. An examination of contemporary illustrations of battles shows similar colours being worn by both sides, with apparently a preponderance of red. This might be a product of artistic licence, making for a more striking picture, but it could equally be that red was actually more popular, being considered a martial colour.

The process of lacing began by fixing the completed rows of scales in their correct relative positions by a single lace that supposedly ran continuously down either side of each section and along the lowest of the top group of holes of the hishinui no ita. An examination of surviving armours shows that it was in fact much more common to use three separate pieces. Because of its importance, this *mimi ito* (border thread) was thicker and stronger than the other lacing and usually of a contrasting colour and pattern. During the Heian period the border thread was white silk decorated with dark-blue chevrons, to which was added later a light blue, forming a pattern known as *takanoha uchi* (hawk's feather). By the Kamakura and Muromachi periods, braids patterned in combinations of white, purple and green, or white, red and green became more popular, the former gaining the addition of dark blue to become the familiar *takuboku uchi* (woodpecker braid) found on most later armours. Some experts maintain that the introduction of the light-green colour did not occur until the Edo period, and that its occurrence on earlier armours is the result of relacing at a later date.

Once the rows of scales were secured in position, the piece was suspended from a stand by a swivel so that it could be turned this way and that, as the remainder of the lacing was put in, always from left to right along each row. Pictures of armourers at work show them using a pair of flat-nosed tongs for the purpose while the ends of the braid were drawn out into a long taper, stiffened by glue, to assist in threading. Some armours from later periods have the braid locked into the holes by small tapering plugs of what appears to be chewed up paper, inserted from the front, but pushed under the lacing so as not to be seen. On the tapered parts of the armour extra lengths of braid were worked in from the widest row, being distributed along it as symmetrically as possible. Sections of the armour which needed to be rigid, such as the do and occasionally the upper rows of the shikoro, had extra leather thongs concealed under the lacing to lock the rows together and prevent them from collapsing into each other.

At the top of the breast, back and shoulder guards, the scales were fastened to metal plates recessed to take them and the joint was covered by a strip of wood, appropriately called *kesho no ita* (cosmetic plate), covered with decorated leather. The whole assembly – plate, scales and strip – was fastened together by gilt rivets, with split copper shanks bent over on the inside. Trapped below this strip and giving a neat finish to its lower edge was a double piping of red and white twill.

Decorative leathers were used extensively, both to cover solid plates of iron, held in

Below: Fabric sock, tabi, dyed in imitation of tsumatagata gawa, one of the many patterned leathers used in the decoration and construction of armour. The big toe is divided to accommodate the thongs of the sandals.

place by *fukurin* (copper gilt edgings), and elsewhere on the armour. All were of a soft, pale suede, either dyed, smoked, or stencilled with patterns. The two former types tended to be used for linings or edgings subject to rubbing; red or blue were the favourite colours if dyed, various yellows and browns if smoked. The smoked leathers could be patterned by pasting paper cut-outs onto the leather before it was smoked to produce a white design on the yellow ground when the paper was removed. For the more pictorial stencilled varieties, the dye was either padded directly onto the leather through a stencil, or a resist was applied to the leather; this left the design in white on a coloured background after dyeing.

During the Heian and early Kamakura periods, the design most often used took the form of Chinese lions arranged into circular medallions, dyed in blue, set in a red diagonal grid of stylized foliage. Later patterns have lions gambolling among rather indifferently drawn foliage in blue or shades of brown with the occasional flower in red, which despite the name 'lion cherry blossom leather' are really meant to represent peonies. Later still, leathers became more pictorial and exhibit a wider range of subjects, including dragons and figures from Buddhist iconography, with the design arranged to fill the space they were to occupy on the armour. Many of these leathers continued in use, becoming progressively more stereotyped into a few basic patterns on the lion-cherry-blossom theme, drawn to a smaller scale more suited to the areas they covered on later armours. One very important pattern deserves mention since it incorporates the date Shohei sixth year (1352), which has led to some confusion. This date was the year in which the pattern was licensed for production, and has nothing to do with when the armour was manufactured; in fact it continued to be made until the end of the Edo period.

The remaining stencilled patterns were more linear, being designed to border the pictorial leathers, and the two were separated by a multicoloured silk piping set into the seam between them. The favourite in the Heian period was red with small groups of white dots at intervals, but on later armours an iris flower growing from the middle of a group of four or six leaves in white on blue became more common. At first these were naturally depicted but gradually they became more stylized, until eventually the pattern became debased and almost unrecognizable.

Left: An Edo period eboshi (tall cap). A similar cap was worn in lieu of a helmet lining in the Heian and Kamakura periods.

Heian samurai wore armour designed specifically for their role as mounted archers and many of its features were dictated by this requirement. Called *o yoroi* (great armour), after the large size of its components, it was to be the only armour considered suitable for the nobility for centuries.

Hachi (helmet bowls) were now almost hemispherical but still retained a slight conical tendency that was to persist for a further hundred years or so. Most were made from overlapping vertical plates, usually eight in number, riveted together along the rear edges by five or six large dome-headed rivets. Because of their often exaggerated size, the heads of these rivets (called *o boshi*, large stars) were made hollow to reduce their weight, giving rise to the alternate name of *kara boshi* (empty stars). One of the terms used for these helmet bowls is *arare boshi bachi*, alluding to the resemblance of the rivets to hail stones. A few helmets which have survived from the Heian period are raised from a single plate, overlaid with strips and fitted with large rivets as reinforcements. Called *ichi mai fuse bachi*, these are the only examples which show that armourers could beat a helmet bowl from a single piece of metal before the middle of the Edo period.

Right: O boshi bachi, a helmet bowl with large standing rivets. Heian period. Note that the rivets are positioned along the edge of the plates where they overlap.

A deep *koshimaki* (plate forming the bottom edge of the helmet bowl) was riveted around the base of the helmet bowl, and at the apex, was a large hole, the *tehen*. The wearer pulled the top of the tall soft hat, worn in lieu of a helmet lining, through the tehen. At first the tehen was rimmed by a shaped iron plate *aoiba za* but later it was also fitted with a *tehen kanamono* (ornate gilt rim). Because the rivets were positioned along the edges of each plate, the large front plate appeared rather bare and was decorated with either a central row of rivets, or by one or more applied iron strips (*shinodare*), emerging from under the aoiba za, and terminating in fleur-de-lis-shaped ends. Positioned on the back plate, which was devoid of rivets, was a gilt ring, *kasa jirushi no kan* (hat-flag ring), from which was hung a silk bow. Originally this ring was added in place of a rivet bordering the back plate, but was soon moved to the central position. As the name suggests, its purpose was to carry a small flag of identification, but it is rarely depicted being worn. Like many details on Japanese armour, the Kasa jirushi no kan was retained for its decorative qualities long after the original use had been lost.

Right: Black lacquered happuri, plate defence for forehead and cheeks, with standing flanges on the cheeks.

A small peak (*mabisashi*) was attached by gilt copper rivets to the front of the koshimaki, hiding the join. It was convex in section and covered with patterned leather held in position by a *fukurin* (decorative rim). To avoid impeding the release of the bowstring, the peak was almost vertical. There were two or, more often, four, holes in the bowl, *hibiki no ana*, through which were knotted leather thongs that provided attachment points for the silk helmet cord which tied under and around the chin. Again, these holes were retained as decoration until the nineteenth century, long after their original function had been lost. Even after protruding rivets were abandoned, four, the *shiten no byo*, were still fitted to prevent a sword from sliding down the bowl and cutting what were, by then, non-existent leather thongs.

The koshimaki also carried a *shikoro* (neck guard) of five rows of tapered scales, giving it a deep conical shape. It reached almost to the shoulders. It was attached by pairs of gilt metal rivets with split shanks, reputedly so that it would tear free if grasped by an opponent; pairs of rivets were used so that in an emergency it could be reattached by a cord. The four upper rows of scales were extended and then bent sharply outwards at right angles, forming the *fukigaeshi*, the distinctive feature found on nearly all Japanese helmets. Its primary purpose was to protect the face from arrows shot at short range after charging the enemy. As soon as the charge was over and the arrow loosed, the samurai wheeled the horse to the right, turning his head in the same direction and bringing the fukigaeshi between his face and the enemy. Because the overlap of the rows was reversed in the fukigaeshi, it also prevented a sword cutting through the lacing between the lames of the shikoro and striking the shoulders. Like the peak, the fukigaeshi were covered with leather, in this case to hide the underside of the scales, and usually had a copper gilt *fukigaeshi no suemon* (chrysanthemum ornament) in the upper outer corner, a decoration that was also applied to the peak and other parts of the armour.

Many samurai are shown in contemporary illustrations wearing an additional defence, the *happuri* (face guard), tied around the brow under the helmet and covering the hel-

Left: Restored and relaced Heian period o yoroi. This type of armour wrapped around the body and had a separate defence for the right side.

met cords. These face guards took the form of a lacquered or leather-covered plate covering the forehead with extensions at either side covering the cheeks. Some had flanges (*yadome*) riveted at right angles to the cheek pieces to act as arrow stops.

Armour for the trunk consisted of four rows of scales called the *nakagawa*, which encircled the whole of the front, left side, and back but leaving a considerable gap under the right arm. Two additional sections made from shorter rows of scales, the *tateage*, covered the upper part of the chest and back. That at the front reached onto the chest and was topped by a solid leather-covered plate, the *muna ita*; the upper edge was shaped at the ends to meet the shoulder straps. The rear tateage terminated in a plate shaped to the back of the neck, the *oshitsuke ita*, from which extended the heavily padded plate shoulder straps (*watagami*). Riveted to the upper surfaces of the watagami were semicircular vertical plates, (*shoji no ita*), which prevented the upper edge of the shoulder guards striking the neck or face during violent action, and protected against circling cuts.

To enable the watagami to be thrown back when putting on the do, the *saka ita* (the middle row of scales in the rear tateage) was laced in reverse and provided with a gilt copper ring from which hung a large heavy silk bow, tied in a special knot. This bow had the double purpose of holding the saka ita down against the pull of the lacing, as well as providing an attachment point for the shoulder guards. Like all do, the o yoroi was fastened to the body by toggles; in this period these kohaze hung on cords attached to the watagami and buttoned into loops anchored to the tateage. These loops were closed by seme

Right: Pictures from a series showing a samurai tightening the draw-strings of the yoroi hitatare and tying on the waidate.

kohaze sliding on them, which locked the loop over the toggles after they had been fastened. This arrangement is the reverse of that found on later armours, where the toggles are always fitted to the muna ita. These fastenings between the watagami and the front of the do were collectively called *takahimo*. Under the left arm, where there was no metal plate, the tops of the scales were wrapped with leather to prevent them snagging on the clothing. The whole front of the do was covered with a large sheet of decorated leather to prevent the bowstring catching on the heads of the scales as it was loosed.

Two small pieces of armour were hung from the ends of the watagami to guard the takahimo and also to some extent the armpits. That on the right, the sword arm, had to be flexible, and consisted of three short rows of scales and a cap plate, and was called the *sendan no ita*. That for the bow arm was a single rigid plate called the *kyubi no ita*. A distinguishing feature of Heian armour is the gentle, lobed shape given to the tops of these plates.

The *waidate* was a secondary defence which filled the gap on the right. It was put on before the do and was tied to the right side of the body by silk cords, one passing over the shoulder the other around the waist. Its upper part was a single leather-covered iron plate which curved with the body and was hollowed at the top for the arm.

Hanging from the lower edge of both the do and the waidate were four *kusazuri*, trapezoidal sections of scales, which covered the lower body and thighs. Those sections at the front and back were attached to the do by lacing, while those at the sides were attached by a band of leather to prevent chafing by the quiver and sword worn at these points. As a slight concession to walking, the lowest row of scales at the front and back were occasionally divided into two sections.

In place of the collar with its attached arm guards that had been worn in the earlier periods, the arms and shoulders were now defended by large, flat rectangular sections of scales called *o sode* (large sleeve). There is some evidence that the warriors during the Yamato period had used shields, but these had to be discarded once mounted archery became the conventional method of fighting. To some extent, sode acted in a similar way to shields; they slid off the arms when they were raised to shoot and hung behind the shoulders, coming into play, like the fuki-gaeshi, as the horse was wheeled round.

The o sode were made of six or seven rows of scales, fastened at the top to a longitudinally curved solid plate, the *kanmuri no ita*. To properly fulfill their role they were fastened by a complex system of cords in such a way that they remained in position yet allowed the arms sufficient freedom of movement for drawing the bow or using the sword. Tied to rings on the ends of the kanmuri no ita were two doubled silk cords with tasseled ends, and a further ring in the middle carried a tie of soft leather. A fourth ring was positioned under the rear edge of the sode, on the third row from the top, to which was tied a single cord. Starting at the top front, the first silk cord and the leather tie were knotted to loops of cord or sewn leather (*gumi wa*) threaded through an elongated metal bead, provided for the purpose on top of the watagami at front and back. The rear cord was tied to the loops of the silk bow on the back of the do. The final cord was tied to the neck of the silk bow, where it hung from its ring. Irrespective of the colour of the armour's lacing, these cords and bows, including that on the helmet, were invariably vermilion; the effect was to create a splendidly coloured detail which matched the lacquered cross knots on the hishinui no ita.

Underneath this polychrome carapace the samurai wore a *yoroi hitatare*, a costume derived from court dress, over a simple kimono and under trousers of white silk. Made of silk brocade, the yoroi hitatare comprised a jacket with voluminous sleeves which had a draw string at the wrist, and a pair of baggy trousers ending just below the knee where another draw string enabled them to be gathered and tucked into the tops of tall, stiff fur boots. The wrist draw strings were tightened, wrapped around the wrists and tied, leaving long loops which were passed over the middle fingers to prevent the sleeves riding up the arms.

No defence was provided for the shins or lower arms until late in the twelfth century, when tubular plate shinguards and an armoured sleeve for the bow arm with an extension over the back of the hand, made their appearance. The inclusion of these new pieces of armour necessitated changes to the way in which the yoroi hitatare was worn. The left sleeve was too voluminous to fit under the armoured sleeve, so it was left to hang down the back, under the armour. Cloth leggings were tied around the shins to prevent the shinguards rubbing, while the boots were replaced by fur-covered shoes called *kutsu*.

Because of their lowly rank, the noble's retainers wore a simpler form of armour, more suited to their role, called a *haramaki* (belly wrap). It was made from three or four rows of scales forming a nakagawa, in this case extended sufficiently to overlap, always with the back over the front, under the right

Left: Trousers from a yoroi hitatare of golden brown brocade. The yoroi hitatare resembles court costume and was worn under armour by nobles of the day.

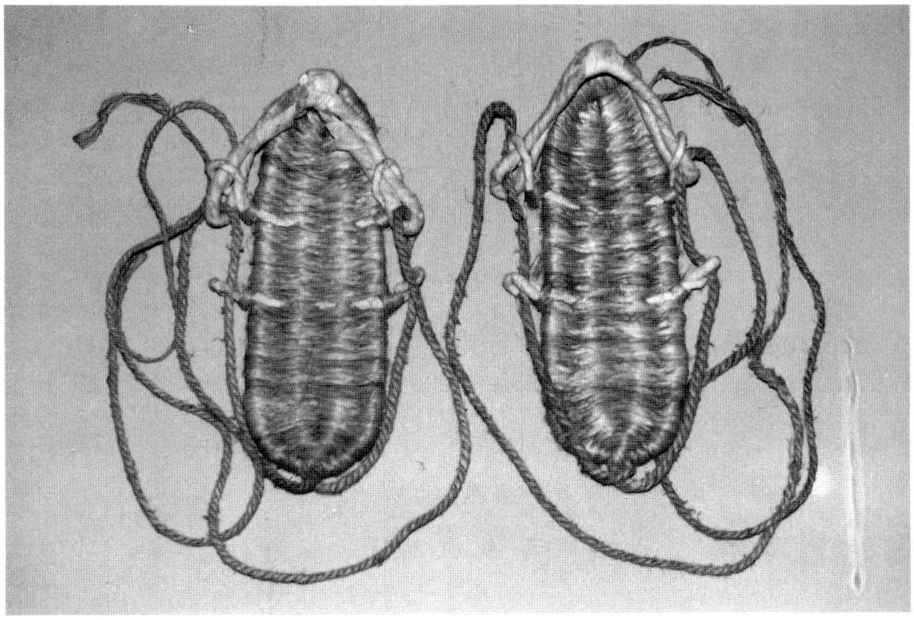

Below: Sandals of rice straw, waraji. This type of footwear, initially worn only by retainers, was adopted by all samurai as fighting on foot became more common. Being disposable, distances were measured in the number of pairs worn out by a journey.

Right: Leather laced haramaki with large shoulder guards. The lacing was originally purple. Heian period.

Far right: Armed samurai wearing an o yoroi. The whole of his equipment was designed with mounted archery in mind.

Below: Brocade kaihan (leggings) were worn under the shin guards.

arm, so obviating the need for a waidate. Tateage were fitted at the front and back with a muna ita, oshitsuke ita and watagami as before, attached by simple braid cross knots to the upper row of scales. Kesho no ita, being too ornamental for retainers, were never fitted. In this instance these knots are properly called *hishi toji* rather than hishi nui, which applies only to those cross knots on the hishinui no ita. Unlike the o yoroi, the takahimo fastenings of a haramaki were attached to the muna ita, usually emerging from the outside, but on one surviving example fitted on the inside so that the cords were less vulnerable. Because a retainer spent much of his time

十ハノ弓

弦ヲ下ヘナシニキリヨリ
上五寸計ノホドヲトリテ
提テ持ヘシ軍陣ニハ丸木
弓本式也雨露
ナドノシメリ
ヲイトウ
叓ナシ

Above: Detail from the Heiji Monogatari Emaki.

Below: Heian period blade fora tachi (slung sword), remounted during the Edo period.

Bottom: Chinese style tachi of the Heian period.

walking or running besides his master's horse, the kusazuri were divided into seven or eight sections to give greater freedom of movement to the legs.

No sode were provided, their place being taken by large *gyoyo* (leaf-shaped plates), which were attached to the watagami by cords so that they hung on the points of the shoulders, giving some protection to upper arms. At least one hinged pair has survived; this reduced the tendency for them to become displaced as the arms were raised. Haramaki were undecorated apart from the decorated leather covering these plates, and the occasional chrysanthemum ornament.

Contemporary illustrations often show retainers without helmets. Instead they wore either a happuri or a simple folded cap of lacquered gauze. Judging by these pictures, retainers wore little under their armour other than a shirt-like garment, with the skirts tucked up into the belt. Many were bare footed, although a few are shown wearing

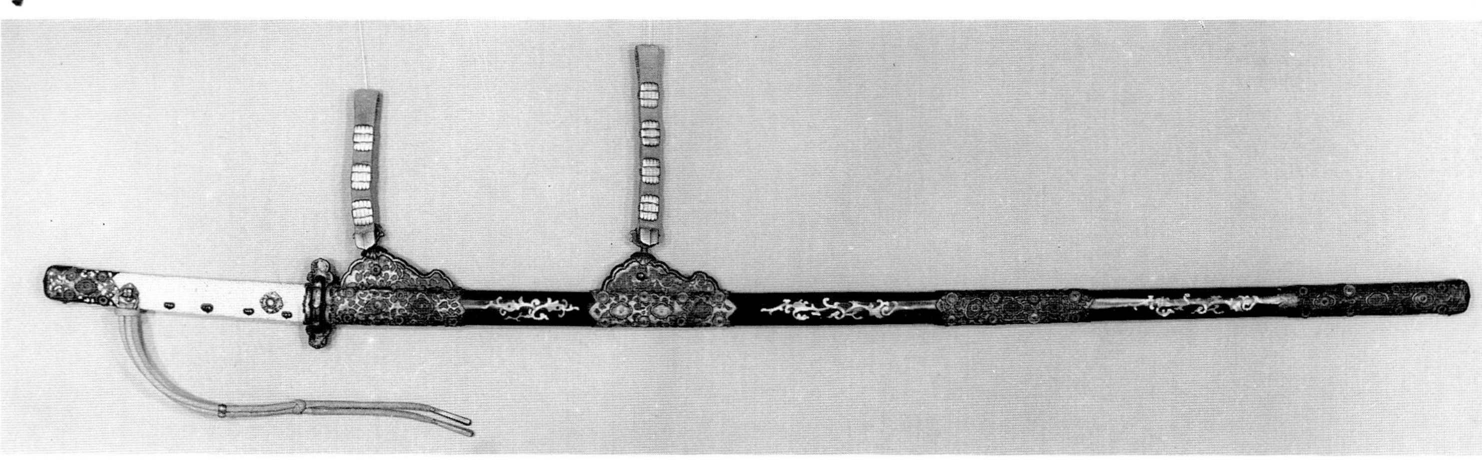

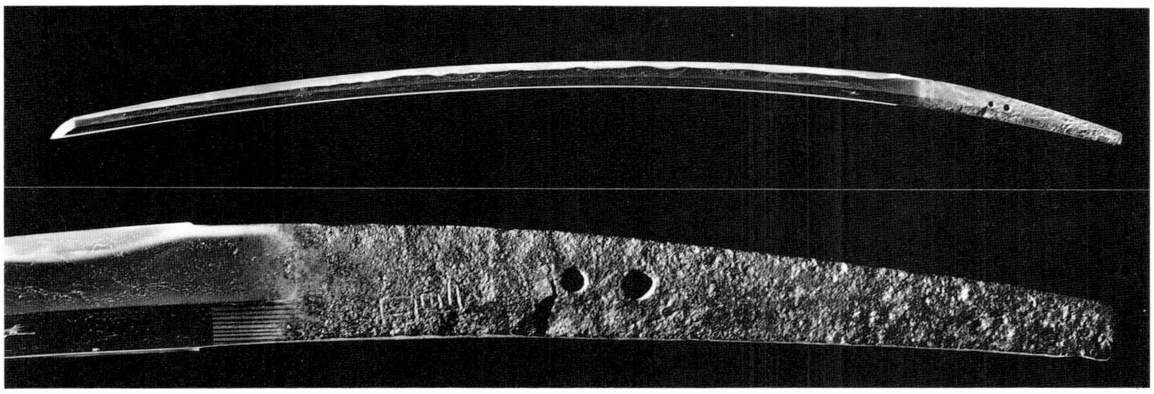

Left: Blade for a long sword in the Yamashiro style by Rai Kuninaga, circa *1330. In this period all long sword blades were made as tachi.*

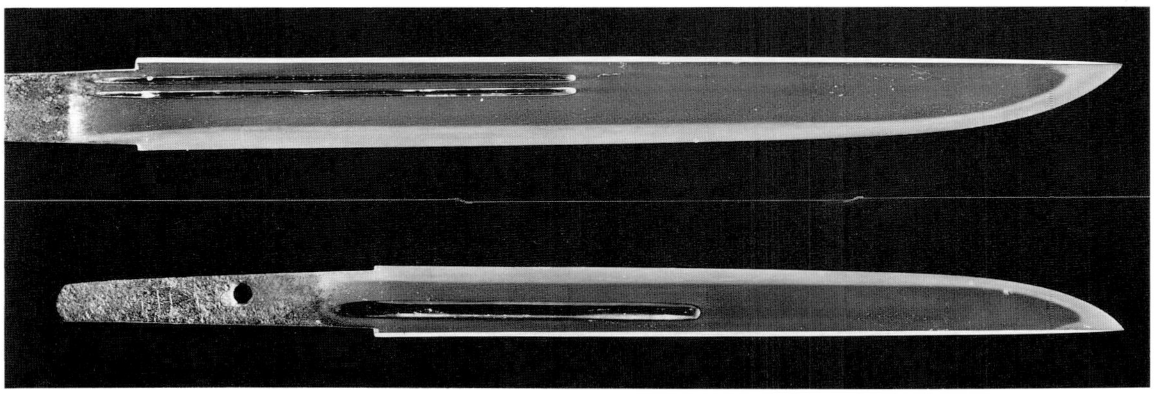

Left: Dirk blade in the Yamashiro style. Signature undecipherable. Most samurai wore a dirk at all times but in war it was only used when unhorsed.

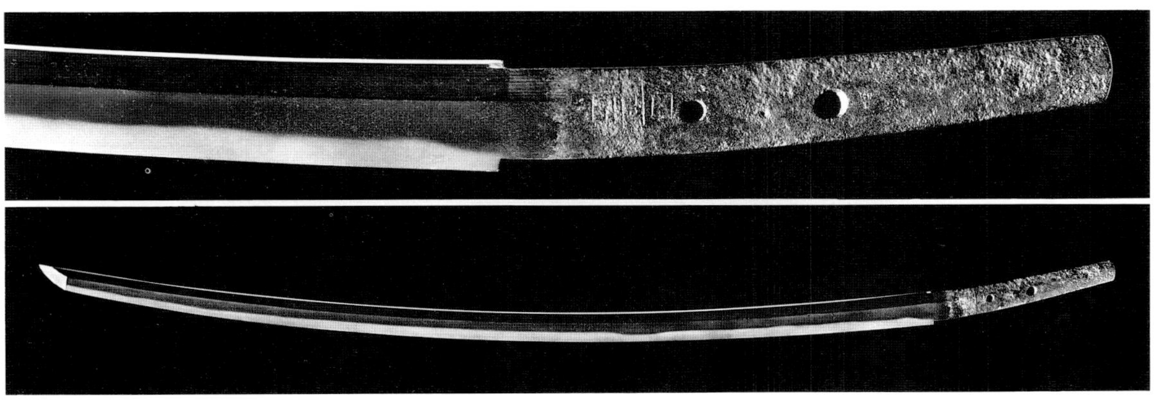

Left: Blade for a long sword in the Yamato style by Kuniyoshi of the Yamato Senjuin group, circa *1300. During the Heian period the long sword was a secondary weapon, used after an initial exchange of arrows.*

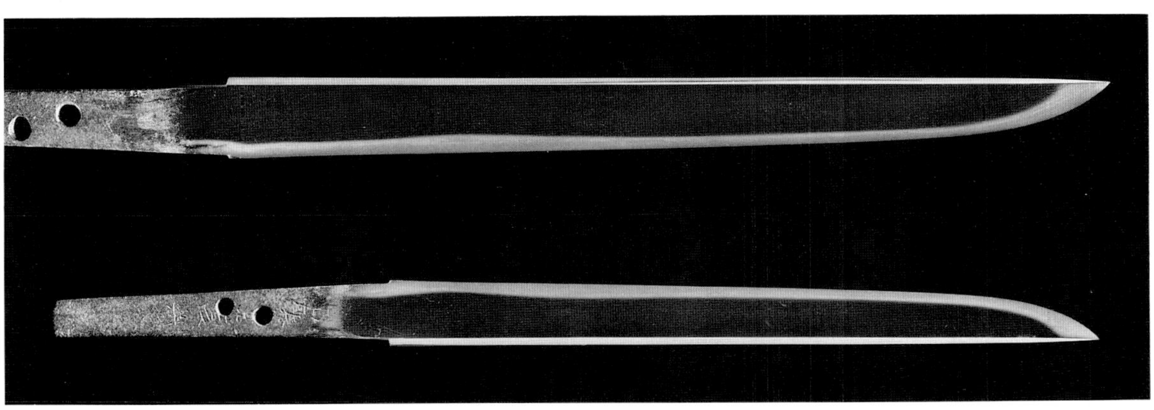

Left: Yamato-style dirk blade signed by Hosho Sadaoki, circa *1360.*

straw sandals. Their equipment was improved, like that of the nobles, when the latter adopted the armoured sleeve, *kote*, for the bow arm. It was not long before a similar though more utilitarian pair of sleeves was introduced for use with the haramaki.

Both nobles and their retainers wore long swords, slung at the left hip edge downwards. These were called *bu tachi* (military sword) to differentiate them from the varieties worn at court. Those worn by the nobles were mounted in gold, silver or copper, as befitted their station. Some had the hilt and scabbard coated with plain black lacquer, *kuro zukuri no tachi*; some were bound spirally with a strip of leather under the lacquer which gave them their name of *hiru maki no tachi* (leech-wrapped tachi) while others were decorated by lacquered designs or by mother of pearl inlay. Those carried by the retainers, *no dachi* (field swords), were serviceable but simply mounted, with plain black scabbards. Both types were fitted with hilts that could be held in two hands, but those used by the nobles from horseback had necessarily to be fitted with lighter blades since only one hand was free to wield them. All nobles and many retainers also carried small dirks with short, flat-sided blades, called *katana*, thrust through the *obi* (sash) on the left front of the body. Nobles used these dirks when they were unhorsed and had to grapple with an opponent. Contemporary illustrations also show a ring-shaped object fastened to the sash alongside the tachi. These were reels of basketwork or leather on which additional bowstrings were carried.

During the Heian period, blade shape and construction reached a state that was so near to perfection that later swordsmiths found it inadvisable to deviate from it. Sword production was mostly concentrated around the home province of Yamato and neighbouring Yamashiro, giving rise to the earliest of the five great traditions of sword making, *go kaden*, in the old sword or koto period. Their blades are characterized by having a very small point section and a gentle, shallow curve, which on early examples became more pronounced near the tang, giving the mounted sword a distinctive upswept hilt. Both areas produced blades that were slim and elegant, as befits the feelings of the age; this is particularly evident in those from Yamashiro.

The following description of the monk Tsutsui no Jomio Meishu in action, from the *Tales of Heike*, gives some idea of the tech-

Below: Screen painting depicting the Taira forces before the Battle of Dan no Ura. This battle saw the Taira totally defeated and virtually annihilated by the Minamoto.

Above: Scene from the Yashima Nana *scroll showing Minamoto Yoshitsune (third from left) in a helmet with kuwagata, with retainers and his companion Benkei (fourth from left, mounted) carrying an assortment of improbable weapons.*

niques for using the long sword at this period:

With his naginata he killed five, but with the sixth it snapped assunder in the midst and, flinging it away, he drew his sword, wielding it in the zigzag style, the interlacing, cross, reversed dragonfly, waterwheel, and eight-sides-at-once styles of fencing and cutting down eight men; but as he brought down the ninth with a mighty blow on the helmet, the blade snapped at the hilt. . .

We have no idea what these styles were but their names seem indicative of sweeping, circular cuts designed to hit with maximum force. Surviving Heian blades are so delicate that it is not surprising that Meishu's broke. An alternative technique practised from horseback was for the sword to be tucked into the crook of the elbow and braced rigid against the body, using the speed and momentum of the charge to deal a slashing cut to the opponent.

A variety of pole arms was carried by both the nobles and their retainers. Paramount among them was the naginata, which by the Heian period had acquired a long blade, widening and curving into a hooked shape at the top. This was fitted into a short shaft some four or five feet (1.2 or 1.5m) long, bound at the top with metal and fitted with a shoe of iron to protect the lower end. The te boko (spear) of the Nara period survived as a straight, ridged blade, about one foot (0.3m) in length, on a short shaft that could only have been used at close quarters for either stabbing or making short chopping cuts.

Kiyomori's attempts to gain power by wooing the court were doomed from the start because the real power now lay in the hands of the warriors scattered all over the country. As soon as they were old enough, the Minamoto, who had been exiled as children, rallied support, particularly in the Eastern plains of the Kanto. Lead by Minamoto Yoritomo, they struck at the Taira in 1180 and launched the country into a war which raged across the whole country and which even Kiyomori's death in 1181 failed to halt. By 1183, the Taira were demoralized and on the defensive as the Minamoto threatened the capital itself. In an attempt to regroup, the Taira snatched the child-Emperor Antoku, and headed to their homelands in the west. However, they failed to move the ex-Emperor, Go-Shirakawa, who was still exercising power from retirement. Encouraged by Go-Shirakawa, the Minamoto set off in pursuit, gaining even more strength as pre-

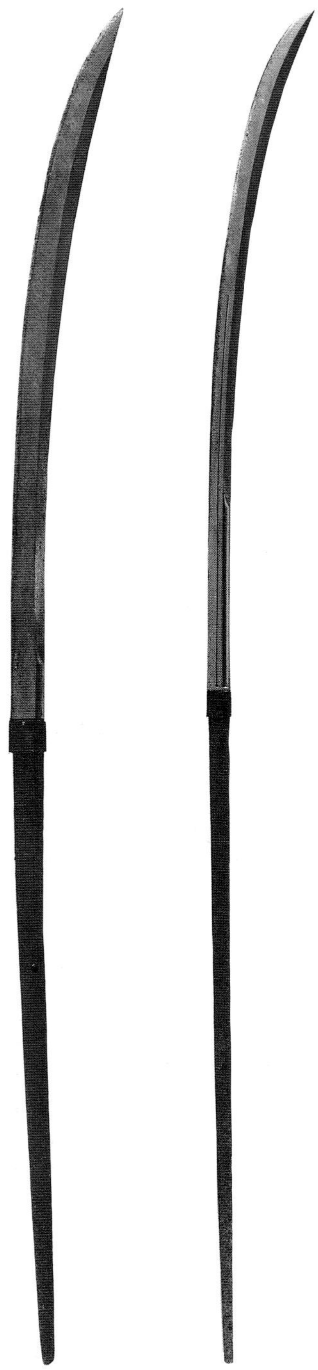

Above: Large naginata (pole arm) blades. The Kamakura period blade (right) reputedly belonged to Benkei; the other dates to the Nambokucho period.

Above right: Nineteenth century print by Kunisada shows Minamoto Yoshitsune being taught swordsmanship by tengu, *mythical birdlike creatures.*

Far right: Camp curtain (jin baku) after which Yoritomo's military council was named. This example bears the mon of the Honda family.

viously uncommitted groups joined what had now become a royal cause.

This terrible episode ended in a battle fought not on horseback, but in ungainly coastal boats opposite the shore of Dan-no-Ura, at the mouth of the Inland Sea. Not only were the Emperor and his retinue drowned, but also the Taira clan was effectively wiped out in the ensuing massacre. Those who did survive committed suicide.

Unlike Kiyomori, Minamoto Yoritomo saw in the courage and loyalty of the samurai an alternative basis for government – what would now be called a military dictatorship. He was still threatened by rival factions, including one led by his brother Yoshitsune, whom he rigorously and ruthlessly disposed of. Yoritomo extracted permission from Go-Shirakawa to appoint stewards and constables in the provinces and took for himself the title, which had existed for centuries but had become an anachronism, of Seii Taishogun (normally shortened to Shogun and meaning Barbarian suppressing Commander in Chief). Avoiding the capital with its temptations and soft life, he set up residence in the eastern town of Kamakura and established an administrative council, the *bakufu*, to deal with military matters. Since the military held all real authority, he effectively transferred

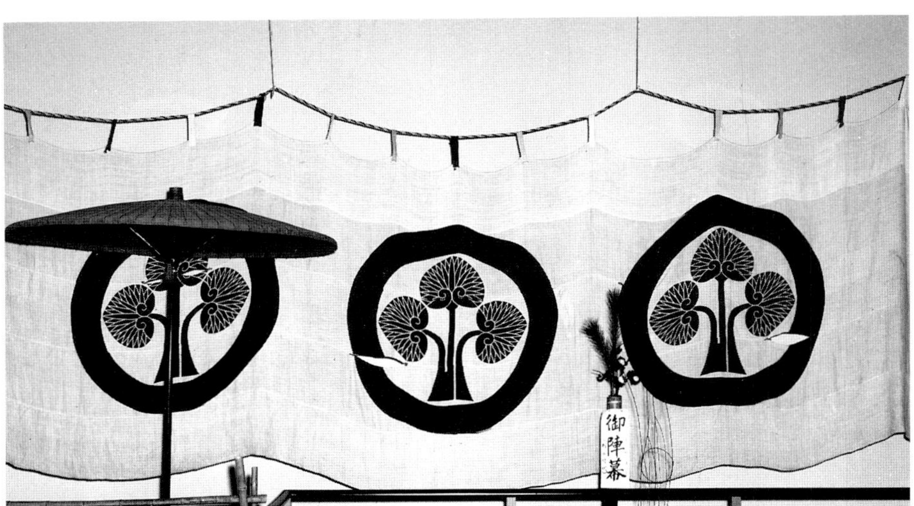

the seat of power while leaving the bureaucracy of the capital in existence but almost completely impotent.

Despite his efforts at eliminating potential rivals, Yoritomo's death in 1199 saw the title pass in succession to his sons who, by comparison with their father, were weak and unsuited to the task. Masa-ko, Yoritomo's widow, prevented further power struggles erupting by gaining control of the Shogun for her own family, the Hojo. Throughout, this period of strife, this family never took the title Shogun for itself, being content to control the country as regents through another series of puppets.

CHAPTER THREE
The Kamakura and Nambokucho Periods

Far right: Painting on a door in Nishi Hongan-ji, Kyoto, of a samurai wearing a horo. This cape-like accessory was thought to have been worn for the awe-inspiring effect it produced as it billowed out behind the wearer.

For the whole of the Kamakura period the country was governed through a tortuous chain of command. In theory, all power came from the Emperor, but in practice he was controlled by at least one retired Emperor, and occasionally two. He in turn delegated control to a Shogun who in his turn was nothing more than a puppet of the Hojo regents. Despite this bureaucratic maze, the country was relatively prosperous. The occasional conspiracy or uprising had little effect other than to transfer, by confiscation, land to the regency, who steadily gained power and influence by giving it to supporters.

Things were not as calm, however, in the remainder of Asia as Genghis Khan and his Golden Hordes moved outwards from their homelands and not only conquered China, but most of Asia and Eastern Europe as well. There is a theory, as yet unproven and unaccepted by Western scholars, that the Khan was none other than Minamoto Yoshitsune, who had managed to escape his brother's depredations by fleeing to the Chinese mainland; certainly the name Genghis when written in Chinese uses the same character. True or not, by 1268 Genghis's grandson Kublai Khan, turned his attention to Japan, which he felt ought to be a vassal, and dispatched envoys to convey veiled threats to this effect. Confident of their position, the Hojo ignored the warning and sent the ambassadors back unanswered, with the not unexpected result of provoking the Khan, who was unaccustomed to such slights, into taking action.

A great fleet of boats, constructed and manned by Koreans and carrying an invasion force of 15,000 men was launched late in

Right: Mounted archer of the Kamakura period wearing an o yoroi decorated with peonies.

1274. The small islands of Iki and Tsushima were taken and the force finally landed at Imazu in Hakata bay, Kyushu. Disembarkation began before the main Japanese force had reached the area, and the few local samurai available had little chance. The Mongols were veteran warriors who fought in closely packed and disciplined ranks, manoeuvering to the sound of drum beats. The traditional ritual challenges made by the samurai before battle were wasted on this enemy. Those foolish enough to charge were hacked to pieces as the Mongol ranks opened and swallowed them. Realizing that there was little they could do, the Japanese withdrew behind nearby ancient earthworks to await the arrival of the main army. They had, however, shown the Mongol leaders that the tactic, effective in previous campaigns, of creating total panic in an enemy force was lost on the samurai. The Mongols did, however, introduce two unfamiliar weapons: crossbows, whose bolts easily outranged the arrows of the Japanese; and explosive shells, which were hurled into the enemies' ranks by catapult. These latter seem to have been an idea suggested by Marco Polo, who was staying at the Khan's court. Far from being the terror weapons the Mongols hoped, explosive shells appear to have caused more alarm among the horses than the Japanese, who made careful drawings of them in the pictorial scrolls depicting their exploits for posterity.

Since the day was nearly over, and fearing night attacks as well as being apprehensive about the weather, the Mongols decided to re-embark, burning and looting as they made their way back to their ships. Their fears were well founded, for that night a storm blew up which, despite the shelter of Hakata Bay, wrenched ships from their moorings and swept them onto the coast, effectively destroying the armada and drowning the greater part of the force. Only a few scattered remnants of the huge army remained to be dealt with the following day and only two are said to have survived to report the outcome to Kublai Khan.

A second invasion was launched five years later, this time with 150,000 men in two contingents; one from Korea and one sailing rather later from China. Once again, Tsushima and Iki were attacked first before the Mongols once again landed at Hataka Bay in late June. This time the Japanese were ready and a long defensive wall had been erected, manned from one end to the other by armies from all over Japan. The Mongols' repeated attempts to secure an adequate bridgehead were repulsed, while other samurai in boats fired or boarded the transports by day and night. With the ships rotting under them and disease rife on board, the Korean force withdrew to await the arrival of the Chinese fleet. By August the great armada was assembled and advancing towards Japan while the Emperor and priests of both Buddhist and

Below: Nineteenth century woodblock print showing pole arms in use during the Gempei wars. The artist has included long-bladed spears, which in fact belong to a later age.

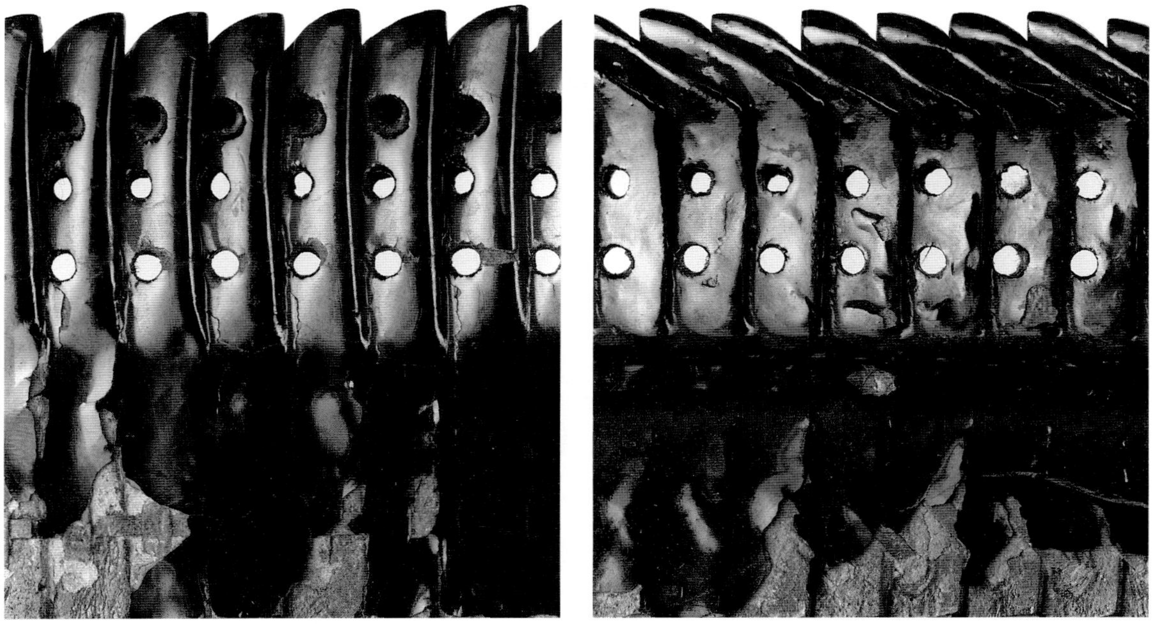

Left: Front (left) and rear of a row of kozane froman Edo period armour. From the Kamakura period the scales were assembled into rows before lacquering, the upper part of each scale being built up with lacquer in front to give a ribbed appearance to the completed row.

Shinto faiths prayed for deliverance. Once again the weather came to their aid; a sudden typhoon of tremendous fury arose and swamped, upturned and smashed the unwieldy transports, causing enormous loss of life. The *kami kaze* (divine wind) subsided as quickly as it had begun, leaving only a fraction of the great armada to limp slowly back to China.

In these brief but telling encounters, the Japanese had their first opportunity to test their equipment and military skills against those of a foreign enemy. It was immediately obvious that the samurai's code of conduct and futile charges were suicidal against an opponent who ignored the rules and shot the horses from under him. His armour, while effective against the arrows and swords of the Mongols provided the wearer was mounted, proved ill-suited to fighting on foot; most of its considerable weight was taken by the shoulders while the kusazuri imposed severe restrictions on walking. Swords, and in particular the points, were said to have broken and chipped against Mongol armour, which contemporary illustrations and descriptions reveal to have been long, skirted coats made from hide and heavy fabric sewn together, worn with iron helmets fitted with leather hoods. Why this should have been a problem when for centuries swordsmen had apparently been cutting through Japanese armour to great effect is a mystery – in all probability they did cut the Mongol armour but became trapped by the layers of thick leather and, being rather delicate, broke as they were wrenched free.

As a consequence of the experience gained during these attempted invasions, dependence on mounted archery went into decline and gradually the horse was relegated to a transport role. Archery became less important, but was never abandoned. The sword and, more especially, the naginata, which had been primarily a retainer's weapon, was taken up by the nobles. A few naginata blades have survived from the Kamakura period. Ranging from some two feet to four feet (0.6 to 2m) in length, they were originally mounted on shafts about four to five feet (1.2 to 1.5m) long. If the *Taiheiki E maki*, a picture scroll of the period, is to be believed, some o naginata had blades six feet (1.8m) long, mounted on proportionately shorter shafts. Like most later blades, these naginata were cut with a complex of short grooves near to the tang, above which the back edge was thinned, but not sharpened, so that the greater part of the blade was a flattened-diamond shape in section. Seen in profile, the curve is slight or non-existent near the tang, becoming more pronounced towards the point. The increase in width near the point gave the blade a rather swollen appearance. As with the majority of Japanese pole arms, the naginata was provided with a tang as long or longer than the blade itself, which fitted into a carefully cut recess in the shaft – a method of attachment that had the advantage of reinforcing the region of greatest stress. Illustrations show that the shaft was oval in section, and retained the metal reinforcement at the top and protective shoe at the bottom as it had in the Heian period. Most appear to

Right: Kamakura period naginata blade.

Above: Detail from Takedori Monogatari *showing fully armed archers and retainers armed with naginata.*

be plainly lacquered, but some are spirally marked, as if they had been wrapped to improve the grip.

Other weapons are occasionally depicted in scrolls, being used by the more flamboyant samurai. One such illustration shows the *kumade* (bear's paw), a species of rake which had a clawed head mounted on a long shaft. A chain is coiled around the shaft, which presumably fastened to the wrist or armour as security against loss in battle. It is shown being used by one horseman in an attempt to drag another samurai from his horse. Very occasionally the *kama*, a species of sickle, was used; it had a straight blade, mounted at right angles to the shaft and sharpened along the under edge. Some were fitted to long shafts, to unhorse an opponent before engaging with the sword or dirk, while others were mounted on a short shaft to be used as hand weapons, to hack and cut at the opponent's armour. The te boko (hand spear) of the Heian period had developed into a true spear with a shaft of about 6 feet (1.8m). It was carried by the lower ranks, and was called *kikuchi yari* after the area in Higo where it was developed. It was still fitted with a short, straight, single-edged blade, prominently ridged to reinforce the point when used for thrusting, but also capable of being used with a cutting action. Contemporary scrolls show some samurai armed with *masakari* (battle axes), fitted with long shafts but, like the kumade and kama, they were rare weapons, carried only by individuals who had developed the special skills needed to use them.

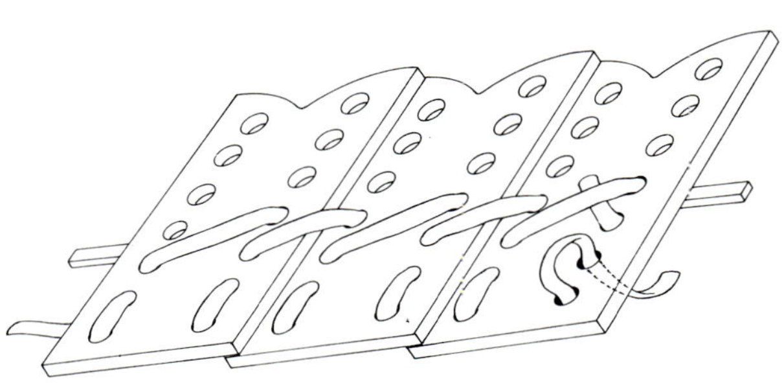

Right: Iyozane laced to a leather thong before lacquering.

The introduction of new weapons and the changes in strategy were accompanied by a series of small but important changes in the way armours were assembled and lacquered, which quite incidentally did much to improve their appearance. Scales, and consequently the lacing, were narrower and lost much of the clumsiness of their Heian counterparts. The appearance was further enhanced by embossing, or moulding outwards slightly, the visible surface of each scale. This made the scales stiffer and gave the completed row a pronounced ribbed look. Scales treated in this way are described as *kara kozane* (hollow scales), and were used for special purposes until the nineteenth century. In general use, however, they were soon superseded by *moriage kozane* (built up scales), in which the relief effect was produced by a build up of lacquer on flat scales, applied after they had been laced into rows. Since this style of scale became the norm, the descriptive prefix was soon dropped and they were, from this period, referred to simply as kozane.

The manufacture of scales, either from leather or iron, was a lengthy and labour-intensive business. Since kozane overlapped each other by a half, a complete armour used several thousand. During the fourteenth century a new technique of scale construction was devised, based on the type of scales and method of lacing that had been used for keiko in the Yamato and Nara periods, which almost halved the number required. These new scales, called *iyozane*, were slightly wider than kozane and punched with two columns of seven holes, instead of the thirteen of a kozane. When assembled into rows, each scale only slightly overlapped its neighbour and hence covered almost twice the area of the same number of kozane. Having no real overlap meant that lacing alone was insufficient to hold the scales into a row. Consequently they were laced onto a strip of rawhide (*kawashiki*) which showed as a distinct rib under the lacquer when the completed row was viewed from behind.

As they were wider than kozane, and had a smaller overlap, the tops of individual iyozane showed as a distinctive feature above the lacing. Armourers experimented by cutting the top edge into a variety of shapes, only three of which occur with any regularity. Usually the upper edge was cut to form a V-shaped notch. Alternatively, it could be cut into a rounded lobe over each column of holes, or shaped so as to resemble two normal scale heads. In the latter case, the scale would be modelled and lacquered to simulate normal kozane construction.

Lacquered articles have been discovered in Japan that can be dated as early as 500 BC, and although lacquer was eventually used in considerable quantities, it was always a valuable commodity, made even more expensive by the labour entailed in its production. To the Japanese its value lay not only in its role as an efficient preservative against the humid climate, but in its long-

Above: Detail of a do made from true iyozane. The hinged bracket is to carry the flag worn on the back of armour.

Below: Purple twill laced o yoroi. The lacing is twill cloth wrapped round tape. Kamakura period.

lasting, lustrous beauty. Unlike Western decorative or protective mediums, whether paints, varnishes or 'japan lacquers', which are complex blends of drying oils, resins and solvents, real lacquer (*urushi*) is simply the processed sap of a small tree, *Rhus vernicifera*, which grows in many parts of Asia. Like rubber, better quality lacquer was obtained by incising the bark of the trunk and collecting the sap in small cups; an inferior grade being obtained from twigs and prunings. After filtering to remove foreign matter, the crude lacquer was gently heated to remove excess water. The finished product was hardened in humid conditions to give a water- and solvent-proof coating that did not scratch or chip easily, and which could be polished to a high gloss.

It was usual to mix pigments with the raw lacquer to enhance its natural dark-brown colour, but the available range was rather limited. Most often it was coloured black, with carbon or, later, iron compounds; a bright-red, with vermilion; or a wide range of brown colours from mixtures of the two. Very occasionally dark-green or blue lacquered objects are found, which involve other mineral pigments since organic colouring matters are destroyed by the lacquer and could not be used. Gold lacquer was frequently used, either produced by coating ordinary black lacquer, while still wet, with gold dust or with leaf, or by grinding the gold dust into raw lacquer to make a kind of gold paint. Silver could be employed in the same way, but its tendency to tarnish to a dull-grey colour made it less popular. This use of precious metals was simulated on cheaper work by substituting tin foil, which when coated with a golden-coloured transparent lacquer looked remarkably effective.

Many elaborate techniques, producing the most varied effects, were invented and used, especially on scabbards, quivers and similar surfaces where the artists strove for novelty while always maintaining their innate good taste. Textured finishes which resisted knocks and felt pleasant to handle were made by incorporating gritty inert materials such as burnt clay or even ground, hardened lacquer into the final coats. Smooth transparent surfaces could overlay the coloured underlayers and enclose within them embedded flakes of metal, mother of pearl or chopped straw, to give finishes of great richness. Realistic imitations of materials like wrinkled leather, bark, bamboo or russet iron were all simulated in this very versatile medium. The russet-iron finish is particularly common on later armours. This fashion resulted partly from the influence of the tea cult with its emphasis on quiet good taste and was partly so that the quality of the metalwork could be seen. A coating of russet lacquer simulated the effect of russet iron without the attendant problem of corrosion.

Lacquering was a long and complex process that began with the careful preparation of the base. Joints in wood had to be filled, and the whole piece smoothed, while metal had to be rubbed with a coarse whetstone to provide a key for the lacquer. A very thin layer of inferior-grade lacquer was applied over the whole surface to act as an adhesive to hold down a layer of cloth or, on cheaper work, paper, which acted as a foundation for the subsequent coats. Further coats of crude lacquer were added to fill the texture of the cloth, each being allowed to harden before being rubbed smooth. Once this base was judged satisfactory, it was levelled and built up with a mixture of lacquer and either flour or burnt clay and sometimes also chopped hemp fibres called *kokuso*. This putty-like mixture was used to produce relief effects or to fill hollows in exactly the same way as a modern finisher would use fillers. When the thickness and surface were judged satisfactory, three or four coats of better quality lacquer were added, each polished to a satin finish with charcoal. Finally, two coats of the best lacquer were added and finished with charcoal dust and ashes of deer's antlers to give the final deep-black lustrous surface.

On most pieces of armour or sword scabbards, the lacquering was now complete but for a more glossy finish a fine coating of special lacquer was applied to give a surface which, while new, was impressive but soon scratched and showed finger marks. If the object was to be coloured or decorated in some other way, further coloured layers or metal dusts, generally being applied over black undercoats to enhance their brilliance, could be applied.

Sakakibara Kozan recommends that decorative lacquering on armours should be carried out by a specialist lacquer artist and not entrusted to the armourer. This suggests that they were accustomed to lacquering their own work, but in view of the complicated nature of the process, it is more probable that each workshop had a lacquer specialist on the staff who could complete the basic processes but who was incapable of fine artistic work.

For a considerable period after the Mongol attacks, there was a general fear of a reprisal throughout the country, as well as considerable discontent among the samurai over the failure of the government to compensate them for their expenses and services. The extensive preparation for the defence of the country had strained the economy, and samurai who had fought petitioned for the traditional rewards for service, which the bakufu just could not provide. The larger landowners away from the centres lost faith in any form of central government, and set up what were almost independent states – foreshadowing later divisions within the country. Sensing this threat, and using yet another squabble over succession as his excuse, the mature Emperor Go-Daigo took the throne and evaded every attempt by the Hojo to unseat him. Outraged, the Hojo resorted to force and in 1333 dispatched an army under Ashikaga Takauji to take the throne by force. Takauji, however, had other plans. Declaring himself initially for the Emperor, he recruited a huge following of samurai who felt cheated by the Hojo, and attacked Kamakura, burning it to the ground. Takauji himself marched on Kyoto (formerly Heian Kyo), killed the bakufu representatives and eventually replaced the self-willed Go-Daigo with a puppet ruler, who granted him the title of Shogun. Go-Daigo took his regalia and fled south to Yoshino in the mountains around Nara, where he continued to reign until 1392 in what became known as the Southern Court, while the Emperors of the Ashikaga continued to rule from the Northern Court of Kyoto.

The whole of this period of turmoil, called the Nambokucho (the period of the Northern and Southern courts), saw almost continual fighting of one form or another as the provincial lords squabbled over land rights. Loyalties lasted only so long as it suited the occasion, being switched from one side to another to take advantage of every opportunity as it presented itself.

However successful the o yoroi had been in the past, it was an impractical armour for use on foot and some nobles abandoned it altogether. Yoroi dating from this period differ in details from those of the Heian period. All were fitted with front and back kusazuri which had a divided hishinui no ita to assist in walking. The shoji no ita attached to the watagami began to swing forwards and the peak of the helmet moved outwards from the vertical – in both cases to give greater protection to the face. The tops of the sendan no ita and the kyubi no ita lost the characteristic gentle, lobed outline of the Heian period and took on a more zigzagged profile. Some armours had the fastening cords threaded through holes in the muna ita, fastening on the inside, aping the haramaki of the retainers. A new innovation was the introduction of the *waka ita*, an additional plate which was laced to the scales of the nakagawa under the left arm to fill what must have been a rather vulnerable gap. The upper edge of this plate, shaped to fit closely to the arm, was held in position yet given some

Above: Rear view of a red laced maru do yoroi, a hybrid armour incorporating the saka ita, shoulder guards and their fastenings from the o yoroi, with the divided kusazuri and overlap under the right arm of the haramaki.

Above: Red and white laced haramaki opening down the back; a very early example of this style of armour. Nambokucho period.

Far right: Green and red laced o yoroi. The colour of the lacing varied to the taste of the wearer. Kamakura period.

degree of movement by small toggles at each upper corner. These toggles were fastened to corresponding loops on the front and rear tateage.

Armours became more of a vehicle for applied ornamentation and decoration. The chrysanthemum ornaments that had been fitted to the leather covering of the fukigaeshi and on the peak of Heian armours were now applied along the hishinui no ita of the kusazuri, the sode and the shikoro. Ornamental plaques of pierced and engraved gilded copper became less stereotyped and were applied to the kesho no ita and the hishinui no ita. They were held in place by gilt rivets; occasionally these represented the *mon* (heraldic device) of the wearer. Further decoration was provided by oversewing the leather cross-knotting on the hishinui no ita, with vermilion silk braid. This emphasized the knots and brought the hishinui no ita into further prominence.

The more practical samurai abandoned the o yoroi and adopted a better quality version of the haramaki worn by foot soldiers. They decorated and embellished it as befitted their rank, and wore it with sode and a helmet. These haramaki were fitted with shoji no ita, an agemaki to which the sode cords could be attached, and the new waki ita under both arms (that under the right arm being of necessity in two parts). Because of their awkwardness, the guards for the fastenings on the do that had been used for the o yoroi were abandoned; they were replaced by a small pair of gyoyo attached to the ends of the watagami to fulfill the same function. A few armours were hybrids between o yoroi and haramaki, having divided kusazuri and the overlap under the right arm like the haramaki, but retaining the leather covering for the front of the do and saka ita of the o yoroi. Like the haramaki, they were provided with sode and a helmet identical to those worn with the o yoroi. These hybrid armours are called *maru do yoroi*.

By the Kamakura period helmets had begun to take on a softer outline. They were almost perfectly hemispherical, with a dozen or more plates with perhaps six smaller rivets in each. Bowls of this shape are called *daienzan bachi* or more simply *maru bachi* (round helmet bowls). This trend towards helmet bowls made with more plates, each fastened by a greater number of smaller rivets, continued throughout the Kamakura and Nambokucho periods. A new and important innovation was the provision of *suji* (small flanges) along the rear edge of each plate, adding considerable strength to the helmet without adding to its weight. Shinodare became almost standard accessories: they were generally of gilded copper rather than of iron as formerly, and built of several layers, each with decorative milled edges. Helmets could be further enhanced by applying the shinodare over plates of silvered or gilded copper, *kata jira*, which occupied the space between the flanges. These relieved the severity of these helmets, acting as a foil to the black lacquer bowl.

Contemporary illustrations show what appear to be the corners of a square of white cloth, or strips of cloth, emerging from between the koshimaki and the shikoro at the sides and back and covering most of the peak

Right: A 32-plate hoshi bachi from the Nambokucho or early Muromachi period fitted with the present neck guard during the Edo period.

at the front – the ends disappearing into the tehen, where they were presumably knotted. This feature appears to be a form of semi-permanent lining, which, if it was tied sufficiently tightly, would lift the bowl off the wearer's head and reduce the concussive effects of a blow. Prior to this development, the inside of all helmets were lacquered but unlined, the wearer's hair and eboshi acting as the only padding. A lining was an improvement in that it made the helmet more comfortable to wear, but it did require that the hair, worn at this period in a queue on top of the head, be undressed before putting on the helmet. Since this change rendered the tehen superfluous, it was reduced in size, with a corresponding increase in the elaboration of the tehen kanamono, which was now made of several chrysanthemum-shaped washers in gilded copper, each of a smaller diameter than the one below.

Towards the end of the Nambokucho period, helmet bowls with standing rivets (*hoshi bachi*) had reached the pinnacle of their development with as many as 36 plates fastened by 15 rivets on each. Of necessity, these rivets had to be thin, appearing long and pointed. Helmets now displayed a profusion of shinodare on the front, back and sides of the helmet bowl in groups of three or five. Where the space between the flanges was too narrow, several plates would be fitted with flush rivets and have the flanges omitted so that larger decorative plates could be fitted. A helmet with four such plates was described as *shiho jiro* (four sides white), or with more, *happo jiro* (eight sides white). The use of the description 'white' in this context refers to the *kata jiro*, now always silvered to act as contrast to the gilded shinodare. The cloth strips had disappeared from illustrations by the Nambokucho period, but some form of completely internal lining was almost certainly fitted, probably made of leather. In later years these linings were generally of coarse hemp, faced with silk or some other fine cloth, shaped by a close spiral of stitches.

As an alternative to shinodare or, more usually, in addition to them, gilt metal rims were fitted over the flanges. These were almost invariably accompanied by *igaki* (small gilt plates with shaped upper edges) fastened between the flanges and just above the koshimaki to form a decorative band around the base of the bowl. In later years, these plates were formed in one with the gilt metal rims, reducing the number of fastenings and, more importantly, the number of perforations for them made in the bowl itself.

During the late Heian period a few warriors had created a sensation by appearing in battle wearing gilded crests. These quickly became standard, taking the form of a pair of flat gilded metal 'horns' of stereotyped shape called *kuwagata*. They fitted into a special socket (a *kuwagata dai*) which was fastened to the peak of the helmet. Early versions are narrow with their upper ends swelling into two pointed lobes that may represent stylized horns – a conjecture based on the fact that very early examples extend from a plate, decorated with the face of a demon, which fastened to the peak of the helmet. This tradition was occasionally continued into the Kamakura period, and later, by embossing the kuwagata dai into a representation of a demon's head. By the Nambokucho period kuwagata became wider and larger, reaching exaggerated proportions in some votive armours, and exceptionally being embellished by engraved decoration.

Accompanying these changes to the helmet were alterations to the shikoro, which now began to broaden out at the bottom to give greater freedom of movement to the arms. Five rows of scales were still normal although there are references in contemporary literature to *san mai kabuto* (three-plate helmets) that can only refer to the number of lames in the shikoro. Since defence against arrows was less of a consideration, the fukigaeshi, while still large, were now no longer bent sharply at a right angle to the shikoro but curved back at a more acute angle to it. In keeping with the trend towards increased decoration, the face of the fukigaeshi might be covered with elaborate gilt-metal ornaments over the decorated leather. A few votive armours were made in which this elaboration was carried to the extreme; almost every available surface, including large areas of lacing on the sode, were covered with the most elaborate pierced and chased metal decorations.

The nobles' custom of wearing the happuri under the helmet became uncommon during the Kamakura period, as the need for protection from arrows fired at close quarters declined. Instead, armour for the lower face, *hoate*, appeared in increasing numbers, becoming even more common during the Nambokucho period. An example of such a mask, covering the chin and cheeks up to the level of the eyes but leaving the nose and mouth exposed, appears in the *Gøsannen Gassen Emaki* – a picture scroll dating from the late eleventh century. No other examples are known from this early period. Developed with the hoate and complementary to it, was the *nodawa*, a bib-like protection for the throat and upper chest, which consisted of a U-shaped plate to which was attached, by an intermediary band of leather, two curved rows of scales. Nodawa may occasionally have been attached to the lower edge of the hoate to form a unit, since, as the hoate increased in popularity, the use of the separate nodawa declined.

Protection for the arms, *kote*, was now universally used and took the form of a fabric sleeve, occasionally of hemp cloth or more usually of gold brocade, to which were sewn lacquered iron plates. The oldest surviving examples consist of large curved plates for the upper and lower arm together with a smaller one for the elbow. These were sewn to the backing by pairs of holes around the edge. A further plate, shaped to cover the back of the hand but having no provision for the thumb, was either sewn to the cuff of the sleeve or hinged to the plate over the forearm, being provided with a loop for the middle finger, and sometimes another for the thumb, to hold it in position on the back of the hand. In keeping with the remainder of the armour, the lacquered surfaces of these plates were embellished by ornaments of gilded copper.

In place of the high fur boots previously worn, *suneate* (shin guards) were now worn with slightly more practical, but still very stiff, fur shoes. During the Kamakura period, suneate were made of three plates hinged together and decorated with applied

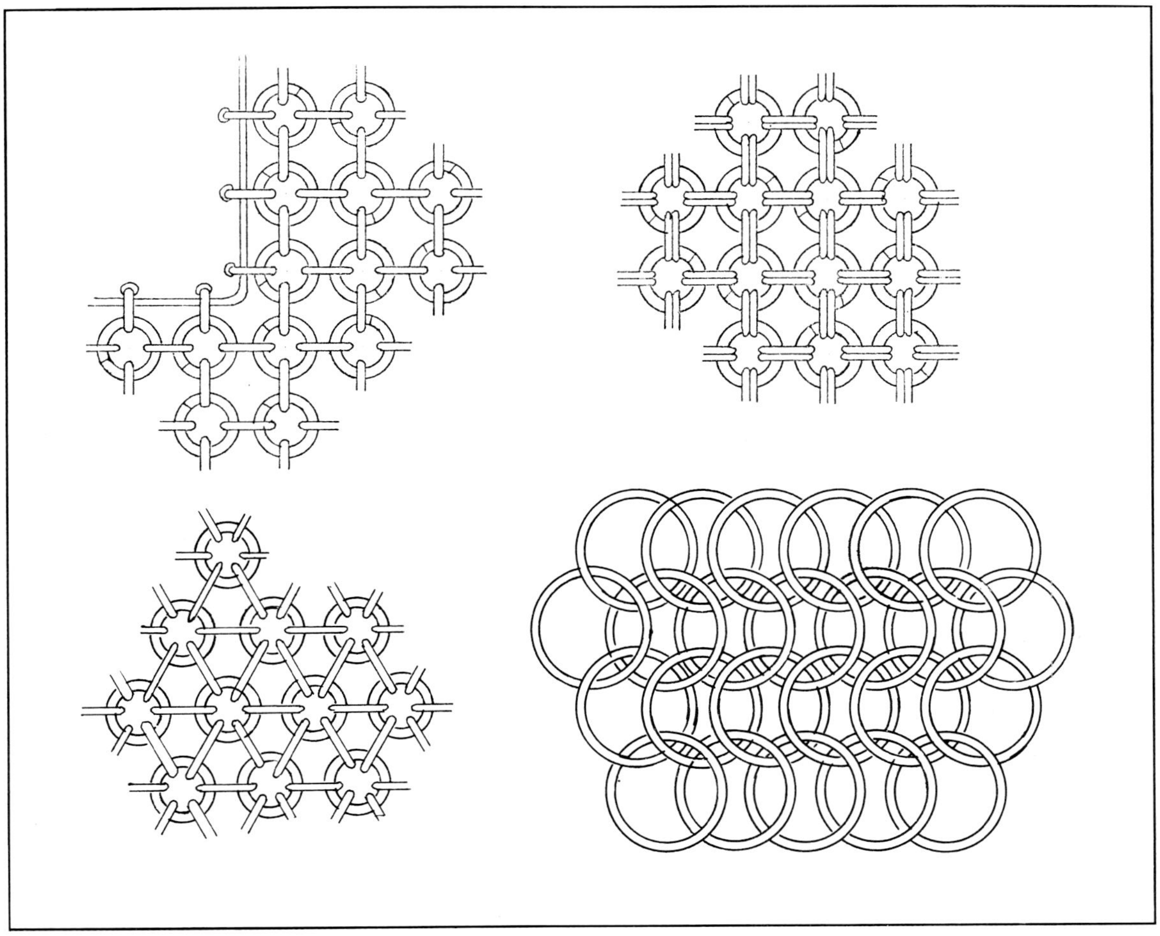

Left: Various types of mail. Top left: So gusari. Top right: Seiro gusari. Bottom left: Asa no ha gusari. Bottom right: Nanban gusari.

Above: Purple leather laced haramaki with tsubo sode (shoulder guards which curve with the arm and narrow towards the bottom). This simple armour was probably made for a retainer. Nambokucho period. The lacing has faded.

gilt ornaments like the plates of the kote. Pictures show they were provided with cords along their rear edges, laced in a criss-crossed manner around the back of the leg. Interestingly though, the oldest suneate surviving (at Gifu and Oita Prefectures), which can be dated to this era, are fitted with cords at the top and bottom to tie around the leg. These simple suneate offered no protection to the knees, a considerable disadvantage for mounted use, and a deficiency which was rectified during the Nambokucho period by adding plate knee guards of considerable size to their upper edge. Suneate fitted with these large knee guards are called *o tateage suneate*, fastened in place by simple ties of cloth or braid which fitted through metal loops riveted to the plates. By this time, the fur boots were being abandoned by all but the highest ranking officers; straw sandals were adopted as being more suitable for use on foot.

The Nambokucho period saw the introduction of mail, which was extensively used to fill the gaps between plates on minor parts of armour. Unlike the situation in Europe, mail was rarely used as the sole defence. Japanese mail construction is unlike any other with the sole exception of a fragment of Etruscan mail now preserved in Paris. It is based on a system of circular links, which lay in the plane of the mail and oval links at right angles to it. Almost all examples are made from wire of good circular section, showing that it was produced by means of a draw-plate. The links were manufactured by winding wire on a mandrel of the shape required, then cutting down the side of the resulting coil with a chisel to form the individual links. Unlike European mail, which was riveted, the links of Japanese mail were merely butted together, relying on the hardness of the metal and the construction to keep them closed.

In most Japanese mail each circular link was connected to four others by oval links, giving a rectangular arrangement, called *so gusari*, having the advantage of being readily connected to plates. Where greater strength was needed the wire could be of a heavier grade, or the oval links could be made of two or more turns of wire to give a type of double or triple mail, called *seiro gusari*. For areas needing a greater degree of flexibility or only light protection, such as the bend of the arm, *koshi gusari* was made by leaving rectangular spaces in so gusari. An alternative construction, based on a hexagonal arrangement of the same types of links, was also used, but not as widely. In its most dense form, *asa no ha gusari*, each round link of mail was connected to three others by the oval links, but variants of lower density were possible. The fact that none of these are especially common would suggest they had little real advantage over the rectangular forms.

Whatever the type of mail used, it was never used alone, being sewn onto some form of fabric or leather backing or, occasionally, sandwiched between layers of cloth. To prevent rusting, and consequent damage to the underlying fabric, mail was always lacquered, generally black even when the remainder of the armour was a more eye-catching colour.

Because the Japanese tended to ride with a high stirrup, the divided kusazuri of the haramaki tended to slip off the rider's leg, leaving the knee and much of the thigh exposed. Several illustrations of the Nambokucho period depict horsemen wearing what appear to be a pair of short baggy trousers over the yoroi hitatare, marked with vertical lines that have been interpreted as splints or plates sewn onto the cloth – which later became known as *kobakama jitate*. An alternative armour involved laced scales, similarly sewn onto a backing, with the lower rows split into pendant sections for greater flexibility, rather like small kusazuri. This style was later called *hodo haidate* after its supposed resemblance to Buddhist altar cloths, which are similarly cut into sections along one edge. Documentary evidence suggests that something similar had been used in the Heian period but there is no indication of the form it took. No examples have survived from either the Kamakura or Nambokucho periods to show exactly what these early leg armours were like. The book *Taiheiki*, dating from the Nambokucho period, mentions *hiza yoroi* (knee or lap armour) – it would seem therefore that this was the customary term used to describe all types of thigh armour until the Muromachi period, when the more common name of *haidate* began to be used.

A mention must be made of the *horo*, a curious device which had a considerable vogue during the Kamakura period but had appeared somewhat earlier. A type of cloth cape, the top fastened behind the shoulders, and flared out slightly towards the bottom. It gathered in and tied at the waist. Pictures of standing samurai show it hanging loosely in a pouch down the back, but when moving on horseback, it inflated with air and ballooned out behind the wearer. Its purpose remains obscure, but was probably purely to intimidate the enemy, although it may have had some protective value when galloping away after an attack. However, one painting casts some doubt over this hypothesis, since it shows a horo being worn over the face and reaching to the horse's head. It obscures the wearer's vision and presumably limits the freedom of movement of the arms. Whether this is the result of a misunderstanding on the

Above: An Edo period reproduction of a nodawa, a defene for the throat and upper chest. The black lacquered plate is iron, the scales leather.

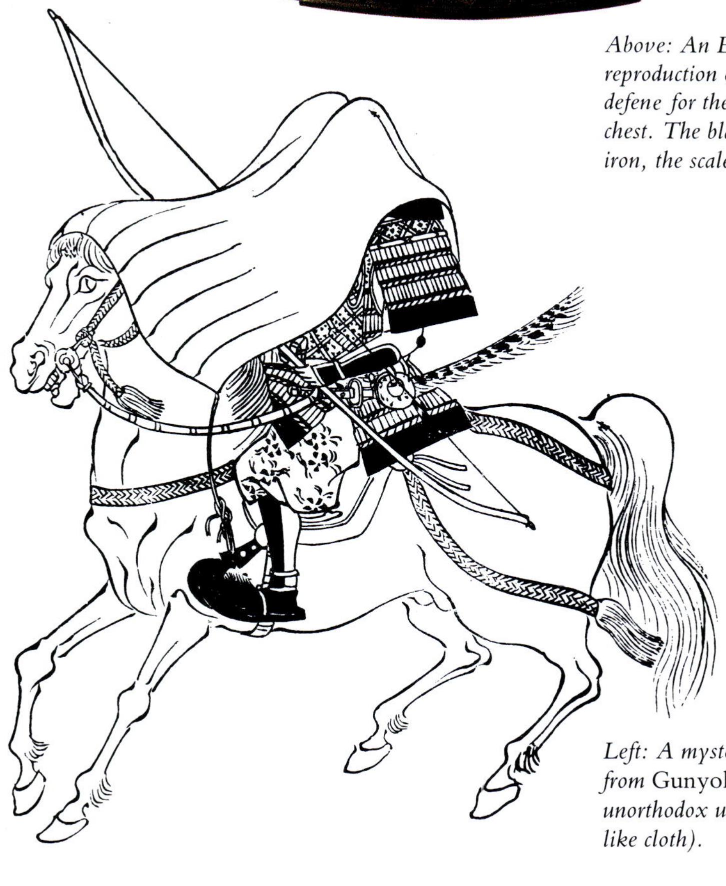

Left: A mysterious illustration from Gunyoki *showing an unorthodox use of the horo (cape-like cloth).*

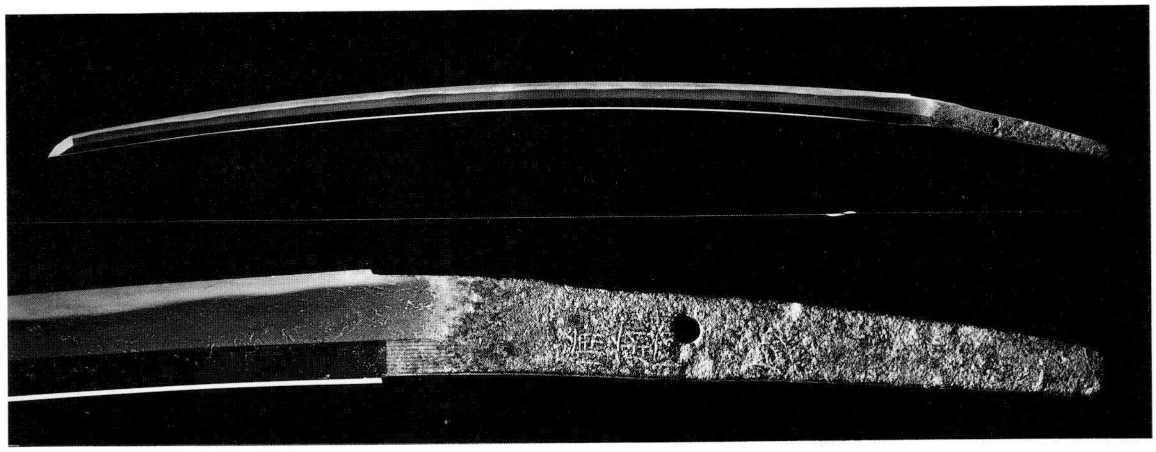

Right: Blade for a long sword in the Bizen tradition; there were more swords made in this tradition than in any other during the Koto period.

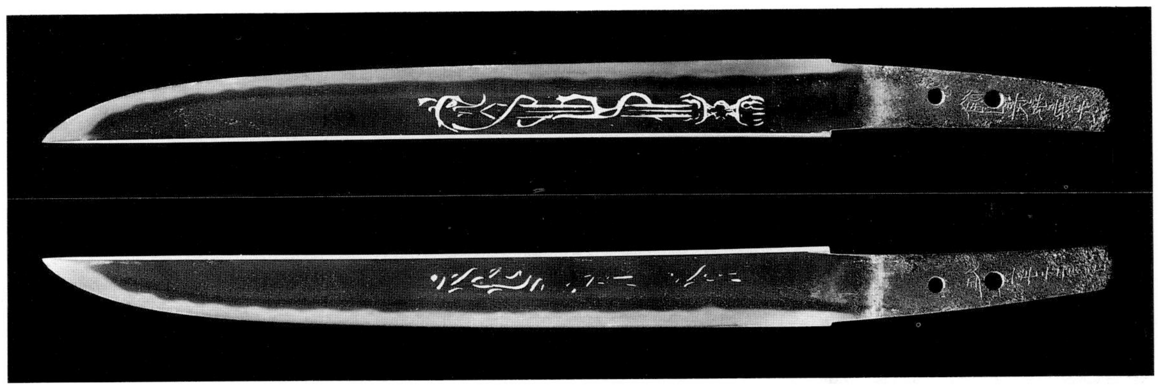

Right: Dirk blade signed Bizen Osafune Kunimitsu and dated 1276.

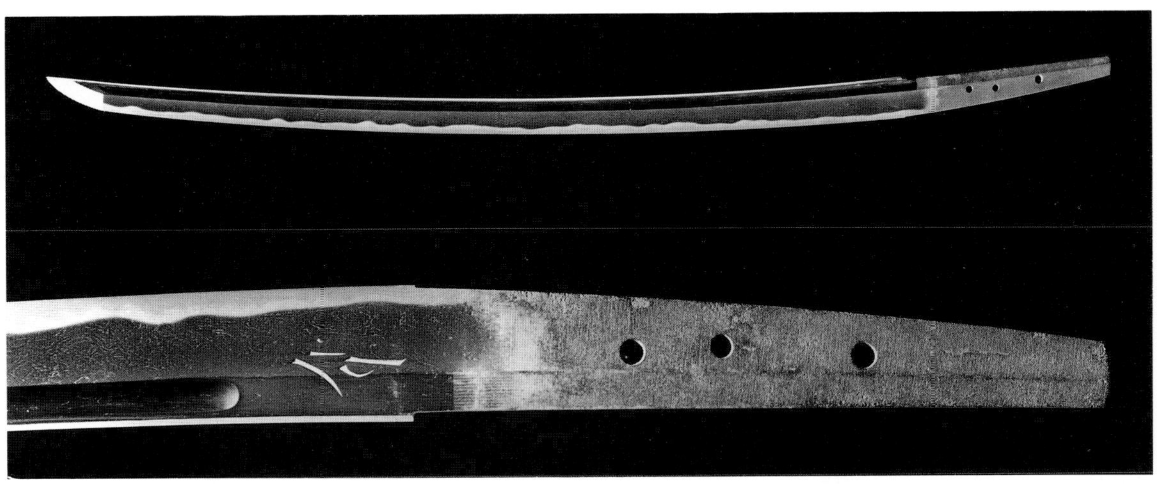

Right: Blade for a long sword in the Soshu tradition decorated with a horimono of a debased sanskrit character.

part of the artist we can only surmise, but the horo was undeniably popular and acquired a considerable mystique in later years, when it was incorrectly revived. Not understanding the principle, these later versions incorporated a framework of bamboo or whalebone to hold the cloth into the shape depicted in old drawings.

While the continuous fighting throughout the Nambokucho period did little to help the prosperity of the country as a whole, it was a period of prosperity for armourers and swordsmiths, and for their suppliers, the producers of iron and steel.

Deposits of iron ore occur widely if somewhat thinly in Japan; mainly in the form of magnetite, a blackish ore and red ferruginous sand. It was the latter that was the first choice of the swordsmiths, but it must always be remembered that a considerable source of metal in ancient times was recycled scrap. In his book on armour making, Sakakibara Kozan states that iron made in Harima and Idzumo was better than that from Bitchu, Hoki, Mimasaki or Iwami and that old saws and agricultural tools were an excellent source of raw material. Masahide boasts in his book that 'there is nò iron that cannot be made into good steel.' But he goes on to say that starting with better quality metal can

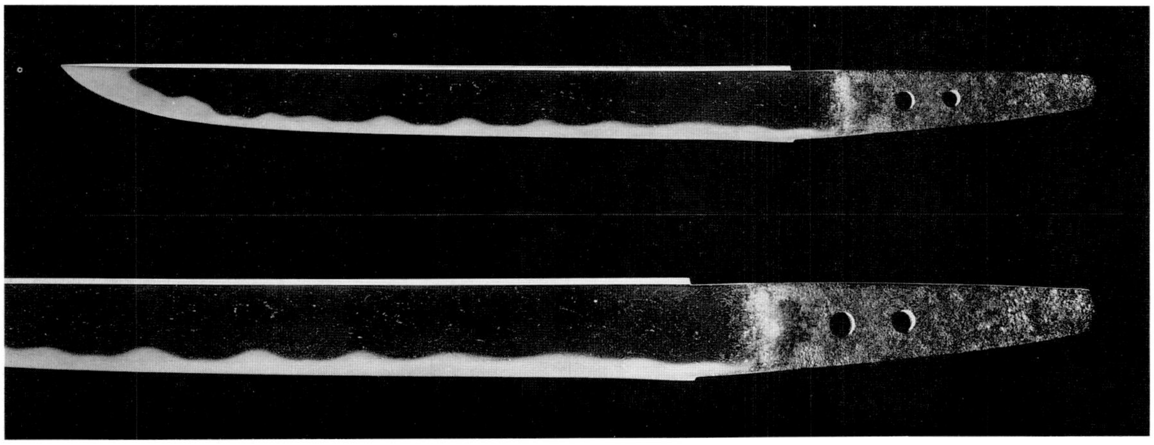

Left: Dirk blade in the Soshu tradition; some of the finest blades belong to this tradition.

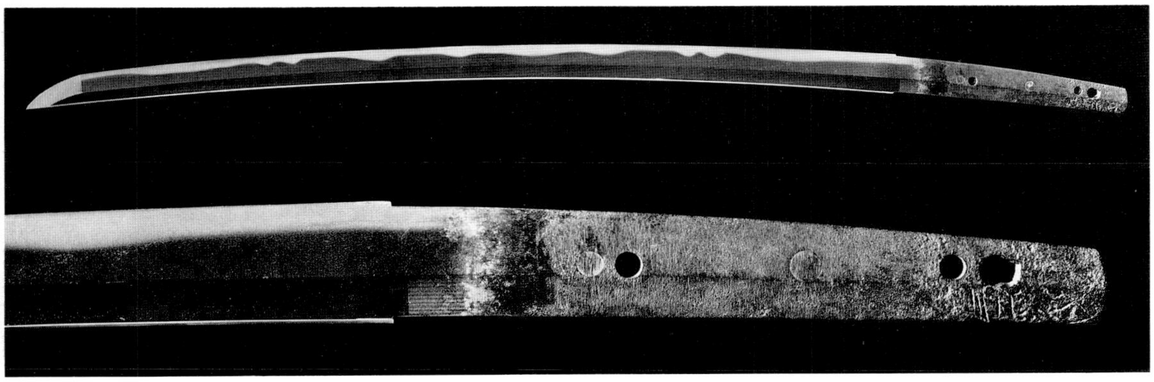

Left: Blade for a long sword in the Mino tradition signed by Kaneuji, circa *1350. This style of sword remained popular into the twentieth century.*

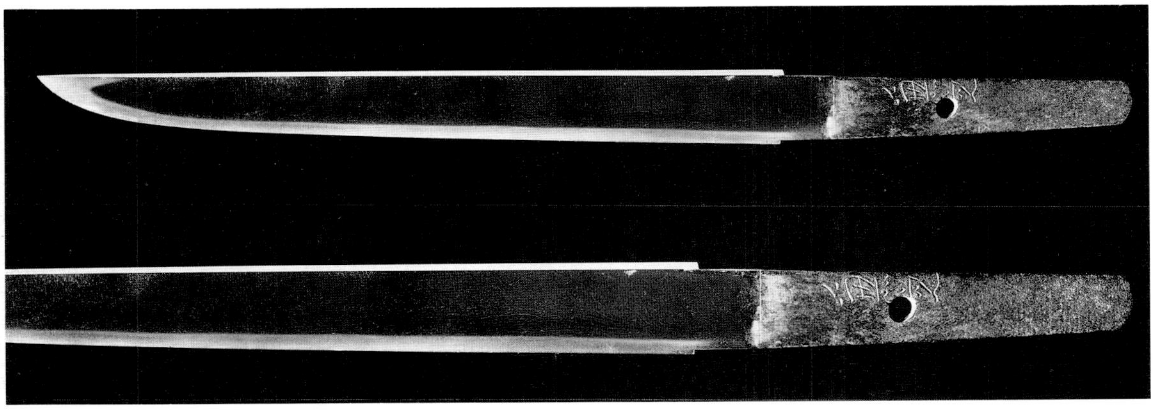

Left: Dirk blade in the Mino tradition signed Kanesada, 1270.

save the smith a lot of time and effort.

Iron smelting was always something of a cottage industry, carried out, during the period for which we have written evidence at least, in a rectangular furnace about three feet (1m) by six feet (2m) in area and some six feet (2 m) high. It was often built into a pit dug into the side of a hill to ease the task of charging, and covered with a temporary shed to give some protection from the weather. The walls of the furnace were of clay, which acted as a flux, helping to promote fusion but also limiting the length of time for which the furnace could operate. Charcoal was burnt in the pit to dry out the soil, and later served both as fuel and reducing agent, being added throughout the firing together with further ore. To maintain a high temperature, air was pumped in through a series of bamboo tubes fitted with cast-iron nozzles embedded in the furnace wall and connected to a second pit alongside in which were housed the bellows, the intervening wall of soil offering some protection from the heat to the men who operated them. At the end of three or four days of successive firings and tappings, from which was obtained cast iron, the furnace was dismantled to obtain the mass of partially fused steel, iron and slag – the raw material of the swordsmith and armourer. In earlier periods, the efficiency of the furnace was such that this bloom was the only product, the temperature being insufficient to effect fusion of the cast iron. This mass could

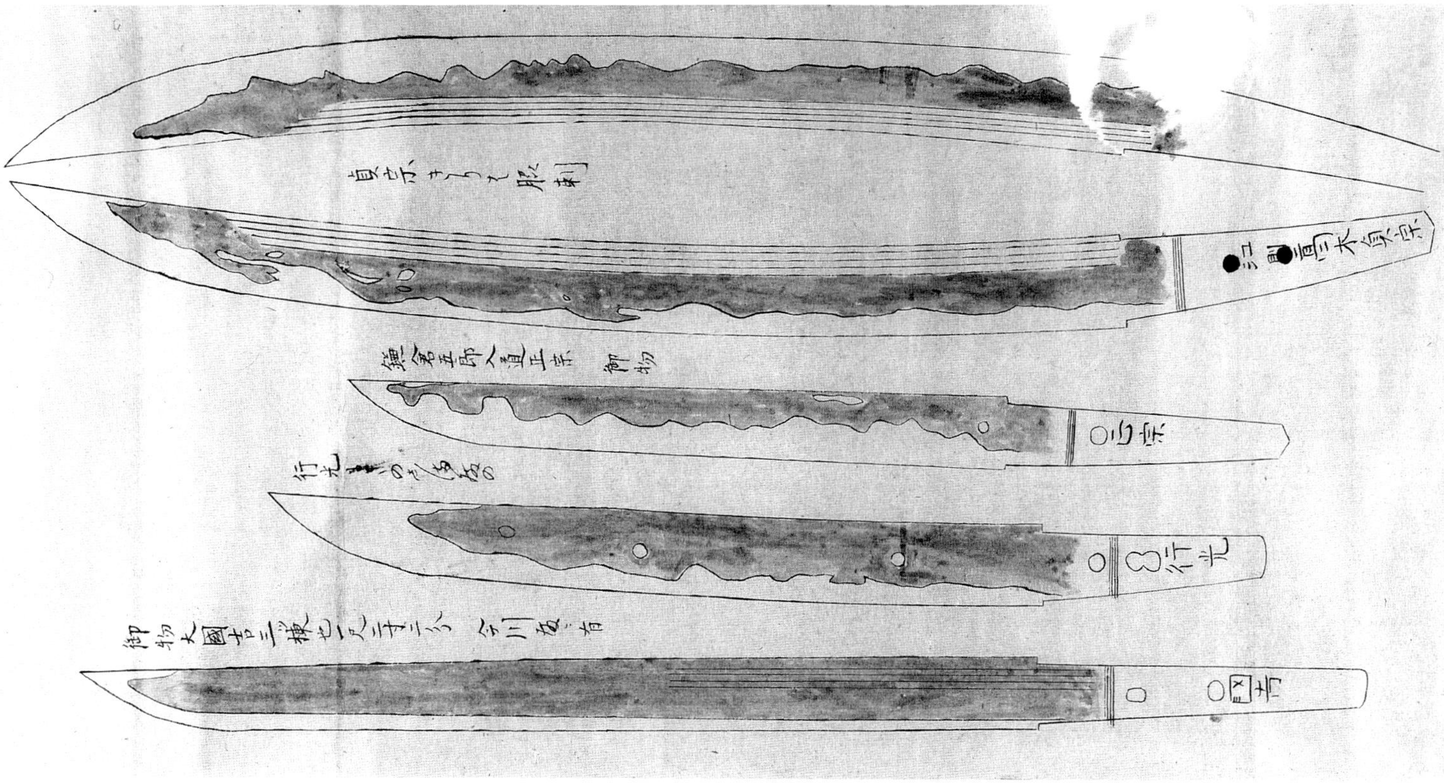

Above: Detail from a scroll of blades by famous smiths. From top to bottom they are by Sadamune, Masamune, Yukimitsu and Kuniyoshi.

be refined by forging to beat out the slag and earthy impurities, but more frequently it was either cut up while still pasty, or thrown into water to fragment and make the selection of the better pieces easier.

To meet the growing need for swords, craftsmen moved to wherever there was a demand, setting up workshops and developing styles to suit local tastes and needs. The provinces of Bizen, Sagami (Soshu) and Mino in particular became important centres of sword making, developing the remaining styles of the five great traditions. Production in Yamashiro began to decline, and in Yamato almost ceased entirely. Many other centres existed of course, but their products show that their techniques were ultimately derived from those of the main traditions.

The Kamakura period witnessed the first golden age of sword making, aided by the recognition given to the craft by no less a person than a retired Emperor. Following the drowning of Emperor Antoku at Dan No Ura, the throne was taken by Go-Toba. After his retirement and, eventually, exile, he devoted himself to the study of swords. Rumour suggested that his hate for the Regent Hojo Yoshitoki, who had forced his exile, was the reason for his interest, but he never exacted revenge. A more likely explanation is that he indulged his passions as a way of staving off the boredom of banishment from the capital. Whatever the truth, he summoned to his palace many of the best swordsmiths of his day, discussing their craft with them, suggesting new ideas and even participating, in a smithy set up in the palace grounds, in the tempering of blades. He is even said to have made blades himself under guidance, several of which still exist.

Lists of the smiths, who attended for one or two months each, show that Bizen was already a leading province in the craft; no fewer than 25 out of the 39 who attended during the years of the second decade of the thirteenth century, came from there. This pre-eminence of Bizen continued throughout the Koto period, which lasted until 1595 – no fewer than 4005 swordsmiths are known to have worked there, compared with 1269 for Mino and 1025 for Yamato. Assuming an average working life for a smith of 20 years, producing, at a conservative estimate, 30 blades of all types annually, Bizen alone would have produced some two and a half million swords during this period, whilst the total for the whole country during the same period would have been nearly 15 million.

It is very difficult to estimate the cost of producing a sword in modern terms, except perhaps in terms of the skilled man hours needed to make it. In the Nara period it took 18 days for the smith to forge a tachi blade, 9 days for the silversmith to make the mounts,

6 days for the lacquerer to make the scabbard, 2 days for the leather worker, with an additional 18 days for labourers. Added to this would be the not inconsiderable cost of the raw materials, making the tachi an expensive production by any standards. A comparable length of time for forging a long blade was noted at the end of the seventeenth century, when the Shogun summoned swordsmiths to make swords at his palace. In each case more than 20 days were required to produce a roughly polished blade. This production time fell rapidly with a shorter blade, a good smith being reckoned to be able to produce a dirk blade in a day and a half.

The enhancement of the status of swordsmiths is reflected by the fact that many of the most famous sported family names, strictly speaking a prerogative of the aristocracy. By the middle of the thirteenth century several smiths were working who have been regarded ever since as supreme masters, and who have never been seriously rivalled. Among them were Toshihiro Yoshimitsu of Awataguchi, Go Yoshihiro of Etchu and, arguably the greatest of them all, Goro Nyudo Masamune of Sagami. Masamune was the son of Yukimitsu and grandson of Awataguchi Kunitomo, who had been chosen to work with Go-Toba. He made a special point of studying under other great smiths in order to become acquainted with as many aspects of the art as possible. Masamune gained such a reputation that he attracted a number of pupils who themselves became famous, the greatest being his adopted son Sadamune, who attracted pupils in his turn. The surviving blades made by these smiths are regarded as treasures to the present day.

Nambokucho swords differ considerably from those of the Heian, principally in their length and robust appearance. The slim, rather delicate blades of Heian tachi were found wanting during the Mongol invasions and internal fighting which followed and were replaced by heavier and longer swords with longer points, which were sufficiently tempered to allow some reshaping if chipped. To add even more strength to this vulnerable part of the blade, the grooves, which were fairly commonly cut just below

Above: Detail from a scroll of famous blades showing a long sword by Masamune. Its elegant shape has been lost because the blade has been shortened. An owner may have shortened the blade to suit his physique or to comply with one of the many edicts during the Edo period.

Below: An unusual no dachi (field sword) mounted like a conventional tachi and dedicated by Hojo Tokimune. Its total length is 5 feet 9 inches (1.77m). Nambokucho period. Swords of this type were too long to wear, so were normally carried.

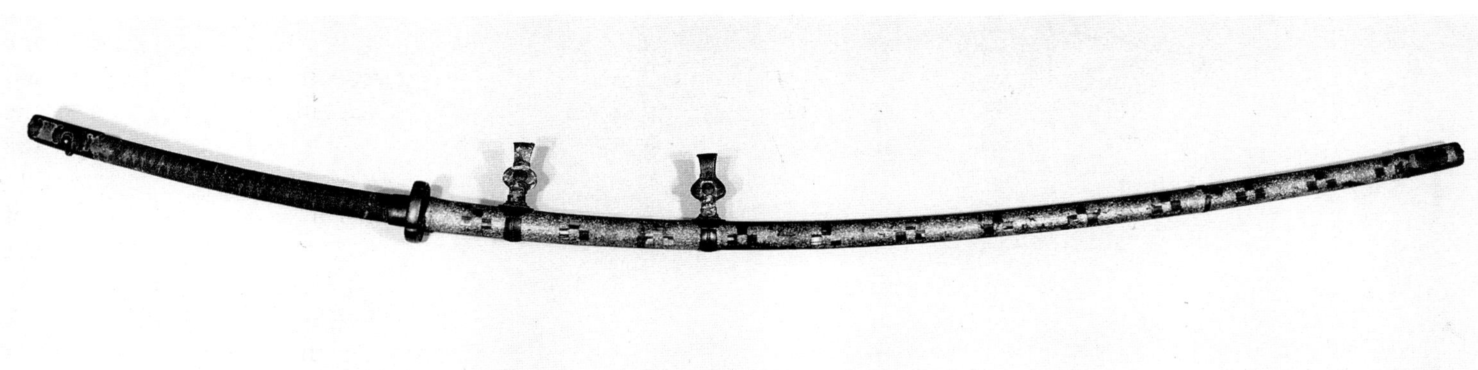

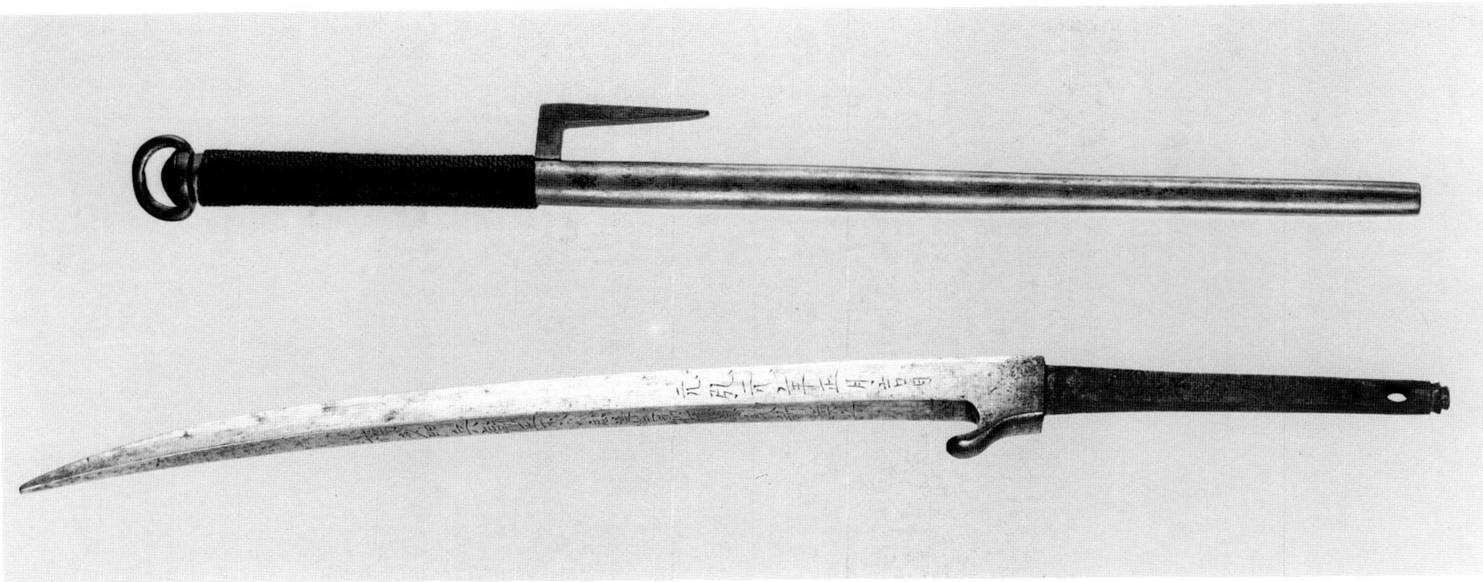

Above: Jitte (top) a club used for parrying swords and a hachiwari (helmet splitter) the latter bearing the signature and date of Masamune as well as that of its maker Shizu Saburo Kaneuji of Mino province. Circa *1730.*

Below: Hyogo gusari tachi. It is 3 feet 2 inches (0.96m) long. Kamakura period. The name hyogo implies a connection between the style of this sword and an official military bureau.

the back to reduce weight, were stopped further back from the point. This tendency to larger, longer blades was taken to extremes during the Nambokucho period with a new type of no dachi with blades of five feet (1.5m) or more in length. Worn slung over the back in plain scabbards, they were carried into action unsheathed and used in much the same way as the two-handed swords of Europe.

The more normal long swords were still worn slung edge downwards from the waist, and the short dirk, with its flat-sided blade, was still carried thrust through the belt on the left front of the body. A few of the surviving dirk blades were designed specifically for armour piercing, as shown by their heavy cross section and acute point. References in contemporary literature confusingly refer to *shito* (stabbing knife), *koshi gatana* (hip sword) and *himo gatana* (braid sword); in all probability they are alternative names for essentially the same weapon, differing only, if at all, in the style of mounting. One variety of dirk that can be identified in paintings is the *ebizaya maki* (prawn scabbard wrapped), so called because the scabbard and hilt were carved with gadroons like the carapace of the crustacean.

Another strange weapon, reputedly devised by Masamune, and invariably bearing his signature in addition to the smith who actually made it, was the *hachiwari* (helmet splitter). Mounted and worn like the dirk, the hachiwari took the form of a curved, pointed bar of steel, having a small hook-like protrusion at the base. Although it could have been used for piercing, the curvature and hook suggest its main use was as a parrying weapon, being held in the left hand while the tachi was wielded with the right.

The hiru maki no tachi of the Heian was still used, together with new varieties with reinforcing strips applied to the scabbard and

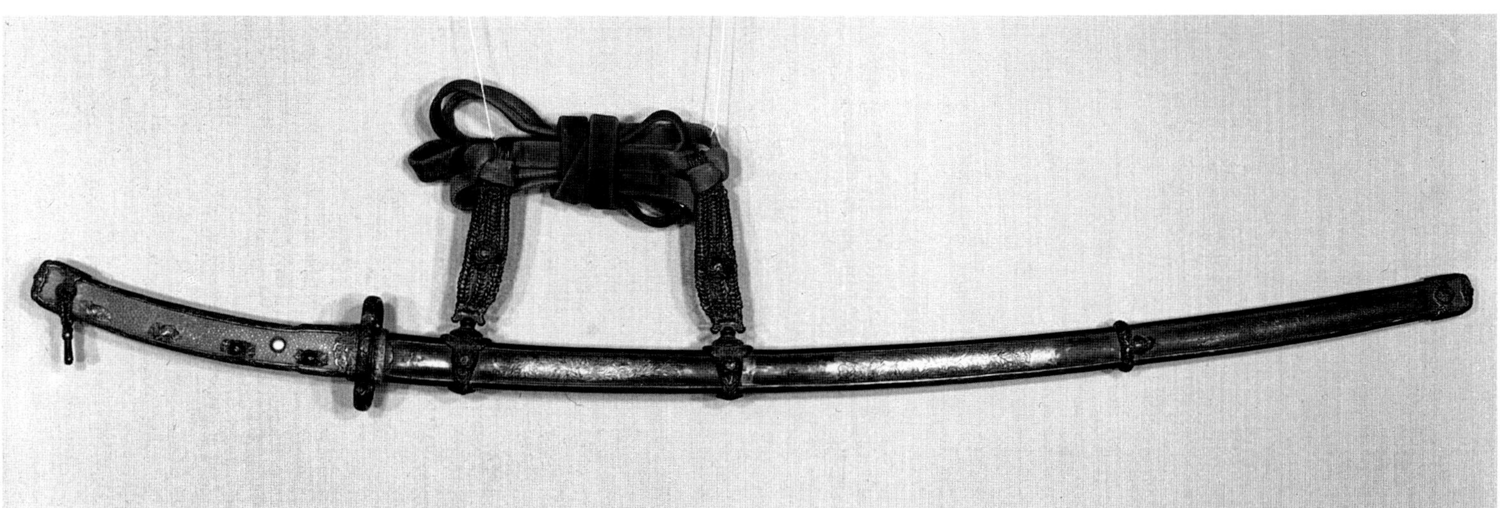

hilt, or with criss-crossed wrappings of leather around the hilt and upper part of the scabbard to improve the grip. This latter type was called *kawa zutsumi maki no tachi* and was provided with a tubular leather cover over the lower part of the scabbard and a leather cover over the tsuba to protect it from the weather and damage in action. It became fashionable to cover the lower end of other types of scabbards with leather or, for the higher ranks, tiger's tail skin.

The components of mounted swords had become fairly standardized and were to continue virtually unchanged as long as swords continued to be worn. Irrespective of the size or style of mounting, all blades were fitted with a soft-metal collar, called the *habaki*, which butted against two shoulders at the junction between the blade and the tang. This relatively insignificant but vital fitting, the only one to belong to the blade itself rather than to the mount, had the dual duty of transmitting the force of a blow from the blade to the hilt, and of providing a seal with the mouth of the scabbard when the sword was sheathed.

Scabbards were generally made of *honoki*, a light straight-grained wood from a species of magnolia whose natural oils acted as a rust preventive. Only occasionally were more decorative woods used – and then mainly for dirks. Some scabbards for field use were fitted with U-shaped metal strips extending the full length at the top and bottom, held in place by gilt rings; the resulting panels at the sides were either lacquered or filled by thin metal plates. One type of sword mounted in this manner can be positively identified as a *hyogo kusari no tachi* (military chain tachi), which was slung from the belt by complex hangers of many fine chains. Whatever the type, all tachi scabbards were fitted with chapes, known as *ishizuke* during the Heian period, but *kojiri* from the Kamakura onwards. Most had at least one *seme gane* (reinforcing band) fitted towards the lower end, which helped to prevent the two halves of the scabbard from separating. The mouth of the scabbard was reinforced by a metal band, below which were two *ashi* (ornate clasps) to which the hangers were attached.

Scabbards for dirks were occasionally fitted with elaborately carved metal mounts matching those of the tachi, but more often they were relatively plain, with perhaps some simple lacquered decoration. They did

Far left: A kogai, an implement which was carried in a pocket on the front of a sword or dirk scabbard.

Left: A kodzuka, a handle of a small utility knife carried in a pocket on the rear of a sword or dirk scabbard.

Below: Kashira (cap of the hilt, top) and a side view and base of the fuchi (reinforcing band at the bottom of the hilt). By the famed Iwamoto Konkwan, these show demons being driven from the house by the throwing of beans.

Right: A pair of gilt-leather-covered gyoyo converted into a purse during the Edo period. These leaf-shaped plates, originally used as shoulder guards on retainer's armours, were later used to protect the fastenings of the shoulder straps.

however gain a new feature in the form of implements carried in pockets in the face of the scabbard. One of these, the *kogai*, carried on the outer face of the scabbard when worn, has attracted more supposition and wild theories as to its use than anything else in the field of Japanese arms and armour. In its usual form, the kogai consisted of an ornamented handle, topped by a small spoon-shaped finial, and a narrow, blunt skewer-like blade; some later versions, *wari kogai*, can be split into two parts along the centre line. These mysterious objects are probably nothing more than toilet implements; the finial being for cleaning the ears and the blade for re-dressing the hair after removing the helmet. The split variety appeared at a similar time to the adoption of the very heavily pommaded hair styles worn during the Momoyama and Edo periods. On the rear face of the scabbard was carried a small general-purpose knife, generally called a *kodzuka*, a term which strictly only refers to its decorative hilt. From this time, these accessories became optional for all short swords.

Hilts (*tsuka*) were also of magnolia wood, carefully fitted to the tang and held in place by a *mekugi* (peg), which at this period was of soft metal with ornate end caps. As silk or leather wrappings became more common,

Below: Hilt of a sword bound in variegated silk over metal ornaments which were intended to improve the grip.

Below right: Folding war fan with gilded paper and iron outer ribs overlaid with dragons in silver.

Right: Nineteenth century woodblock print showing a samurai in battle standing on a fallen pavise and carrying a trophy head in his teeth.

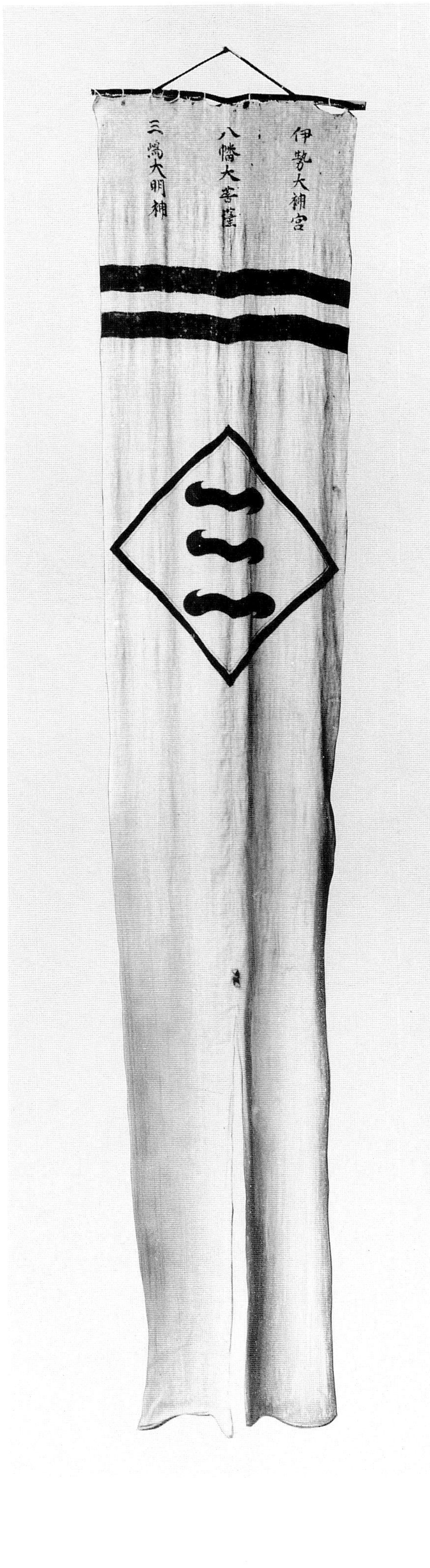

Right: Banner of hemp cloth about 11 feet 6 inches (3.5m) long. Muromachi period.

the peg lost its decorative ends, becoming a tapered piece of bamboo or horn. The whole outer surface of the hilt was covered with *same*, the skin from the back of several species of ray found in the China Seas. After cleaning and preparation, the skins reveal creamy-white bony nodules which vary in size with the size of the fish and the position they occupy, being most pronounced in a concentrated patch just behind the head. The size and regularity of these large nodules dictated the price of skins; they were sometimes so valuable that they were ornately wrapped in brocade and given as presents.

Fittings for tachi hilts invariably included a pommel, *kabuto gane* or *kashira*, shaped like the chape, and a reinforcing band at the base called the *kuchi gane* (mouth metal) or, later, the *fuchi*. If the scabbard had metal-reinforced edges, the edges of the hilt were also fitted with them. Small nails with ornate heads, often in the form of mon or rice bales, were inserted into the hilt both as decoration and to assist the grip, their place being taken by larger ornaments, as the use of bindings over the same became more common. Katana hilts were similarly fitted with pommels and were reinforced at the base; these were sometimes bound but in this period they were more often fitted with a wide metal band, *do gane*, carrying raised ornaments on each face.

Only the tachi was provided with a tsuba (hand guard). A flat disc, it had raised thickened edges, and a lobed outline and was held in place between the habaki and the hilt. It was protected by one or more decorative washers, *seppa*, on each side, which were occasionally expanded to cover most of the face of the tsuba.

Having learned lessons from the methods used by the Mongols, the samurai began to appreciate the advantage of tactics in war and to acknowledge the potential of the common foot soldier. Battles were no longer haphazard scrambles for glory and reward; now the troops were carefully orchestrated in tactical manoeuvres based on Chinese military texts. Lines of infantry armed with pole arms were deployed against cavalry, protected against arrows by *tate* (portable wooden shields). These shields figure prominently in illustrations of battles, and were made almost exactly like their counterparts, the pavises, of Europe – even to having a hinged prop at the back, and being decorated with heraldic

Left: War fan with black lacquered papers decorated with a mon in gold, used for directing troops.

Below left: Sode jirushi, an identification flag worn tied to the shoulder guard. Nambokucko period.

Below: Menuki in the form of male and female dragons. These ornaments were fastened under the binding of sword hilts to improve the grip.

symbols on the front. Heraldic banners, *hata*, in the form of long streamers of cloth some two feet (0.6m) wide attached to a cross bar of bamboo at the top, were used to indicate rallying points. These designated the allegiance of the troops.

Commanders now took a less active role in the actual fighting, being positioned with their guard on vantage points where they could direct the movement of their troops, generally by means of a *gunsen* (war fan). In later periods, these fans were often made with gilded or black papers decorated with a red sun fastened to heavy iron sticks, enabling them to be used as a weapon in an emergency. There was also a non-folding fan, which was a more or less rounded plate of wood, leather or, occasionally, metal, mounted on a handle; the plate was lacquered with the user's mon or with a perpetual calendar showing inauspicious days.

Arrayed in ranks under fluttering pennants of brilliantly dyed cloth and wearing multi-coloured armours, the samurai of the period fought battle after battle in support of one or other of the courts or, more often, for land and the wealth it brought. For the remainder of the population it mattered little who held title to the land they farmed; life was hard.

CHAPTER FOUR

Civil Unrest: the Ashikaga Shogunate

Far right: Reproduction of a Muromachi period o yoroi. It was made by Masuda Miochin Ki no Muneharu in 1860 and presented to Queen Victoria by the last Tokugawa Shogun.

Unlike Yoritomo, who sensibly moved away from Kyoto, the Ashikaga fell into the old trap of setting up the Shogunal Court in the capital. Doubtless they felt it necessary to keep a close eye on the Emperor during the Nambokucho period, but the pleasurable life in the capital appealed far more to Ashikaga tastes than a spartan existence in some provincial backwater. The Ashikaga built magnificent palaces in the Muromachi quarter of the city, giving the name to this period of Japanese history. They spent lavishly, encouraging artists and craftsmen to return to Kyoto to provide the luxury goods they demanded. To pay for this extravagance, unprecedented taxes were levied on farmers; at times over two-thirds of their yearly production was demanded, forcing many to borrow money or pawn belongings to exist.

From the shores of southern Japan and in particular the islands of Iki and Tsushima, pirate-traders had carried out profitable raids on both China and Korea for many years. Answering Chinese requests, the Ashikaga crushed this enterprise and set up official trading operations to import even more luxuries to satisfy their taste for high living. The organization of this and other schemes was delegated to the monks of wealthy monasteries, who acted as advisers and civil servants to the Shogunate. In exchange for brocades, porcelains and other luxuries, the Japanese shipped raw materials and arms, principally appallingly low-quality sword blades, in their thousands.

For the first time, discontent was evident among the lower classes, who up until now had tolerated their lot with surprising good humour. Prior to the fifteenth century, battles and skirmishes had caused some local damage to crops, or had resulted in the burning of a village, but, by and large, the samurai had ignored the peasants and had been ignored by them in return. The burden imposed on the peasant farmers by the be-

Below: Painted screen showing an attack on a fortified mansion. A horseman on the left wears a red dyed horo, which billows out behind him as he charges.

haviour of the Ashikaga, and by those lords who aped their lifestyle, was something that could not be ignored and which touched on everyone's lives. Organized by the *ji zamurai* (local squires), the agricultural community formed themselves into groups called *ikki* for mutual protection and, when forced, retaliated. On several occasions these groups besieged the capital and succeeded in forcing the government to cancel all debts owed to money lenders, and on one occasion even defeated a bakufu army.

To counter these insurrections, the lords built up their armies, even recruiting members of the peasant classes, provided they could equip themselves with arms. These low ranking infantry were aptly named *ashigaru* ('light foot', in the sense of 'light infantry'). Poorly armed and even more poorly led, these unfortunates were motivated almost entirely by the promise of loot rather than by any sense of loyalty, and proved of little value to the commanders of the time.

Even as late as the fifteenth century, o yoroi were still being made and worn by a few high-ranking samurai, but were now anachronistic, and were usually worn only on ceremonial occasions. In battle most samurai wore a development of the simple haramaki-style armour, which wrapped around the body and obviated the need for a waidate.

Since the late Heian period, the necessity for vigil had given rise to the need for a form of protection that could be worn with, or under, everyday wear. The need had been met by a simplification of the haramaki, called a *shita haramaki* (under belly wrap) or more commonly *hara ate* (applied to the belly). These light armours corresponded exactly to the front part of a haramaki, but the nakagawa stopped under the left arm instead of continuing around the body and it had an abbreviated waki ita as on the right. Since there were no watagami, straps were attached to the waki ita and were worn crossed over the back fastened by toggles to loops attached to the muna ita. This fastening was supplemented by cords fastened to the lower rear edges of the nakagawa that tied around the waist. Early versions were normally fitted with three rudimentary sections of kusazuri covering little more than the hips, but a few were made with sections of normal length. In the Kamakura and Nambokucho periods, considerable num-

Above: Page from Gun Yo Ki *showing foot soldiers equipped with utsubo. These enclosed quivers are shown covered with cloth dyed in distinctive patterns that may have served as a means of troop identification.*

bers of these very simple do were produced for foot soldiers, who wore them with simple kote and a happuri. Both scale and plate versions for use by troops, and more decorative versions for wear over normal clothes, continued to be made well into the Edo period. They differed from the earlier ones in having the separate kusazuri modified into a single downward-tapering section that covered only the lower abdomen.

For a short while the original name haramaki continued in use to describe an armour opening on the right. However, this type of armour took the name *do maru* (body round) when an entirely new style of do evolved from the hara ate. Taking the old name, haramaki, this style was produced by extending the sides of the hara ate around the body, complete with further sections of kusazuri, to form a do having its opening down the centre of the back, where it fastened by braid ties. These extensions of the nakagawa meant that the rear tateage and the oshitsuke ita had to be split, each half being fitted with a padded watagami in place of the cross straps. Having the opening at the back caused something of a problem with the fastenings of the sode, since there was nowhere to fit the silk bow on the back. One solution was to provide the armour with a narrow centre plate, *sei ita*, suspended from the oshitsuke ita by toggles and tied in at the waist by the waist cord. Most examples of these back plates are fitted with a section of kusazuri that overlapped those attached to the do and a silk bow, enabling the sode to be fastened in the traditional way. More rarely, this plate consisted of only two rows of scales and a top plate; it was just long enough to carry the ring and its bow, but offered no protection from the middle of the back downwards. Other armours seem to have had neither form of back plate, being fitted instead with small rings on each half of the oshitsuke to which the cords from the sode could be tied.

Many haramaki and most do maru continued to be provided with the same o sode that had been designed originally for the o yoroi, together with the wagumi and, in the case of the do maru in particular, shoji ita as well; the latter being particularly necessary when the arms were lifted over the head when using a sword or naginata. O sode were, however, cumbersome and greatly impeded the free movement of the arms, having been devised originally to act as static shields. More satisfactory versions were introduced, fitted closer to the shoulder and moving with the arms when they were lifted rather than slipping off them. This was achieved by forming the kanmuri no ita into a curve and turning its upper edge at right angles to form a standing flange that guarded the neck and, incidentally, obviating the need for the shoji no ita. Like o sode, this top plate was covered with leather held in place by a gilt fukurin and was fitted with a kesho no ita over the scale heads. The remainder of the sode differed depending upon the type. Those designed for haramaki had the rows of scales continue the curve of the kanmuri no ita and tapering towards the bottom, giving rise to their name *tsubo sode* after their supposed resemblance to a jar. The other, which appears to have been worn indiscriminately with either haramaki or do maru, had lames which became progressively flatter and wider towards the bottom and hence were called *hiro sode* (spreading sode). The ring which on Heian period sode had been fitted inside the rear edge to take the rear cord was replaced on all sode by an elaborate kogai kanamono, attached over the lacing on the fourth row of scales. Apart from this minor improvement, the attachment cords, and the method of fastening these sode to the do, remained unchanged.

The traditional style of armour (now called the do maru) and the new haramaki differed in several small ways from those made earlier. The lames of the kusazuri had an inwards curve at each end, making them fit the legs better and giving the region below the waist a bell-shaped outline. This was achieved by lacing a strip of hide to the back of the scales as they were assembled into rows before they were lacquered. Armours also began to develop a slight constriction at the waist, achieved by tapering the scales in the lower rows of the nakagawa. This transferred little weight from the shoulders to the hips unless, as was sometimes done later, the wearer wore a layer of padding under the

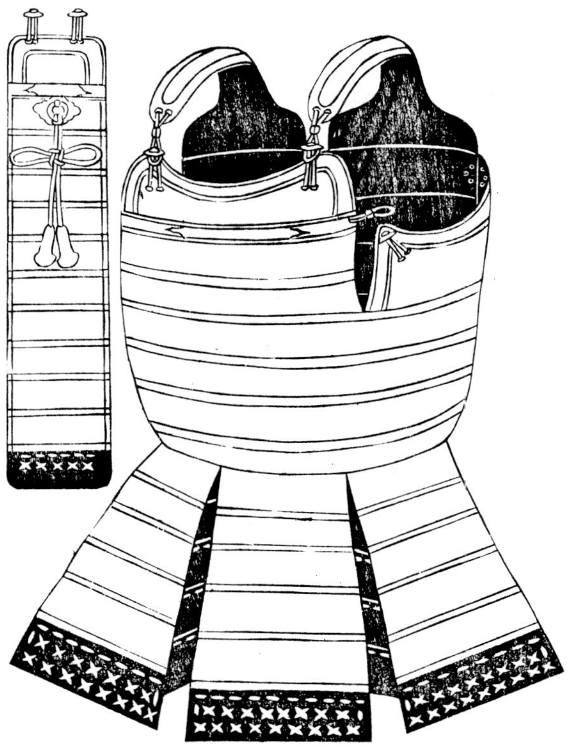

Left: Drawing from Gun Yo Ki *of a Muromachi period haramaki with the opening down the back. The narrow plate is the sei ita (lit back plate) which covered the opening.*

Below: A posed photograph from the late nineteenth century accurately depicts samurai of the Muromachi period. The kneeling page wears a hara ate, covering only the front of the body, and holds a signalling conch.

Right: An Edo period reproduction of a haramaki incorporating a helmet bowl by Saotome Iyetada.

Far right: Sei ita (plate covering the opening of the haramaki) from a Muromachi haramaki. The bottom part covers the trunk and is of leather-laced iyozane, the remainder of kozane, smaller scales, laced with silk.

Do maru (Kamakura/Nambokucho period)

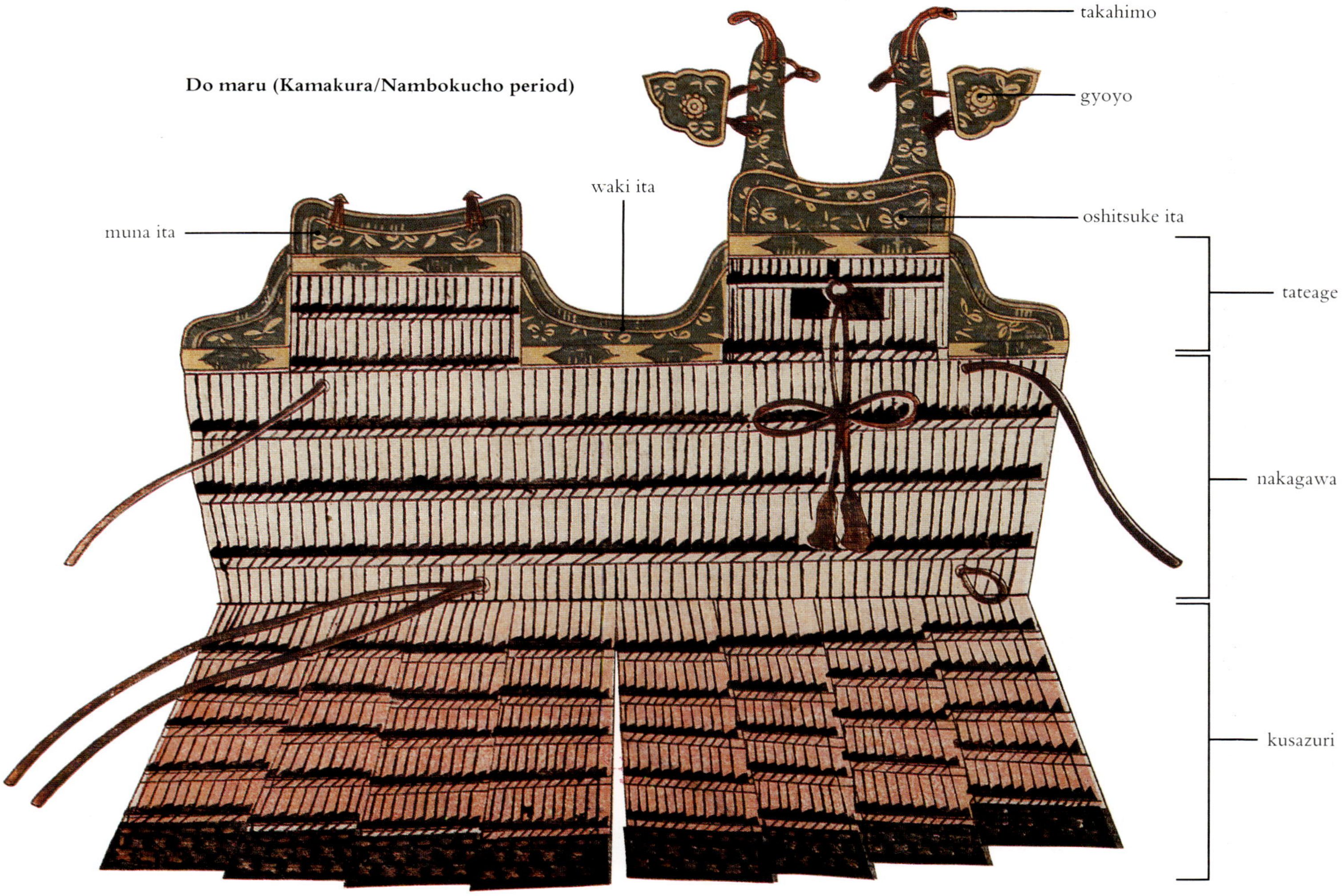

trousers of the yoroi hitatare. Some armours were made entirely of iyozane, others used a mixture of both iyozane and kozane, employing the former for the nakagawa and the latter elsewhere. One strange form of both do maru and haramaki appeared; it was covered entirely with plain, smoked leather held in place by cross knots on each row of scales. These armours were called *kawa zutzumi do maru* or *kawa zutzumi no haramaki* (leather-wrapped armour), and since few survive, they cannot have been popular – probably because they were rather dull compared with the elaborate colours and patterns of lacing that were now popular for more conventional armours.

As helmets were now invariably fitted with a permanent lining, they were made larger, to keep the sides of the helmet itself away from the head. A further consequence was that either three or four rings were riveted to the koshimaki to provide attachment points for the helmet cord, which could no longer be attached high inside the bowl. Reputedly, the increase in the space between the lining and the bowl reduced the concussive effects of a blow as well as making the helmet more comfortable to wear.

The extremely elaborate helmets of the Nambokucho period were replaced by more sober helmets. The rivets were countersunk into the surface of the plates and then lacquered over. Decoration was confined to a gilt tehen kanamono, fukurin and igaki, with usually three shinodare applied directly to the

Above: An unusually early kawa zutsumi do maru. In this type of armour the entire outer surface was covered with smoked leather. Nambokucho period.

Above left: Blue laced do maru with o sode, now considerably faded. Kuromachi period.

Left: Akoda nari kabuto by Miochin Iyetsugu (1558-1591), who worked in Sagami. The koshimaki has been modified to take the present neck guard at a later date.

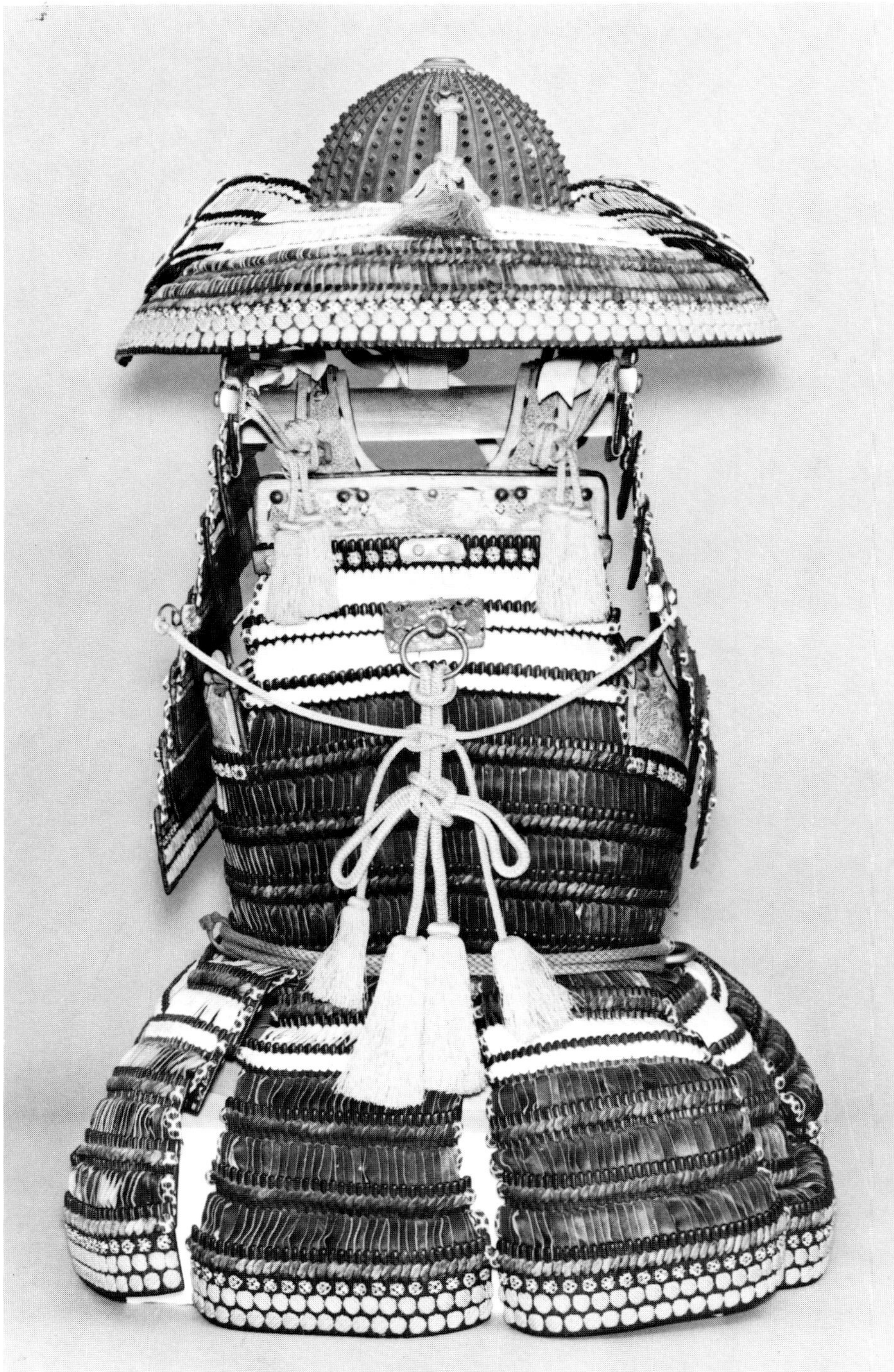

Above: Rear view of a blue and white laced do maru with large sleeves. The wide, spreading neck guard and the fukigaeshi bent backwards to lie along it are typical of the fashion of the time. Muromachi period.

lacquer on the front plate and two others on the back plate. Any helmet bowl in which the rivets were no longer visible but the flanges remained prominent are described as *suji bachi*. As the era progressed, the swelling of the bowl increased, particularly at the back, the tehen tilted forwards slightly and the area round it was slightly depressed. The shape resembled the top of the recently introduced pumpkin, and hence these helmets were called *akoda nari kabuto*.

The peak, which now projected forward at a considerable angle, continued to be covered with decorated leather but was almost completely hidden by the enlarged kuwagata dai fastened to it by gilt-headed rivets. An extra socket, the *haraidate* (prayer stand), became a standard addition fitted centrally between the curved sockets for the kuwagata, the combination being called *mitsu kuwagata dai*. In many cases the central crest took the form of a stylized straight sword blade of the type used in Buddhist ritual, and when it did, its socket was elaborately shaped to represent the stylized thunderbolt hilt normally fitted to these swords. For other crests, the haraidate was a simple rectangular tube having its outer face decorated en suite with the other kanamono on the armour.

Continuing the trend that had started during the Kamakura and Nambokucho periods, the shikoro continued to spread, until in its extreme form it was almost horizontal – *kasa jikoro* (named after the umbrella-shaped hat worn by farmers). Although it allowed the arms to move freely, it left the head and neck vulnerable at the sides, so some had an extra protection fitted underneath the shikora. These *shita jikoro* were generally flat rectangular scales laced to a cloth backing, which hung down like a curtain close to the head. At least one helmet survives where the shita jikoro is of more normal construction but is shaped closer to the head, fitted rather incongruously below the regular one. The fukigaeshi continued to be formed from all but the hishinui no ita and was now bent so far backwards that they all but lay flat on the shikoro itself.

Armour for the face became more common in the later Muromachi period, but was by no means universal. When no mask was worn, the upper chest and throat were protected by a nodawa. The hoate contined to be the most popular type of mask, covering the chin and cheeks to just below the eyes, but an abbreviated version, the *hanbo* was also available which covered only the chin and angle of the jaw. Masks were now provided with two or three rows of scales, curved to fit around the throat. Called *yodare kake* (baby's bib), it hung outside the do, filling the gap above the muna ita and obviating the need for a separate nodawa. For those wanting more protection, similar masks, called *me no shita ho* (below the eye mask), were available provided with a nose piece; on most examples this could be removed to convert it into a hoate. Wrinkles, moustaches, imperials, whiskers, beards, and even gilded or silvered teeth were added

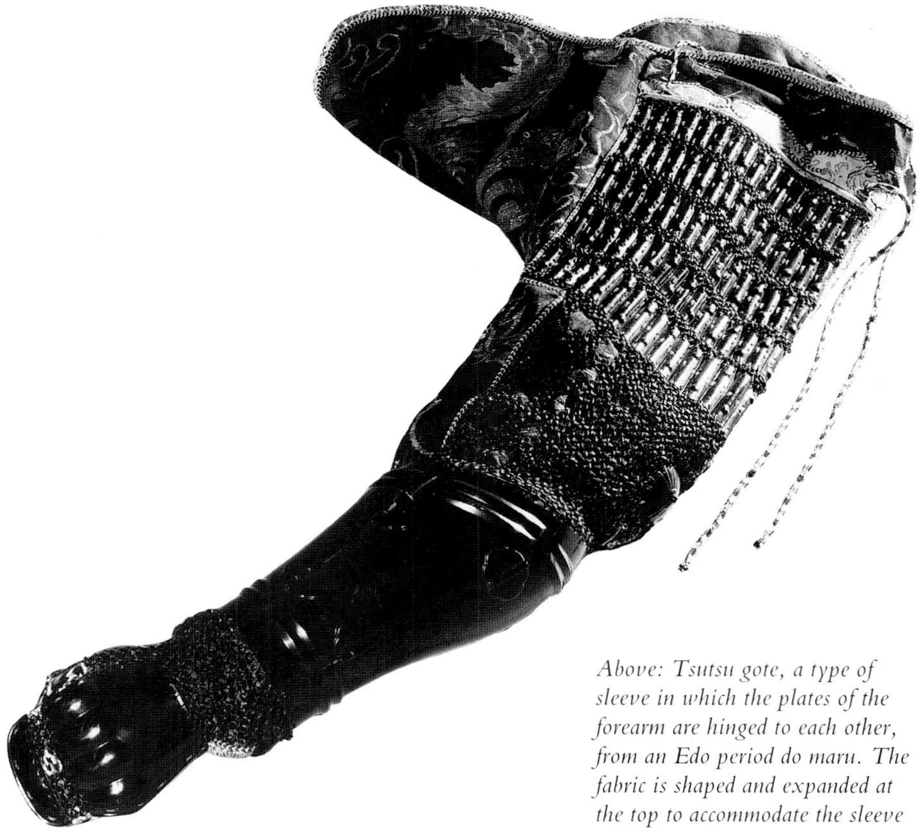

Above: Tsutsu gote, a type of sleeve in which the plates of the forearm are hinged to each other, from an Edo period do maru. The fabric is shaped and expanded at the top to accommodate the sleeve of the brocade costume worn underneath armour.

to masks to enhance their warlike appearance. Most were lacquered red inside, supposedly to impart a reddish, warlike hue to the features, but since the interior could not be seen when worn, this theory is rather dubious.

Very occasionally a full face mask, *so men*, was worn. One of the few to survive is a black-lacquered example. A combination of a happuri with a hoate, it can be separated at the temples, leaving a T-shaped opening for the eyes, nose and mouth. Another covers the face completely, but is just a skeleton framework fretted from a single piece of iron. The first of these examples still retains its yodare kake, and the holes in the latter show that one was originally fitted.

These *men gu* (face armour) were made either from iron or leather, the important feature being that they fitted the face properly. As an aid to comfort, they were provided with a hole or a tube under the chin to drain away perspiration. The helmet cord was tied to hooks on the cheeks and long projecting studs under the chin. This was found in practice to be a much more secure method of fastening the helmet than when the cord was tied directly to the chin. The lower lip and chin protrude in an exaggerated way on many masks, not only to make them more grotesque but also to form a groove which prevented the helmet cord from becoming dislodged. A great number of different methods were devised for tying helmets; these varied from a simple cord tied under the chin, to complex arrangements involving up to five rings on the helmet, the cord looping from them and the hooks attached to the mask in all manner of ways – advocates of each method claiming it had special advantages in battle.

A considerable number of complete armours survive from the Muromachi period

Below: Nineteenth century woodblock print showing retainers of the Takeda family dressing for battle.

Above: Men gu (face armour), from various periods. Top row, me no shita ho, which cover the face and nose below the level of the eyes; middle row, hanbo which cover only the chin and lower cheeks; bottom row nodawa, defences for the throat and upper chest.

Right: Masks covering the whole face were never very common. This example is signed Kojima Munenao, a Miochin smith who worked in the late eighteenth century.

which show that armour for the limbs was developing to keep pace with that for the head and body. The kote were now based on fairly tight-fitting sleeves, *iyeji* (foundation), having a core of hemp cloth stiffened with unripe-persimmon juice, lined with thin silk and covered on the outside with linen, hemp or brocade. All three layers of fabric were bound together around the edge with leather or braid edging. The sleeve was laced up the inside of the arm by a cord so that its fit could be adjusted over the under garments. Onto this base was sewn the defensive metal work, which at this period was of two types. One variety generally had three large plates over the forearm, hinged or sewn to each other with braid, and called *tsutsu gote* (tubular kote). The alternative variety was made up from a varying number of narrow splints connected by mail, and was called *shino gote* in reference to the shape of the leaves of bamboo grass. This term occurs in the book *Moko Shurai*, which suggests that this style had been used in the Kamakura period, but no illustrations or examples survive to show what these early versions were like.

Both varieties of kote were provided with a handguard, *tekko*, which was embossed for the knuckles, and which was extended by a strip of mail and a further small plate to cover the first joint of the fingers. Also joined by mail was a shaped plate for the thumb prolonged by another tiny plate. Loops of cord or braid were provided, generally threaded through the mail joints, through which the middle finger and the thumb were passed to hold the tekko in position. A further cord, fastened with a toggle just above the wrist, prevented the weight of the sleeve dragging on the hand.

The upper part of both types of sleeve was covered with mail into which were set plates whose number, size and arrangement varied considerably. One special type that came into use towards the end of the period, particularly for use with the better quality haramaki, had the whole of the upper arm covered by a small plate sode sewn permanently into position. To allow it to fit close to the arm, the plates of this sode were hinged in two places, the lowest lame being cut off at an angle to allow the elbow to bend. Because these kote resembled those shown being worn by the Buddhist divinity, they were called *bishamon gote*. All types of kote were provided with a small domed plate, *hiji gane*, over the point of the elbow and a capping plate, *kanmuri no ita*, divided into three by hinges or mail to fit the shoulder, and flanged for stiffness.

Prior to the late Muromachi period kote had been put on before the do, being held in place by cords or ties of cloth under the opposite armpit or across the chest. While this method continued to be used, towards the end of the period kote appeared which formed part of an abbreviated jacket, *sashinuki gote*. Some had a standing armoured collar, *tominaga sashinuki gote*. Others had the fabric foundation trimmed to the edge of a capping plate with holes for cords, carrying small toggles that fastened to loops on the underside of the watagami; this transferred some of the weight of the kote to the armour rather than directly to the body.

Armour for the upper legs also underwent considerable development during the Muromachi period, encouraged by the improved techniques developed in the use of pole arms. At the start of the period, an arrangement that had first appeared late in the Nambokucho period was perfected in which rows of kozane were arranged to encircle the knee and lower thigh. This type of haidate took the form of a divided apron of fabric, reinforced with leather to take the weight of the armoured portion. Along the lower edge of

Below: Hodo haidate (defence for the thighs with the lower part divided into sections) from an Edo period reproduction of a do maru.

Bottom: Shino suneate (shinguards) of splints connected by mail. The centre shino is hinged across under the tie to avoid rubbing the instep. Edo period.

Above: Illustration showing the kote (armoured sleeve) being tied around the body under the opposite arm.

each section of fabric was sewn three curved rows of scales, the upper row being laced in reverse for flexibility. When worn, the scale sections were tied above and below the knee so as to completely encircle the leg. This restricted movement to such an extent that this form of defence had only a limited vogue. It was superseded by a flatter arrangement of kozane, still attached to an apron-like fabric support, hung in front of the thigh and knee and only loosely fastened behind the leg by a narrow band of fabric. Initially, the scales were in several rows, the lower ones subdivided as they had been during the Nambokucho period, but by the mid-Muromachi they were replaced by continuous rows of iyozane (larger scales), laced in reverse so that they overlapped downwards. This arrangement was lighter and easier to make.

On their lower legs, most samurai continued to wear some form of o tateage suneate (shin guard with knee plates), which by the middle of the Muromachi period was sometimes supplemented by an additional plate covering the back of the leg. An alternative, lighter form made of splints, like the corresponding kote, now made its appearance. These *shino suneate* differed from the plate variety in that the shino on the inside of the leg only extended to mid-calf, the lower part being replaced by a patch of leather, *abumi zuri no kawa*, to prevent damage to the stirrup leathers. Some had the defence for the knee omitted, when they were known as *kaihan suneate*, but most are fitted with them, in the form of a standing section of *kikko* or brigandine made from small hexagonal plates quilted between layers of fabric or leather. All samurai now wore straw sandals over soft leather ankle socks which had a separate big toe to accommodate the thongs of the sandals.

The swords and other weapons carried during the Muromachi period consisted of a mixture of the older styles of the Kamakura and Nambokucho periods, and other newly devised varieties. Most still wore the kawa zutzumi no tachi, although an alternative, *ito maki no tachi*, appeared in which the hilt and upper part of the scabbard were wrapped with silk braid in place of leather. One innovation that started early in the period was for the dirk or short sword worn edge upwards through the belt to be increased in length and to be worn as an alternative to the tachi. At first these *uchi gatana* (striking or piercing sword) were relatively short, with light, relatively straight blades averaging about two feet (0.6m) in length. These were more suited to thrusting than the longer, curved blades of tachi. As their utility became recognized, they were made longer and sturdier, being

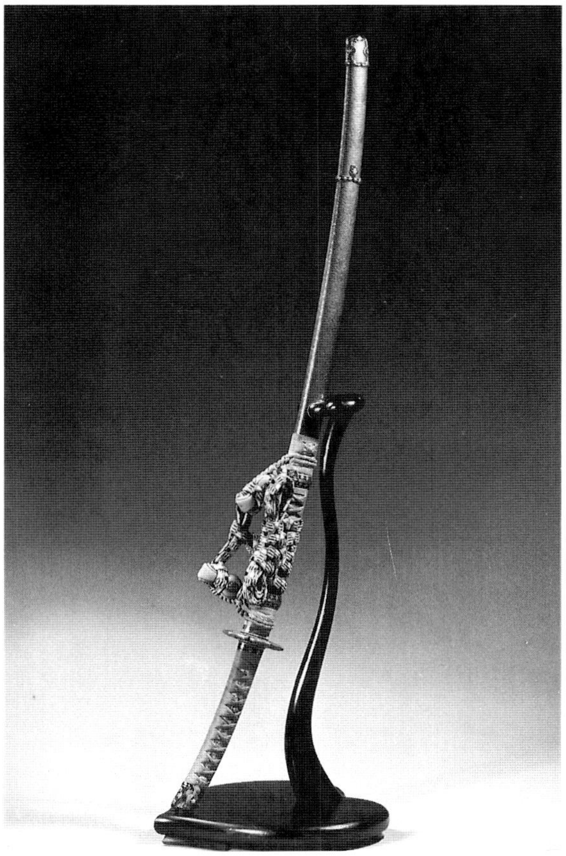

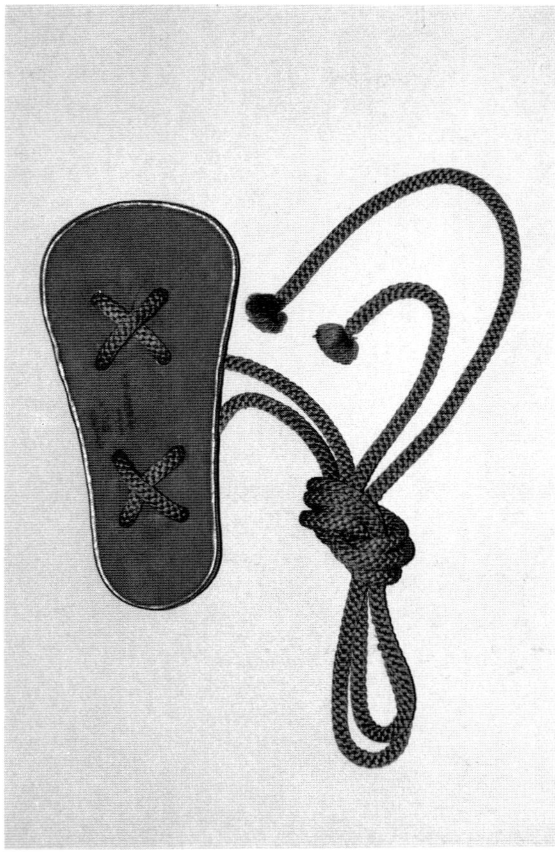

Far left: An ito maki no tachi on a tachi stand. This type of sword has the hilt and upper part of the scabbard bound with silk. Edo period.

Left: A koshi ate or sword carrier. Momoyama period.

mounted in a similar way to the tachi but without ashi and sometimes without tsuba. Like dirks, they were fastened to the belt by a strong braid, threaded through a slotted protrusion on the outer face of the scabbard a few inches below the mouth, called a *kurigata* (chestnut shape). So popular did this style of sword become, that it was eventually adopted as standard wear when in civilian dress, accompanied by a short sword, chiisa katana or wakizashi, mounted in a similar way. Some samurai, whether because of poverty or design, had tachi made with removeable ashi so that they could be worn as uchi gatana. Others wore uchi gatana fastened to a sword carrier, koshi ate, edge downwards in the manner of a tachi.

It is not known why this form of sword mounting became so popular; it may be that it was simply more comfortable to wear, as the sword was held firmly to the body and did not bump against the hip when riding or walking. This was also the case when the sword was carried in a koshi ate, since it was tied closely to the waist. Having the hilt in a fixed position meant that the hand could be guided straight to it when the need arose to draw the sword quickly, rather than having to fumble, as would have been necessary for the hilt of a tachi, which swung on its hangers. Since the Japanese always removed the long sword when entering a house, leaving it in a rack placed for the purpose by the

Below: Sword guard of russet iron pierced with a design of sickles and a pagoda.

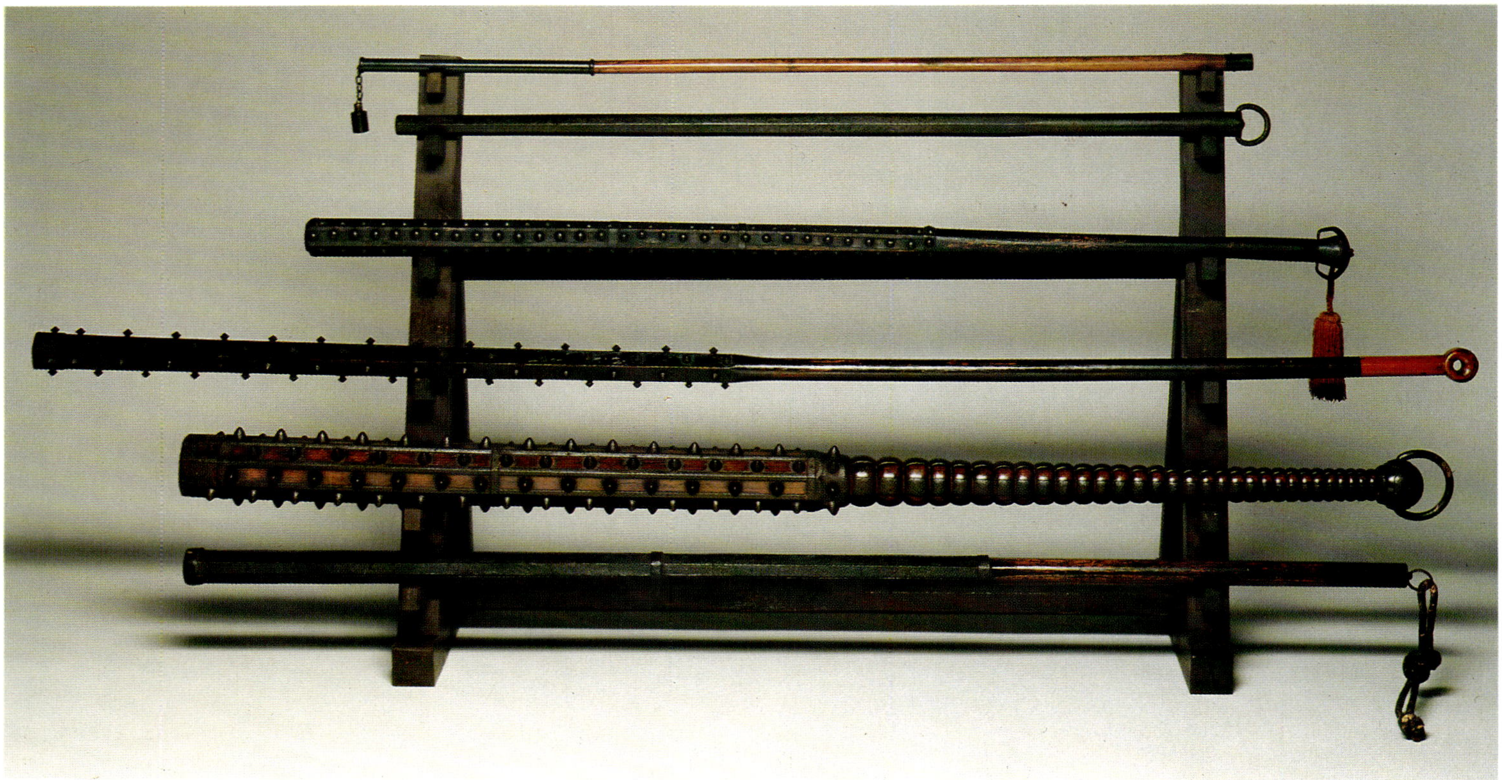

Above: Various types of club. The top example contains a weighted chain which can be flicked out at an enemy.

Below: Pole arms. The bottom two are fitted with parrying bars.

door, the answer may be much more prosaic. The tachi was tied to the belt by its cords, and had to be untied to remove it. An uchi gatana, on the other hand, could be slipped from the belt, or repositioned in it, in just a few seconds.

Those with the strength to do so went into battle carrying the huge no dachi, but most preferred one of the varieties of pole arms. Naginata were still popular, but they had slightly smaller blades than previously, mounted on proportionally longer shafts. In

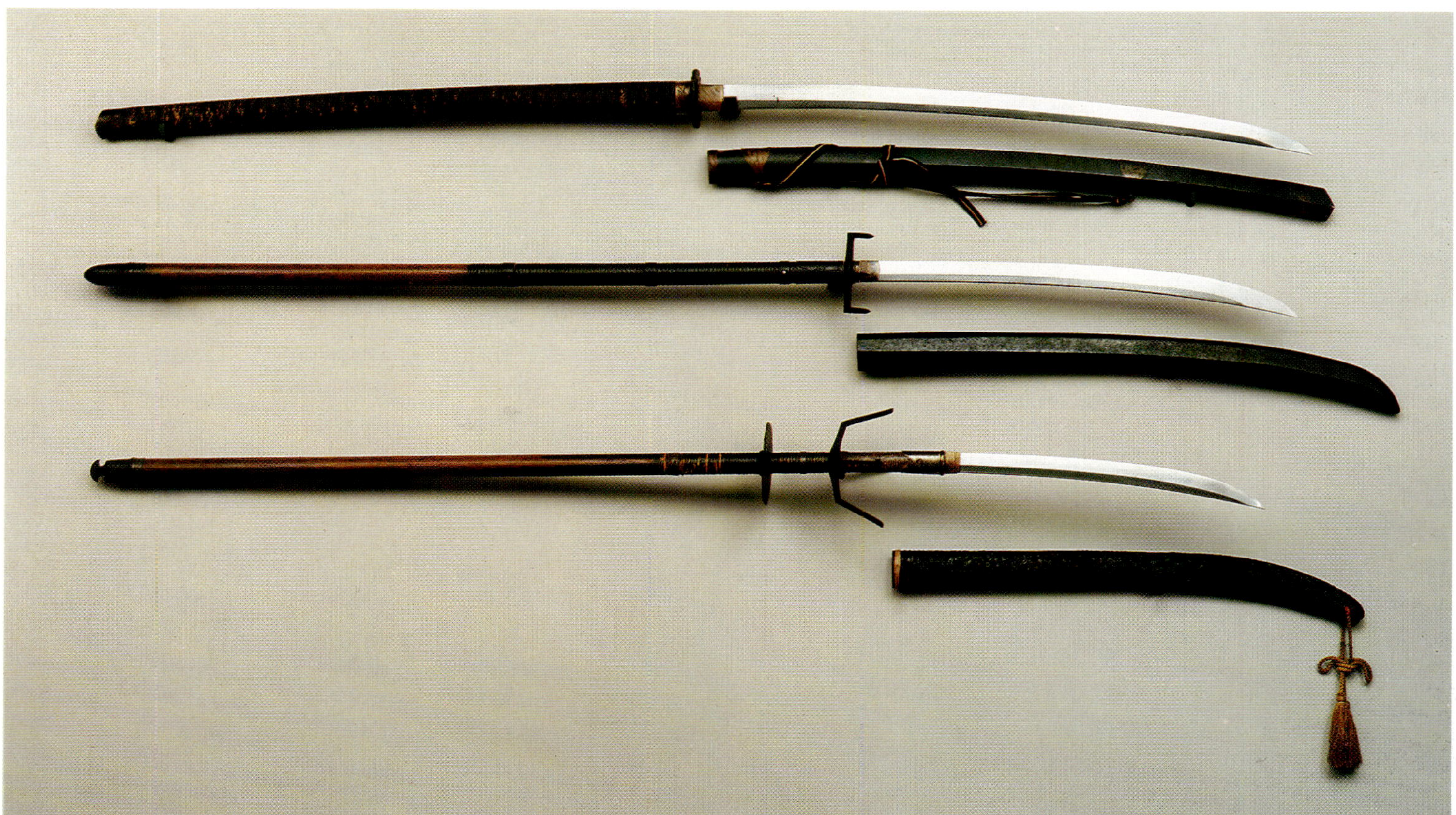

Far left: Utsubo of exaggerated proportions. These quivers offer the arrows complete protection from the weather.

Left: Saika bachi having hinged plates to guard the temples. Helmet bowls of this type, made at Saika on the Kii peninsula, are characterized by the chrysanthemum-shaped plates applied to the top of the bowl.

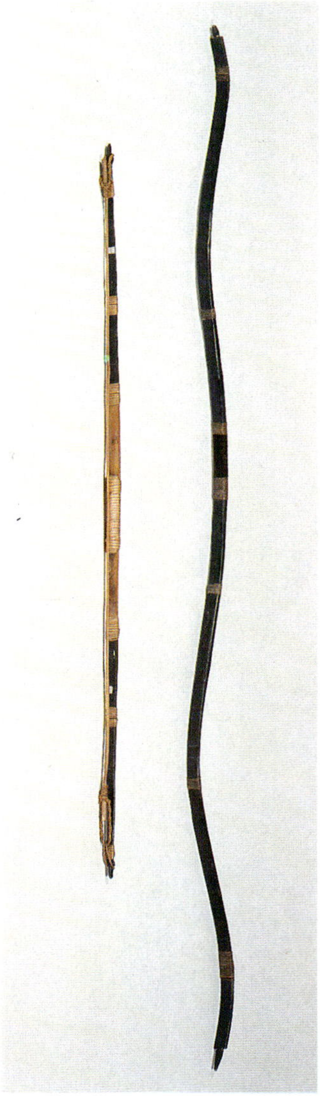

Below: Two bows. The bow on the left is a han kyu, or half bow, for use in restricted spaces.

common with all pole arms of the period, naginata shafts now sported several ornamental reinforcing bands around the region enclosing the tang of the blade, below which was a bulbous binding of cord that acted as a hand stop. In use, the hands are continuously slid along the shaft of the naginata, and reversed on it, as different defensive stances are adopted. During these manoeuvres the hand stop acted as a tactile indication to the upper limit of the shaft. It was now usual to lacquer or otherwise decorate only the part of the shaft above the hand stop (the part of the shaft that had to be split to cut the socket for the tang of the blade); the lower part was generally of polished wood.

A few kumade and kama were still being used, but as in all periods they were rare weapons, used only by a small minority. Similarly, a few of herculean stature carried clubs of iron or wood, *kanabo*, of tapering octagonal section, about five feet (1.5m) long, and frequently studded for most of their length. No doubt a blow from such a weapon would have been devastating, but their sheer size and weight would suggest they were meant more for intimidation than for serious use.

A weapon similar in many respects to the naginata appeared around the middle of the Muromachi period. Called the *nagamaki*, some authorities consider it merely a variant of the no dachi. The apparent similarity between the names is illusory; naginata means 'mowing down sword' while nagamaki means 'long wrapping' and refers to the fact that many have their shafts wrapped in a criss-crossed manner, like a sword hilt. In shape, the blades of the nagamaki resembled a large, heavy sword blade, sometimes thinned along the back edge to reduce weight. It was fitted to a short shaft about four feet (1.2m) long and was generally provided with a tsuba or other protection for the hand. Modern enthusiasts who have attempted to use them describe them as clumsy, ill-balanced weapons with little to recommend them. Despite this they enjoyed a considerable vogue extending into the Momoyama period, being favoured by Oda Nobunaga for his front-line troops.

By far the most common pole arm carried was the *yari* (spear). Fitted with a head which was a flattened-diamond shape in section, its length could vary from six inches (15cm) to three feet (0.9m) or more. Unlike the naginata and nagamaki, which had oval shafts to assist in directing the blade, spear shafts were round or multi-faceted, lacquered in the upper part and reinforced with metal rings. Most shafts were of oak, but one formerly in the author's collection was built from wedge-shaped pieces of bamboo, glued together in the manner of a fishing rod. The total length of yari during most of the Muromachi period was a modest six or seven feet (1.8 or 2.1m), but towards the end of the period, foot soldiers were armed with longer spears as a defence against horsemen.

Archery continued to play its role in all Muromachi battles. The power of the bow had been increased by surrounding the wooden core with bamboo on all four sides. A new type of quiver, the *utsubo*, appeared which all but ousted the old ebira. It was enclosed, offering better protection from the weather to the arrows. Most utsubo were more or less cylindrical containers with a rounded upper end and a lidded opening in the side near the bottom. They were worn on the right hip and held in place by straps and cords; the lid was swung aside as the arrows were taken out downwards. When not in use the lid was held shut by a strap. Later utsubo varied considerably; the upper part swelled outwards like a balloon in some, others were elaborately lacquered or covered with fur. However, during the Muromachi period they were plain utilitarian objects, worn with a cloth cover decorated with stripes of colour or with mon. These covers may have acted as troop identification on the battlefield as well as providing protection.

Right: Oki tenugui kabuto, a type of helmet with almost vertical sides to the bowl and top plates which extend beyond the back of the bowl. The applied flower shaped plates suggest the work of the Saika Haruta armourers.

A curious weapon that survives in considerable numbers made its appearance at the end of the Nambokucho period and became more common during the Muromachi period. The *uchi ne* originally took the form of a very short spear, with a shaft that was only about a foot (0.3m) long and a small but heavy three- or four-sided blade. At close quarters it could be used for stabbing or thrown in the manner of a dart, while for longer ranges it could be held by the point and thrown in a similar way to a knife. Later versions were fitted with exaggerated fletchings to stabilize their flight, and a nock (frequently of ivory) which, because the weapon was a missile was purely decorative. Those that survive from the Edo period generally have a tasselled wrist cord through the shaft near the nock, indicating the tendency to use them more as a stabbing weapon than as a missile.

Unlike the swordsmiths, whose names have survived both on blades and in the literature of the Heian period, reference to armourers is remarkably scarce. Even the name *kanko* (armour person) that was used during the Kamakura and Nambokucho periods has a slightly derogatory implication. By the Muromachi period, however, the situation began to change with the introduction of the more complimentary name, *katchu shi* (armour craftsman) and isolated references to groups of armourers with names like Yuasa, Handa and Gennai appear in contemporary literature. In the book *Sekiso orai* by Ichijo Kaneyoshi, the name 'Wakito' occurs with reference to a group of armour makers, while in *Oninki* an armour is referred to as being a Koizumi yoroi. Koizumi and Wakito are suburbs of Nara, suggesting that there was already a concentration of armourers working there.

Two groups, the Haruta and the Iwai, share the distinction of being the first armourers that can be positively identified in Japanese records. Almost without doubt, the Haruta was the first group to start signing its work and it is probable that it is the same group as the Handa mentioned above. Such signatures, at first chiselled only inside the back plate of helmet bowls, had been preceded by quality control marks in the form of single characters, occasionally applied in red lacquer. Once the practice of signing helmets became common, the *ukebari* (lining) was provided with a vertical slit at the back so that the inscription could be read.

Towards the end of the Muromachi period the Haruta group was known to be based at Nara and it was probably responsible for the Koizumi armour mentioned above. At this time it specialized in making akoda nari kabuto, and continued to make them long after other, more practical, helmets had been adopted by other groups. Because of this adherence to the older style of helmet, the group suffered something of a decline in popularity during the sixteenth century, although it managed to maintain its appointment as armourer to the Shogun. At some period towards the end of the fifteenth century some of the Haruta moved to Kii and flourished by adopting the methods and styles being developed there. Unfortunately little is known about this branch, since it rarely signed its work, much of which can best be described as sturdy if not elegant.

Also working in Nara were the Iwai, about whom even less is known than the Haruta. During the Muromachi period members of this group seem to have been general armourers, but by the Momoyama and early Edo periods they were making armour for the Shogun himself, and for presentation by him, specializing in armour made of hardened leather. The mainline Iwai later became renowned for lacing and tailoring metalwork made by other groups, although a few helmets survive that show it could still make armour itself. Many more members of this group are known to have dispersed to different parts of the country to work as part of the retinue of various *daimyo*.

Towards the end of the fifteenth century a few tentative moves were made that were to transform traditional manufacturing techniques. Apart from minor cosmetic changes to the shape, and the number and size of rivets, helmets were still being made in essentially the same labour-intensive fashion as in the Heian period. An early example of a helmet made and preserved in Tosa province, shows that the armourers there were conscious of the problem and had found a solution; a solution which, although relatively insignificant at the time, was to be extremely important later. Because the shape of this new helmet was, in contrast to the akoda nari, contoured close to the head, it became known, not unnaturally, as the *zunari kabuto* (head-shaped helmet). Of the greatest simplicity, its main constructional element was a long plate running from front to back over the crown of the head, riveted to a rather wide koshimaki at each end, with two further plates filling in the gaps at each side. A simple peak whose lower edge arched over the eyes was riveted directly to the koshimaki in front. In the case of the surviving helmet, a small pair of kuwagata are held in place by these same rivets. An illustration of ashigaru by Tosa Mitsunobu shows the zunari kabuto being worn with a shikoro of cloth, marked as if quilted, but probably meant to represent mail. This is the first example of helmets being made for munition armour, *okashi gusoku* (lent armour), designed for low-cost production.

Below: A saika bachi, a multi-plate helmet made in Saika, decorated with the typical flower shaped plates of the Haruta armourers.

Above: Oki tenugui kabuto of considerable weight devoid of ornament.

Other armourers in the town of Saika on the Kii peninsular were also beginning to experiment. Their inspiration is said to have been a strange helmet washed out of the banking bordering the sea shore, a story which may have an element of truth because their initial productions bear more than a passing resemblance to the tsuki mabizashi kabuto of the Yamato period. What finally emerged were *saika bachi*, differing in detail from each other, yet recognizably related. The helmet bowl was rather higher than a hemisphere and circular in plan. It was made up of about eight vertical plates riveted to a wide koshimaki at the base and had a large, domed, circular plate with a multi-lobed outline at the top. Surmounting this were several more iron plates with a chrysanthemum-shaped outline surrounding the small iron rimmed tehen. All of the rivets involved had small rounded heads fitted with a washer of iron marked with radiating lines, *za boshi*. Many examples had no peak as such; instead the koshimaki continued across the front as a separate piece, cut out over the eyes and embossed with wrinkles and eyebrows. A few examples have small additional plates hinged above each temple, forming a sort of built-in happuri (a feature that also occurred on helmets represented on some haniwa.)

Another form of helmet bowl, whose inspiration can only be guessed at, was also produced by the Saika smiths. It was called *oki tenugui bachi* because it resembled the thin cotton towel worn under the helmet to absorb perspiration. There is some evidence that these helmets may have originated with the Tosa group since the book *Ken Mon Zatsu Roku* describes them as being similar to the *tosa zukin kabuto*. Since *zukin* can be translated as a hood or turban, this reference may be describing a similar but now unknown form of helmet; a view reinforced by the fact that they were called *zukin nari* (hood shaped) during the Edo period. The helmet bowl of the oki tenugui kabuto had the koshimaki extended upwards to form the sides of the helmet, and was capped by two plates, curved downwards at the front and sides only, riveted together along the centre line. These top plates were attached solely along the front and sides of the helmet, leaving the rear edge overhanging the koshimaki and often with a distinct gap beneath, which may have added considerably to the comfort of the wearer in the humid climate of Japan. Once again there was generally no separate peak, the front plate being embossed and fitted with applied eyebrows. Some examples were fitted with a narrow brim riveted around the koshimaki, which turned up at the front to form rudimentary fukigaeshi, while others were repoussed with a groove; in both cases these features were probably added to stiffen the sides and particularly the back since it gained no support from the top plates.

Neither the saika bachi nor the oki tenugui bachi was provided with the usual fittings for crests since generally neither had a peak to which they could be fitted. Instead they had simple iron hooks, *tsunomoto*, riveted to the brow, which in the case of the oki tenugui bachi were frequently double pronged.

So popular did these helmet styles become that the Haruta smiths who moved to Saika took up their production and abandoned their favourite akoda nari. Essentially, their products were very similar to, although perhaps rather more refined than, the rather brutal helmets of the indigenous smiths, and can be distinguished by the applied large diamond or flower-shaped plates, sometimes pierced so as to leave only an outline. These decorative plates became almost a trademark of the Saika Haruta; they used smaller ones under rivet heads in place of the more usual round washers of za boshi.

In the first year of the Onin period (1467), an argument between two families of nobles broke out in the capital. Other nobles joined sides and a prolonged war broke out, fought almost entirely in the city itself. This urban war continued for a total of some 11 years, gradually dying out as the participants lost their sense of purpose and drifted back to their provinces. Some idea of the scale of fighting can be gained from the fact that a single lord turned up with 20,000 men to support one faction; little wonder that a great part of Kyoto failed to survive.

On their return to their homelands, many of the nobles found their domains had been usurped, or divided up among those they had left in charge. Those with the means to do so fought to regain their possessions while others had little alternative but to accept the situation. Fighting flared up throughout the country as the more ambitious saw their chance to gain land and status. This unique situation is summed up by the phrase *geko-kujo* (those below overthrowing those above). It was a time of rapid rises to prominence by minor members of the nobility and the equally rapid decline into obscurity of previously important personages. Throughout the remainder of the fifteenth century, and for the whole of the sixteenth, the country experienced almost perpetual warfare, giving rise to the name *sengoku jidai* (The Age of the Country at War).

As the scale of fighting, and the numbers involved in it, increased, the demand for arms and armour rose to unprecedented heights. Scale armours that had served the samurai well over the centuries suffered from defects that became more and more apparent as the magnitude and duration of the conflict increased. Armours had evolved into rich costumes, valued almost as much for their appearance as for their defensive qualities. With their subtle colour schemes and often lace-like metal decorations they were totally unsuited to the rough-and-tumble of the long campaigns that were such a prominent feature of these wars. Sakakibara Kozan's analysis of the situation sums up these disadvantages admirably:

A large quantity of lacing is a disadvantage. When soaked with water it becomes very heavy and cannot be quickly dried; so that in summer it is oppressive and in winter liable to freeze. Moreover, no amount of washing will completely free the lacing from any mud which may have penetrated it, and on long and distant campaigns it becomes evil smelling and overrun by ants and lice, with consequent ill-effects on the health of the wearer. It is also easily damaged because it will retain a spear instead of letting it glide off harmlessly.

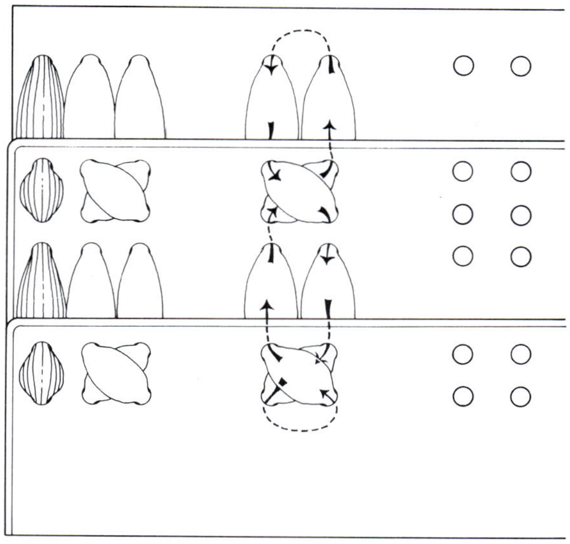

Left: Sugake lacing was adopted as a means of reducing the amount of braid used in the construction of an armour. Large quantities of lacing became heavy when soaked and harboured dirt and vermin on long campaigns.

Below: Dark green kebiki sugake laced do maru. Sugake lacing (see diagram above) can be seen on the kusazuri.

Left: Karuta gane tatami do. These armours of mail and plates sewn onto a fabric backing dispensed with lacing entirely. Since they could be cheaply produced, and folded for storage and transport, they were widely used for arming common soldiers.

Above: Karuta gane tatami kabuto inscribed in red lacquer 'medium size'. This inscriptian suggests it was for issue to low-ranking troops.

Below: Tatami hitai ate, a minimal helmet usually worn by foot soldiers, fitted with a hood of kikko and hair.

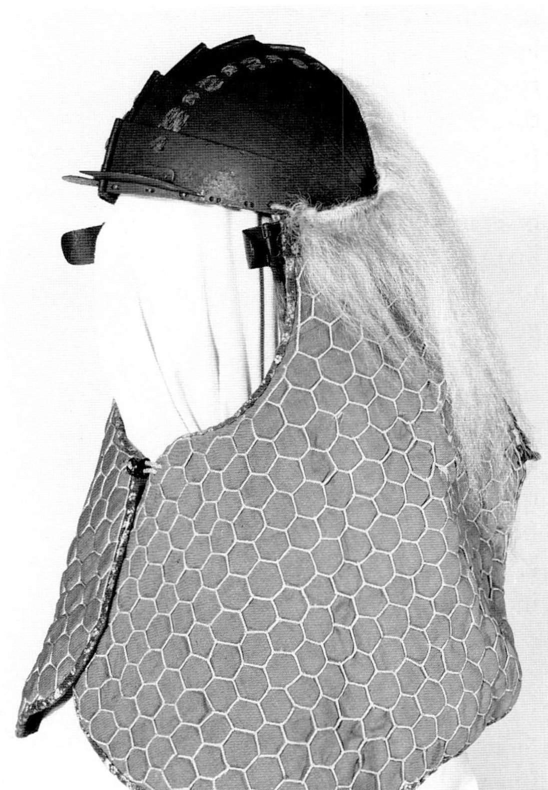

What Kozan fails to say, but what is equally important, is that its production involved immense amounts of labour, which could only be afforded by the very wealthy. Armourers, their order books full, struggled to keep pace with the demands placed on them. Not only were the samurai demanding armour, but commanders were also faced with the problem of providing something for the ever-growing numbers of ashigaru being recruited. In the past, when ashigaru had been relatively few in numbers, many had been left to look after their own interests, and a battlefield provided a plentiful supply of spare equipment. This *ad hoc* approach could hardly be countenanced when a whole army needed equipping. Inevitably the answer lay in the abandonment of scale construction altogether and its replacement by plates, but there were many who showed a reluctance to abandon such a well-tried system without first exploring every alternative.

Reducing the amount of lacing was a step in the right direction and could be achieved without changing the method of construction at all. In the traditional *kebiki* (drawn hair) style of lacing, each length of braid connected adjacent rows of scales by alternating from one to another, horizontally from left to right. A new technique was devised called *sugake* (simple hang) lacing in which the length of braid was threaded vertically up the rows of scales from the lowest to the top, then back again, giving the appearance of a pair of laces, cross knotted on each row to lock them in position. These double columns of lacings could be spaced along the rows, keeping the total amount to a minimum. A rare variation of this technique was *mitsu suji gake*, which used groups of three adjacent holes rather than pairs, laced in the same way with an additional length of braid running vertically down the centre holes. In a few cases armours were made of kozane, laced in the sugake style, with all the unused holes filled in with lacquer. While this reduced the lacing problem, it did nothing to reduce the initial labour involved in making the scales. Another method that was tried was to use iyozane, with the completed rows wrapped in lacquered leather and pierced only where needed for the sugake lacing. In this case there was some saving in time since each iyozane covered almost twice the area as a kozane, with the added advantage that there was also a considerable saving in weight.

Above: Chochin kabuto, a helmet which collapses flat for storage, extended, and (below) closed.

While these experiments were being tried, others dispensed with lacing altogether and made armours from small plates sewn onto a fabric backing with the gaps between them filled with mail. Both do maru and haramaki versions of these were successfully created. By hinging the few large plates such as the muna ita and watagami, the whole armour could be folded into a compact package for both storage and transport. They were called *kusari do maru* or *kusari haramaki*, and further differentiated into *karuta gane do* and *kikko gane do* depending whether they were made from rectangular or hexagonal plates respectively. Because they could be folded, all types were known by the generic term *tatami do* (tatamu being the verb to fold). A few were of high quality and obviously made for men of rank, but most were cheaply made munition armours, issued to troops from stores when needed. The fact that many have sections of kusazuri omitted at the back shows they were not all meant for the humble foot soldier; perhaps they were for lightly armoured cavalry which could be deployed rapidly over rough terrain.

All types and qualities of helmets are found accompanying these do, but for munition armours, a simple hood of mail and plates fitted with a nominal shikoro was considered adequate when cost was a consideration. One such helmet in the author's collection has a slit at the back for the wearer's hair and is inscribed inside in red lacquer 'medium-large size'. Even cheaper was the *hitai ate*, a simple plate, shaped to fit the forehead and sewn to a band of cloth which could be tied around the head. This defence obviously derived from the happuri of the Heian period, and was later elaborated and extended further onto the head, by providing it with a peak and making it of two or more plates, riveted loosely at the temples so that it could be collapsed for storage. In this more developed form, called *tatami hitai ate*, it was often sewn to a hood made of mail or of kikko to offer some protection to the remainder of the head and neck.

During the early Edo period, a novel folding helmet was made to accompany tatami do. The most usual type has the bowl divided horizontally into overlapping rings fastened together with sugake lacing, and arranged so that it can be locked in an extended position to a pivoted curved strap by a turn button.

Far left: O yoroi, traditionally from Tamba province. The helmet is decorated with shinodare applied to the front plate, and is fitted with the characteristic spreading neck guard (kasa jikoro) of the Muromachi period. The tsurubashiri gawa, leather cover to the front of the do, is printed with the Buddhist divinity Fudo.

Below: Dark blue laced mogami do. This type of armour was constructed of horizontal strips of steel, individually hinged. Edo period.

Above: Detail of the sei ita (back plate) of the armour opposite showing the unusual treatment of the lacquer and typical lobed Momoyama style kanamono. The rivets holding these ornamental plaques in position are engraved with the owner's mon; the character 'ju' in a circle symbolizing the Christian cross.

More sophisticated versions have spring-operated studs on each section that snap out and lock over the tops of the plate below as the helmet is extended, the taper of the rings stopping both types from extending too far. Because they resemble the familiar paper lanterns, these helmets are called *chochin bachi*.

While tatami do had solved some of the problems of traditional armours, they suffered from a lack of rigidity which offered almost no protection against the force of a blow. Large rigid sections were needed to dissipate the energy over a wide area. One solution to this problem was to replace the rows of scales with strips of steel, fitted with hinges to enable the wearer to put it on. Called *mogami do*, these armours were of either do maru or haramaki style, with each strip forming the nakagawa divided into five curved pieces joined by hinges in line with the edges of the tateage at front and back. Irrespective of whether they were laced in the kebiki or sugake style, most had the tops and sides of the plates turned outwards to a small flange, against which a narrow, round beading was modelled with lacquer. Continuing the traditional method of construction, each of these strips was individually lined with leather, which was held in place by the leather ties that fastened the strips of the nakagawa rigidly to each other. These armours were fitted with kusazuri, sode and shikoro which matched the construction of the do; they were made from strips of plate, lacquered and laced either in the kebiki or sugake style.

Even though the mogami style of construction continued to be produced as long as armour was worn, the multiplicity of small hinges, and the rather delicate internal ties which really held the do together were serious weaknesses; further developments were needed before plate armour could be said to be superior to that made from scales.

Right: Mogami haramaki of Naito Yukiyasu, a Christian Daimyo exiled to Manila for his beliefs. This reassembled armour clearly shows the individually hinged plates in the do that characterize this construction. The helmet is an etchu zunari kabuto with the central plate overlapping the brow plate and the lower plate of the neck guard cut with a straight edge at the bottom.

CHAPTER FIVE

The Evolution of Modern Armour

Far right: Detail from a folding screen showing the siege of Osaka Castle.

As the fifteenth century drew to a close, fortunes and reputations were gained and lost with a bewildering rapidity. Those with sufficient courage or guile prospered while the weak and indecisive went under. Gekokujo was at its height, with long-established families sinking into obscurity, while newcomers rose to positions of power and prominence.

A typical example of how minor figures achieved fame and fortune is shown by an incident which arose after Ashikaga Masatomo instructed his son to join a monastery. Not having a religious leaning, the son's response was to murder his father and assume control of the family's domain. From indignation or, more likely, using the incident as a pretext for action, an obscure samurai called Ise Shinkuro launched a successful attack on the son, gaining control of the province of Izu in the process. Like so many in his position, Shinkuro changed his name, choosing Hojo, in an attempt to gain respectability, joining a monastery under the adopted name of Soun. He then set about acquiring the neighbouring province of Sagami, inviting the local lord to a hunt. Needless to say, the lord, not the deer, was the quarry, and Soun emerged with the fortress town of Odawara added to his acquisitions. Using more conventional tactics he completed the conquest of Sagami before passing the task of further expansion to his son and grandson. By the mid-sixteenth century the family were powerful land owners with most of the eastern plains of Honshu under their control. With such treachery and military aggression almost commonplace, it is hardly surprising that the demand for the trappings of war was at an unprecedented level.

Having once acquired land, those who rose to power employed every means they

Right: The main tower of Hamamatsu Castle, which served as an observation platform.

Below: Hamamatsu Castle – a corner tower. Castle building reached a climax in the sixteenth century at the height of the civil wars.

could to hold onto it, indulging in an unprecedented spate of castle building. Fortresses and strongholds, often little more than temporary stockades or fortified houses, had been built since Yamato times, but by the Muromachi period they had begun to take on a more permanent character, developing into castles, sited to take maximum advantage of the terrain. The golden age of castle building occurred during the sixteenth and early seventeenth centuries, indeed the period is named after a castle. Enormous works at Osaka and Edo were built with multiple towers, moats and outworks extending a mile or more on each side. Natural defensive positions such as hills or mountain crags were the first choice of location, but lakes, rivers and even the sea were exploited for their defensive possibilities. When size and the site permitted, the enclosed area was divided into a series of compartments on different levels and separated by gates and bridges to confuse the enemy should he gain entry. Once inside, his progress was impeded by one obstacle after another and he was constantly assailed by the arrows of the defenders. In some castles, these 'killing grounds' take on the character of a maze, and abrupt changes of direction are required to reach the heart of the stronghold.

The basis of these structures was a series of platforms of rammed earth, faced with cyclopean masonry that rose in a sweeping curve, often directly out of the moat, and becoming vertical or even overhanging slightly towards the top. On these bases were built the walls of stone or wood that divided the interior. Towers and arrow loops were incorporated where needed to provide defence to the flanks and to cover the areas within. The various gates were sometimes surmounted by towers, usually a single storey high, from which the defenders could pour missiles down onto the attackers. As a precaution against fire, the gates were often plated with iron and the timber structure of the tower, like the other structures of the castle, was heavily plastered. At the heart of

Below: Scene from the film Kagemusha *showing a commander with his pages and personal guards controlling troops from a vantage point.*

the defence was the main tower, with perhaps subsidiary towers connected to it rising in storeys of decreasing size, with sweeping roofs and overhanging gables. Although it looked impressive, the tower had little military value; it was essentially a command post and watch-tower during a battle. The tower at Osaka stood on a base about 100 feet (30m) square and 50 feet (15m) high; the tower itself was three storeys high, which added another 40 feet (12m) to the total height. The towers were used for storage and similar purposes; the main living quarters were more or less conventional buildings erected in the various courtyards within the walls.

Very few castles were taken by direct attack, but when attempting such an assault, the Japanese used siege equipment similar to that of Europe. The attackers constructed all manner of portable shields and movable towers to enable them to approach the walls. Moats were filled with brushwood fascines, and hooked scaling ladders were employed to scale the walls. Despite these aids, starvation and betrayal were responsible for far more capitulations than any amount of heroic fighting. In one castle the mats covering the floor, normally stuffed with rice straw, were filled instead with dried edible roots which could be taken up and boiled in an emergency.

During the first half of the sixteenth century armourers all over the country continued the break with traditional methods of construction that had begun towards the end of the Muromachi period. Faced with the unprecedented demands being made on them, they were more than ready to adopt the new techniques and novel styles that are now called *tosei gusoku* (modern armour). This important transition did not happen suddenly, nor did the new armours being produced necessarily show all the features that are now associated with the concept. Haramaki and do maru were still being made for the few who wanted them, but these were very much in the minority and most samurai chose the more practical, if sober modern armours.

Below: Scene from the film Kagemusha *showing foot soldiers armed with spears.*

Freed from the constraints of tradition, the armourers conceived a bewildering array of new types of armour that remained in production side-by-side with the older styles until armour was finally abandoned altogether during the nineteenth century. This blossoming of inventiveness coincided with the emergence of new groups of armourers during the late fifteenth and early sixteenth centuries to compete with the long-established Haruta and Iwai groups. Among the first, and by far the most important, were the Miochin, followed later by others, among whom the Saotome group must be singled out because of the extremely high quality of its work.

Much of what has been written about the Miochin is based on writings of the Edo period, and in particular a genealogy of their own creation, designed to enhance their respectability by claiming a long pedigree and association with the famous. In fact, the Miochin were comparative latecomers to the craft; the first independent mention of them as a group is in *Gozuisin Sanjoki*, published in 1506, where they are recorded as being makers of bits for horses. Another reference from the same period, in *Kebukigusa* confirms that they were bit makers and adds that Yamashiro was the centre from which they worked. Even as late as the early Edo period, the *Wakan Sansaizue* lists both the Ichiguchi and Miochin as being makers of horse bits. This association with bits is substantiated to some extent by the large numbers of tsuba signed by Miochins, and especially with the name Nobuiye. These tsuba, which date from the Momoyama and early Edo periods, are of well-forged iron and are decorated with punching and piercing – both techniques that were used in the making of the cheek plates for bits. These tsuba were probably a subsidiary product made when the demand for horse equipment was low.

Considerable doubt remains as to which of these bit makers first turned to making armour, but several helmet bowls survive from the 1450s that show features suggestive of later Miochin work. They are signed 'Yoshimichi' and 'Takayoshi' but these two never used the name Miochin in their signatures. The first to do so was Miochin Nobuiye who, according to tradition, lived from 1485 to 1564. Judging by the quantity and rather varying quality of work signed with this name, it is more than likely that there were several people who used it – almost certainly unconnected with the group who made the tsuba. Some of these helmets may be the work of pupils, since it was common for them to use their master's name as a mark of respect. This practice (called *okkake mei*) was carried out with the noblest of motives, and with no intention to defraud, but has been responsible for much confusion over attributions ever since. Equally, the master often signed the work of his students if its quality was such that it did not discredit the workshop.

According to Yamagami Hachiro's *Nihon Katchu no Shin Kenkyu* Nobuiye's first signature dates from 1510, when he was 25 years old. The Miochin genealogy states that he was born in Shirai and later moved to Osumi, and was originally named Yasuiye. At some point early in his career he is sup-

Below: A high-sided, flat topped 62-plate suji kabuto by Miochin Nobuiye.

Below right: A 62-plate suji kabuto by Miochin Nobuiye. The neck guard is decorated by a silk frill copied from the ruffs of the Europeans.

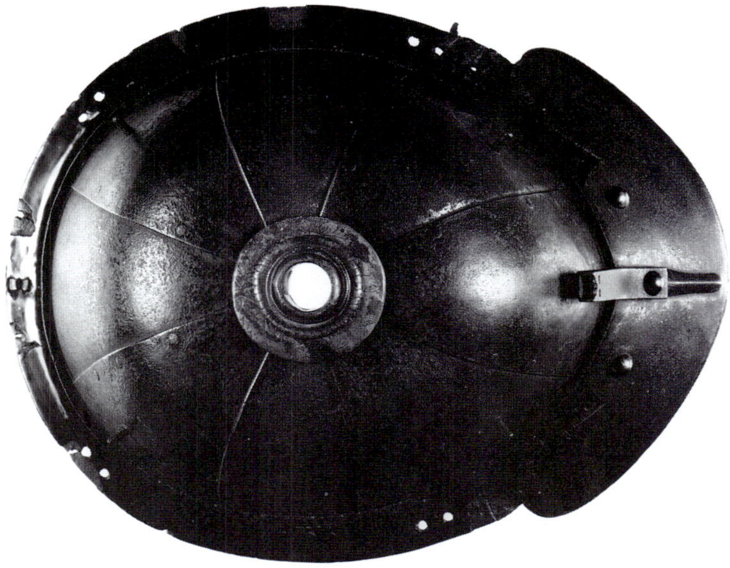

Above and above left: Eight-plate helmet bowl of heichozan form (high sided, flat topped) by Miochin Yoshimichi.

posed to have made a fine helmet for Takeda Harunobu (later Takeda Shingen), a well-known warrior-daimyo, who granted him the right to use the character 'Nobu' in his name in recognition of the quality of his work. Unfortunately there is no evidence for this whatsoever; no Miochin helmets appear in the inventory of the Takeda family's possessions after Shingen's death. There is, however, a Nobuiye helmet inscribed in red lacquer as belonging to Shingen, but this inscription is considered to have been added during the Edo period, probably by the Miochin. The whole episode appears to be little more than an attempt to enhance the reputation of the group by association with the famous.

What cannot be disputed is that the Miochin, and Nobuiye in particular, completed the development of a style of helmet, evolved from the akoda nari, that particularly suited the fashion of the time and the type of warfare then being conducted. These high-sided suji bachi were egg shaped in plan, with steeply sloping sides that flattened rather suddenly towards the top, giving the bowl the appearance of having a distinct 'shoulder'. Many were made from either 32 or 62 vertical plates, but other configurations were not uncommon. Devoid of superfluous ornament that might be damaged in action, they were even left unlacquered, but given a controlled coating of rust, to show the excellent quality of the metalwork. Even decorative leathers were eschewed in favour of a plain steel peak, fitted with a simple iron haraidate held in place by the centre one of *sanko no byo* (three iron rivets), which fastened the peak to the koshimaki. Nobuiye characteristically shaped the haraidate so that it lay close to the front plate of the helmet, and filed its top edge into a cusped V-shape, below which are two holes arranged vertically. He also shaped and fitted the peak in such a way that its centre was slightly lower than the outer edges when viewed in profile. As on most helmets, the vestigial holes (hibiki no ana) and their protective standing rivets (shiten no byo) were added, slightly higher than halfway up the sides.

Second only to Nobuiye and perhaps even more imitated, was Miochin Yoshimichi, whose products, while very similar, differ in

Below: A 32-plate heichozan kabuto fitted with an ichimanju jikoro (neck guard in which only the top plate is curved in section) by Miochin Ki Yasukiyo. The waved outline of the plates and the rivets hammered over on the outside are unusual. Late Edo period.

Above: An unsigned goshozan suji bachi of the type produced by the Haruta smiths. Helmets of this type are higher at the back than the front and have the rivets countersunk under the lacquer.

Above right: Ko boshi kabuto signed 'Saotome Iyetada.' The profusion of rivets, while demonstrating the skill of the maker, added considerable weight to the helmet.

having the haraidate standing rather more forward, off the front plate, and pierced with two holes arranged side by side. Yoshimichi's peaks also differ from Nobuiye's in that the centre is higher than the outer edge when viewed from the side. Miochin work was in great demand and inevitably many of the group subsequently moved away to establish their own sub-groups in different parts of the country, sometimes dropping the name Miochin in favour of another. Once the Miochins had shown the way, the Saotome, Haruta and other groups began to produce their own versions of the high-sided helmets, in varying qualities and with slight regional variations.

On some of these helmets, particularly those produced by the Miochins and Saotome, standing rivets were reintroduced; but in an unprecedented profusion that far exceeds the number needed to hold the plates together. Sometimes as many as 22 *muku boshi* (pointed rivets) were fitted to each plate, each carefully graded in size, becoming smaller towards the tehen, and exactly aligned in perfectly straight rows. A typical 62-plate *ko boshi bachi* (small-rivet helmet bowl) might incorporate over 2000 rivets, so closely spaced as to almost hide the surface of the bowl itself. Apart from demonstrating the consummate skill of their makers, it is difficult to see what advantage these helmets possessed; the number of holes needed in each plate and the increase in weight can only have been detrimental. Despite this, they were popular helmets, produced by the very best armourers and incorporated in high-quality armours.

The profiles of these helmets differ depending upon the makers and the taste of their clients. With their love of intricate terminology, Edo period armourers classified them according to the shape of the top and the angle it made with the line of the koshimaki. Those still showing a vestige of the high back of the akoda nari (called by them *reiseizan*, mountain top heaped up) were known as *goshozan* (rear victory mountain); when flat on top they were called *heichozan* (level top mountain), or when higher in front

Below: A zunari bachi, typified by the longitudinal plate over the centre of the head, fitted with a crest in the form of a fan paper with the character 'yama' (mountain) torn out of it. It is signed by Saotome Iyetada.

zenshozan (fore victory mountain). Those higher than a hemisphere were called *koseizan* (high built-up mountain), or if the tehen region was depressed, *tenkokuzan* (heavenly valley mountain). Although whimsical flights of fancy designed to impress customers, these names do provide a basis for classification in the absence of anything better.

Hineno Hironari and his brother Yajiuemon, both high-ranking samurai from the province of Mino who took a great interest in the design and construction of armour, developed and popularized the zunari style of construction which had originated in the province of Tosa. The *hineno zunari bachi* that resulted was higher and rather more swollen at the back than the original, with the front overlaid by a brow plate that curved outwards at the base to form a peak. A similar helmet manufactured somewhat later in the province of Etchu was favoured by the Hosokawa family; it differed in construction in

Above left: A typical Hineno zunari kabuto with fittings for crests at the top and front. Zunari helmets of this type have the central longitudinal plate riveted under the brow plate and the lower edge of the neck guard shaped to the shoulders.

Above: Harikaki kabuto, a helmet bowl decorated by a light superstructure of wood, paper, leather and lacquer, in the form of a stylized cap folded back on the head. Momoyama period.

Left: Eboshi nari kabuto, a helmet shaped to resemble a tall cap. Momoyama period.

Right: Etchu zunari bachi decorated with dragons and clouds in overlay. This bowl has never been mounted but the armourer has indicated the position for crest holders at the front, sides and top. Late Edo period.

Below: Gold-lacquered zunari kabuto, a style of helmet developed in Tosa, overlaid by mail. Momoyama period.

having the central plate over the crown overlap the browplate rather than being riveted underneath it. Because these helmets were made of a few simply shaped plates, zunari bachi could be made from heavier-gauge metal and harder steel than more conventional multi-plate helmets. For this reason, better quality versions of this style of helmet became popular with men of high rank and, because they could be made by far less skilled craftsmen, they were the first choice for cheap armours, and were turned out in their thousands from thin metal. Being rather plain in appearance, many zunari kabuto were decorated with coloured lacquer or were covered with hair, bristles, feathers or textured leather. Others relieved the severity by adopting all manner of exaggerated *tate mono* (crests) fitted to the front, sides, top and back of the helmet.

These crests, which were applied to all types of helmets, were often little more than silhouettes of metal, wood or leather, gilded, lacquered, or decorated in some other way. A few, however, are masterpieces of wood carving, embellished with lacquer, hair and other materials. When fitted to the front of the helmet they were called *maedate*, if at the sides, *waki date*, on top *kashira date* or at the back *ushiro date*. The subject matter was sometimes heraldic, but just as often appeared to have been chosen at the whim of the wearer and could depict almost anything.

Hineno Hironari is also credited with what must be the ultimate in helmet decoration, the *harikake bachi*. Using a zunari helmet bowl as a base, fantastic creations in wood, rawhide and paper were built up and subsequently lacquered; these represented anything the imagination could conceive. Since this superstructure was light, size was not a limitation and a few flamboyant samurai appeared on the battlefield wearing helmets that towered several feet above the head or extended several feet from side to side. The subjects represented were legion, ranging from animals and plants to everyday objects and even abstract ideas. Edo period books list hundreds of varieties, ranging from rather conservative copies of hoods and caps, to helmets in the shape of 'peeled winter cherries', 'curled sea slugs' or even the improbable 'helmet in the shape of a snow storm'. However absurd some of these now seem, they were undoubtedly popular in their day and sufficient survive to show the artistry exercised by their makers.

Zunari bachi were not the only simple helmets produced and once the idea had been established that efficient helmets could be made of a few plates, other constructions, the simpler the better, were explored and exploited. Particularly popular were those fashioned in the form of a court cap, *eboshi nari kabuto*, or the closely related helmet shaped like a catfish's tail, *namazu o kabuto*. Both types were made of two plates riveted around the edge at the front, top and back, and opened outwards at the bottom for the head. In common with most simple helmets, they were generally fitted with a brow plate and concave peak combination, in the zunari bachi style, with a small inner plate bridging the gap across the brow to which the helmet lining was sewn. All non-regular helmets, that is those that are neither hoshi bachi nor suji bachi, are generically classified as *kawari bachi* (novel or peculiar helmets).

To accompany the zunari and its fanciful variants, the Hineno devised a new form of shikoro that fitted closely to the neck, falling in a slight concave curve to a bottom plate shaped to the shoulders. The makers of the etchu zunari bachi produced a similar arrangement, but it had a straight edge to the bottom plate. Unlike previous shikoro, only the top plate (*hachi tsuke no ita*) was extended and bent outwards to form rudimentary fukigaeshi, usually decorated with the owner's mon. Some however, abandoned fukigaeshi altogether since they no longer served any useful purpose. Others, called *ite jikoro*, had removable or hinged fukigaeshi which could be taken off or swung out of the way when using a bow. These close-fitting shikoro became so popular that other types of helmet were modified to take them; the angled flange of the koshimaki was clipped into tabs, so that it could be bent vertical.

Above: A haruta kawari kabuto in the form of a head wearing a court cap. Helmets were made in unusual styles to make the wearer distinctive in battle.

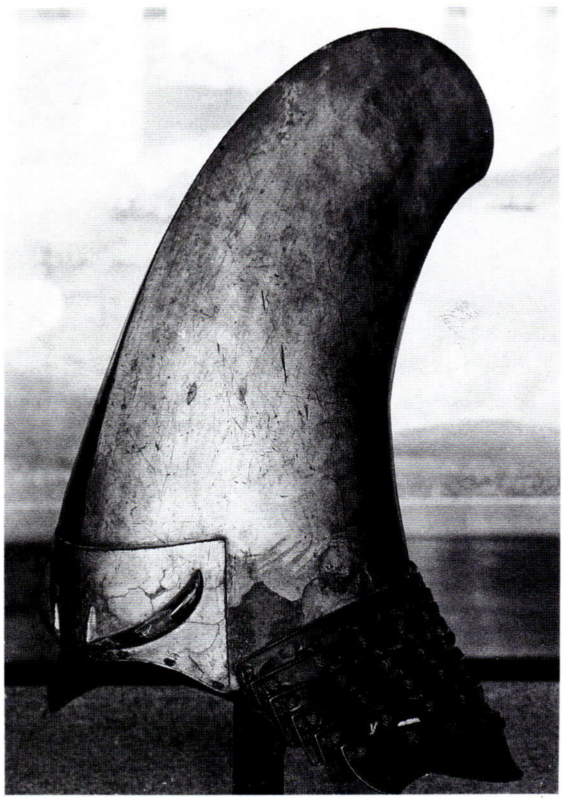

Left: Embossed kawari bachi, an unconventional multi-plate construction, in the shape of a Chinese cap. Momoyama period.

Far left: Naga eboshi kabuto, a helmet in the form of an exaggerated tall court cap.

Right: Six-plate hoshi bachi (helmet with prominent rivets) decorated with dragons in overlay. Kaga work of the Momoyama or early Edo periods.

Far right: Me no shita ho, a mask covering the face and nose below the eyes, of russet iron signed with the words 'Ki Yasukiyo, a pupil of Miochin Muneyasu, made this'. The surface treatment of lines is called sujichigai yasurime.

Below: Harikake kabuto, a helmet with a built up lacquered superstructure in the form of a cap worn by priests of the Nichiren sect.

When not fitted with this close-fitting *hineno jikoro*, helmets were provided with neck guards of more or less rounded outline, the fukigaeshi was formed as a prolongation of the top plate. If all the plates were curved in section it was called a *manju jikoro* (dumpling shikoro), either *o manju* or *ko manju* depending upon its size. If only the top plate was rounded, the remainder being more or less flat, it was called *ichimanju jikoro*; one variant of this form had all the plates except the top one divided into three sections covering the sides and back. Called *gessan shikoro*, this gave great freedom of movement, but was never very popular since the smaller sections offered less protection from a blow. As the hineno jikoro required a vertical koshimaki, it was no longer possible to fit the iron rings for the helmet cord. In their place, cord loops were threaded through holes in the koshimaki and the shikoro, in three, four or five places depending upon the way the owner tied his helmet cords.

Armour for the face, men gu, was now standard and could be either a hoate, hanbo or me no shita ho according to taste. Very few so men were made, except as demonstrations of the armourer's skill, since they restricted the vision far too much to be practical. Whatever the type, they came in all manner of forms; heavily wrinkled or smooth, with or without teeth or facial hair, lacquered or russet iron. Some smiths adopted the standing flange (yadome), which had been used on the Heian period happuri, to guard the helmet cords. All masks were now fitted with a throat defence (yodare kake) as a matter of course, which was either

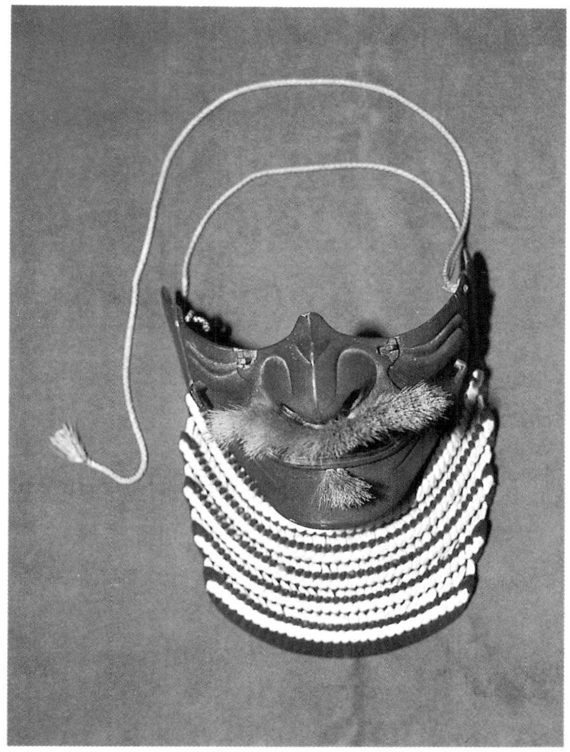

Far left: Me no shita ho with hinged throat defence.

Left: Russet lacquered me no shita ho with a throat defence that extends upwards following the line of the jaw.

laced directly to the mask or to an intermediate band of leather (*komori tsuke*). Nodawa were almost totally abandoned as their function was now superseded by the yodare kake of the mask and the modifications that had been made to the do.

Although practical, plate construction was dull, and many samurai still favoured kebiki lacing, not infrequently for the whole armour, but at least for the *gessan*, as the kusazuri were now called. In order to retain some of the advantages and ease of manufacture of plate construction, armourers devised a way of simulating scales using lacquer. *Kiritsuke kozane* (cut-out and applied scales), as they were called, were produced by shaping the upper edge of a plate like a row of scale heads, piercing the plate with holes for lacing, then modelling the surface into a series of vertical ribs with kokuso, before the final lacquering. Properly done, the effect is remarkably realistic, only lacking the deep undercuts between the heads of the scales. A similar method was used to produce *kiritsuke iyozane*, most of which are virtually indistinguishable from a real row of such iyozane scales wrapped in thin leather under the lacquer. In many cases, the makers of kiritsuke

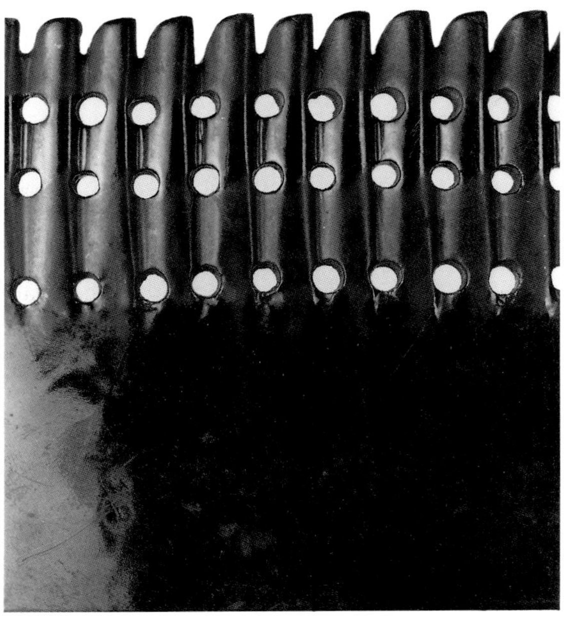

Far left: Kiritsuke kozane, plates covered with lacquer to simulate small scales.

Above: Plate cut out for kiritsuke iyozane and pierced for imitation lacing. The pairs of holes along the lower edge are for internal ties which held the do rigid.

Left: A plate pierced for sugake lacing, where pairs of laces are spaced along a plate or row of scales.

Above and above right: Front and rear views of a tosei do ('modern' armour) from Gun Yo Ki.

iyozane even went as far as fitting a kawashiki, held in place by imitation lacing fastened through two rows of holes drilled along the centre line of the plate. When lacquered, the sewing and the ridge formed by the kawashiki on the inside added considerably to the realism; only the rigidity of the solid plate betrayed the true method of construction.

Complementing the new styles of helmets, armourers devised a whole range of do which most samurai found preferable to the old do maru and haramaki for use in the field. Much of the terminology changed during this period. The muna ita (plate covering the top of the chest) was now called the *oni damari* and the oshitsuke ita (plate covering the top of the back) was called the *boko no ita*. In *tosei do* (modern do) the number of rows of scales, or their plate equivalents, in the nakagawa increased to five. This not only improved the protection for the lower abdomen but also allowed the do to sit more firmly on the hips. For this latter reason, tosei do can also be called *tachi do* (standing do). Similarly, an additional row was sometimes added to the front tateage to improve the protection given to the upper chest. This emphasis on covering a greater part of the body, almost certainly a result of the increased use of straight-bladed spears, is also reflected by changes to the plates covering the top of the chest and those under the arms. Both plates had their upper profiles modified to fit closer to the throat and arm respectively, and were given a rolled out upper edge, which acted as a stop rib to prevent weapons sliding off into the body. Whereas protection for the neck had previously been provided by the shoji no ita and the shikoro, it was now usual to fit a *tate eri* (armoured collar) usually of kikko, but sometimes of mail. On the inside, these collars were extended in the form of a padded yoke across the upper back and over the shoulders, making the armour considerably more comfortable. The watagami also gained minor defences for the shoulder in the form of *kohire* (little fin), made of either scales, plate or brigandine, fastened along their outer edges. These helped to cover the gap between the watagami and the top of the kote or sode, now exposed to a downwards cut by the introduction of closer fitting shikoro.

Whatever the type, many tosei do were provided with a pouch, *hanagami fukuro* (nose tissue bag), either on the left front, just above the waist, or attached behind one of the front gessan. As its name suggests, it was used to carry paper handkerchiefs and other small necessities when armed. Because the uchi

gatana was more popular than the tachi, those pouches situated on the front of the do had the double function of protecting the lacquer from contact by the tsuba of the swords. Where a pouch was not fitted, it was sometimes replaced by a simple pad of fabric or leather to serve the same purpose.

As tactics improved and the co-ordination of large numbers of troops became important, identification on the battlefield grew in importance. In the Muromachi period, warriors had sometimes worn a streamer attached to a stick in the haraidate. It now became common practice to equip each member of a company with a flag or other identification called a *sashimono*, worn in a holder attached to the backplate of the do. To accommodate this fitting, the back of the tosei do was shaped with a slight vertical groove over the spine. Various arrangements were introduced for attaching the sashimono. Most commonly, a bow-shaped metal bracket (*gattari*), with a square or round holder at its centre was pivoted to the boko no ita. Some gattari are ingeniously hinged in

Left: Byo toji okegawa do, an armour of horizontal plates fastened by prominent rivets. The purpose of the hinged hook attached at the waist on the right is unknown. (Lacing modern.)

Below left: Rear view of a hon iyozane nuinobe do, an armour made in two parts and joined by a hinge under the left arm and laced with sugake lacing.

Left: Nuinobe do fitted with a sashimono of paper plumes. This device was worn for identification on the battlefield.

Right: Attachment for the sashimono, the identification emblem attached to armour.

Far right: The war standard of Honda Masashige. The Honda family came to power in the sixteenth century. Momoyama period.

the middle so that they could be removed from the pivots when not required. Alternatively the bracket might take the form of a wooden plate, lacquered or covered with leather and tied by thongs to the boko no ita. Into this upper socket was inserted a lacquered wooden tube (*uke zutsu*). The lower end fitted into a metal cup (*machi uke*) riveted or tied to the lower edge of the do.

The sashimono worn by common troops generally took the form of small flags of silk, hemp or cotton, dyed and printed with mon, stripes or other devices and flown from a bamboo pole some three or four feet (0.9 or 1.2m) long which fitted into the uke zutsu. The upper edge of the flag was supported by a horizontal rod pivoted to the pole in such a way that the flag remained extended and visible, even in windless conditions. Company commanders and other officers frequently wore alternative sashimono, perhaps large fabric or gilded paper feathers, sunbursts or other emblems of gilded wood or leather.

Even larger ensigns and war standards, *uma jirushi* (horse emblem) were positioned at strategic places on the battlefield to act as rallying points during the action and were carried as identification when marching. Many of these standards incorporate long, coloured ribbons hanging from a finial decorated with a mon mounted on a pole about eight feet (2.4m) high. Other commanders chose large gilded fans, gourds and other objects similarly mounted. Commanders still carried fans with which to direct the movements of their troops; these were even more necessary since the wearing of masks made speech difficult. A new form of insignia, indicating rank, was introduced; it took the form of a tassel of hair or paper, often gilded, which hung from a short baton. These *sai hai* were either tucked into the sash or hung from a ring (*sai hai no kan*) provided for the purpose on the right breast of the do. A second ring, supposedly for a towel but more probably simply to balance the appearance of the do, was added to the left breast on some armours; this became virtually standard during the Edo period.

The new types of do were subdivided and named by the armourers, with their usual passion for terminology, on the basis of what are often quite minor differences in construction. In an attempt at some form of order, laced do will be considered first.

Hon kozane maru do were tosei versions of

the do maru made with the nakagawa extended by an additional row of scales. The equivalent haramaki was unpopular and all but unknown. When made of iyozane with sugake lacing, but in the style of a do maru, they were simply referred to as *iyozane do*. Much more popular and more convenient armours were made by dividing the maru do into two parts under the left arm and fitting a long hinge from the waki ita to the waist. By making the pins of these hinges removable, the do could by split into two separate parts, facilitating storage and transport. A much less common arrangement was to omit the hinge and fasten the two parts of the do by a tie at each side. These *ryo takahimo do* are most commonly, but not exclusively, found as munition armours, since they could be adjusted to accommodate a wide variety of sizes. The use of the term takahimo in this context refers to the ties for the side openings of the do, the term *aibiki* now being used for the fastenings between the watagami and oni damari.

Do made of true scales but divided into two sections by a hinge were given the name *hon kozane ni mai do* (true-scale two-section do). When the equivalent do was made from imitation scales, they were called *kiritsuke kozane ni mai do*. Iyozane do divided in the same way were called *hon iyozane nuinobe do*, or simply *nuinobe do* if of false scales. (The term nuinobe was used by armourers in several contexts and means literally 'extended sewing'. Why this appellation came to be applied to this style of do is unknown, but it illustrates some of the difficulties encountered in attempting to translate the vague terminology used.) A variant of these laced do had the upper and lower parts laced in different styles; the usual arrangement was to have the nakagawa laced in kebiki and the tateage in sugake. This armour is called *dangae do* (changed rows do) because of their banded appearance.

Similar do to all of the above were produced with four hinges, positioned below the edges of the tateage at the front and back. Since they could be divided into five sections (front,,left side, back and two overlapping sections under the right arm) they are called *go mai do*. These were subdivided on the basis of whether they were made from true or false scales in exactly the same way as ni mai do. A

Far left: War standard in the form of two gilded umbrella shapes. These heraldic devices acted as rallying points on the battlefield and were a prominent feature of Momoyama warfare.

Left: Sai hai, a commander's baton, of paper strips on its display stand.

Left: Iyozane do gusoku. In this construction the rows of scales are continuous around the body and had to be sprung open to admit the wearer, imposing a considerable strain on the structure. Momoyama period.

Above right: Blue laced hon kozane ni mai do gusoku, an armour of 'true' scales in two parts which is joined under the left arm by a hinge.

Above far right: Light blue laced yokohagi okegawa do gusoku. In this type of armour the plates forming the do were fastened by countersunk rivets and lacquered over. (Helmet cord modern.)

rare construction had the plate under the left arm divided to form a *roku mai do*. These were generally fastened by ties at each side, becoming *ryo takahimo roku mai do*, but an example formerly in the author's collection was fitted with a hinge as well as ties, enabling the two left sections to be joined.

More popular, and certainly more economical to make, were do which abandoned lacing and scales, or their imitations, and replaced the scales by plates. Most common were the various forms of do in which the separate strips of plate from which they were made were visible. When these strips were horizontal and fastened with countersunk rivets, that is, without visible fastenings, they were called *yokohagi okegawa do* after their supposed resemblance to a coopered bucket with hoops around it. Most of these are ni mai do, but they were also made in go mai do form. If fastened together in a visible way, different names were used which described the fastenings: *byo toji yokohagi okegawa do* or *byo kakari do* had prominent rivet heads, sometimes in the shape of *mon*; *kasugai do* were made from plates fastened to each other with a type of staple; *hishi toji yokohagi okegawa do* or simply *hishi toji do* were fastened with cross knots of metal, silk or leather; *uname toji yokohagi okegawa do* or *uname toji do* were fastened with simple horizontal sewing.

An alternative construction, usually of go mai do form, was made with the plates arranged vertically, called *tatehagi okegawa do*. In most examples the front and back sections consisted of a large central plate extended by a narrower plate at either side. An important derivative of this type of do was devised in the Yukinoshita area of Kamakura, and called therefore a *Yukinoshita do*. Date Masamune invited Miochin Masaiye and his family to Sendai to make armour in this style for both himself and his troops. During his stay in Sendai, Masaiye introduced changes and brought the style to its fully evolved form. Yukinoshita do were made of five sections which tapered towards the waist. The front and side sections were made of single plates while the back was normally constructed of vertical plates like a tatehagi okegawa do. Each section was provided with hinges riveted to the outside of the plate, unlike other do which had them on the inside, with only the knuckle visible. A distinguishing feature was the oni damari, either in one with the front plate, or riveted solidly to it, pierced with three holes for the aibiki instead of the more usual four. Hinged to the boko no ita were plate watagami with simple flap-like gyoyo hinged to their ends which hung over the aibiki. Plate kohire were provided, hinged to the outer edges of the watagami. Because all parts were hinged, they could be totally dismantled into more or less flat components for easy storage and transport, and quickly repaired or replaced if damaged. During the Edo period, this style, with slight variations, was called *kanto do, sendai do* or *oshu do* because of its popularity in these areas.

All types of okegawa do could, and usually did, have the upper plates of the front tateage and the oni damari laced in some way to introduce a certain degree of flexibility. One plain russet iron yokohagi okegawa do formerly in the author's collection had the two upper plates of the front tateage and the lower plate of the nakagawa in front, fitted with rivets sliding in slots in the adjoining plates as an alternative to lacing; exactly the same method of introducing fexibility as was used for European armours. Plate do, but particularly okegawa do, could have the edges of the component plates left plain, decorated with metal rims, or shaped into an undulating outline. Once again Edo period armourers devised extremely fanciful names for these shapes, only a few of which occur with any degree of regularity and are worthy of note.

When the plates of the do were not visible but lacquered smooth, or made from a single plate of iron or leather, the term used is *hotoke do* (alluding to the Buddha, that is, unblemished). Alternatively, the whole front of an okegawa do could be covered with a sheet of leather to give a *kawa zutsumi do* having a similar appearance. These smooth-faced do, as well as the tatehagi okegawa do with their wide front plate, provided a perfect vehicle for decoration in lacquer or damascening in gold or silver, and many were so treated. Others showed cross knots on the smooth surface, purely as decoration since the plates were in fact riveted under the lacquer. This variety is called *hishi toji hotoke do*. Alternatively a hotoke do could be provided with a laced portion to allow some flexibility. When this lacing is at the bottom it is called *koshi tori hotoke do*, or if at the top, *mune tori hotoke do*.

Finally, mention must be made of a range of do embossed in imitation of the human torso. Since these do resemble the guardian statues outside Buddhist temples, they are collectively called *nio do*. Most were made from a single plate, either embossed or modelled with kokuso with breasts, ribs and spinal protrusions that simulate human conditions from extreme emaciation to a comfortable rotundity. Individual varieties are named after divinities whose bodies are depicted in art with the same amount of flesh. A variant of this style, of which at least one example has survived, is called *katahada nugi do* (bared shoulder do) representing a partially emaciated body, lacquered in a flesh colour, which has the lower part and left

shoulder draped in sections of scales laced in different colours to represent clothing.

All types of do were fitted with gessan in seven or more sections. These were almost invariably laced to the do in the kebiki style, irrespective of the other lacing. This lacing was long, which gave great freedom of movement to the legs but left a considerable undefended region that was only partially covered by the thick padded outer belt (*uwa obi*). Some samurai increased the protection of the hips by having a series of mail covered cloth flaps (*koshi gusari*) sewn onto the lower edge of the do under the lacing, as additional security. The gessan themselves generally matched the construction and lacing of the do, but were often of rawhide rather than steel to save weight. To maintain the curved shape of the leather plates a curved iron rod, (*shikigane*) was laced to the back before being lacquered. Most do had gessan constructed of five plates in each section, but very long versions with up to eight plates in each, which reached almost to the knees, are occasionally encountered.

Worn with these do were all manner of

Above left: Yosekake sugake odoshi ni mai do, a two section do with the lacing arranged in vertical bands.

Above: Hon iyozane nuinobe do. The style of construction and lacquering and colour of the lacing varied according to the owner's taste and pocket.

Far left: A flamboyant armour incorporating a hishi toji okegawa do of horizontal plates fastened by cross knots and a kawari kabuto (unconventional helmet). The shoulder guards too are unusual in being made of kikko, a type of brigandine of hexagonal plates sewn between layers of fabric.

Left: Dark blue leather laced armour having an okegawa go mai do with both mune tori and koshi tori (five part do of horizontal plates with sections of lacing at the top and bottom). These sections of lacing introduced a degree of flexibility into what would otherwise have been a rigid and uncomfortable do. Armours are traditionally described by the colour of the lacing, but most have now faded.

sode, chosen both to complement the armour and to signify the status of the wearer. Generals and others of high rank continued to wear the impressive o sode or hiro sode of an exaggerated size. Those lower in the social scale wore a more practical size of hiro sode, or a new type called *tosei sode*. These were only slightly curved, rectangular in shape and of modest size. Tosei sode were designed to be hung from the fastenings of the kote, rather than being hung from the watagami, and had simple cord loops for the purpose fastened through holes in the top plate. In most cases, they were stiffened with

Above: Mid-blue laced go mai do gusoku. An inscription on the do records that this armour was made to the order of Nakagawa Mochinori, a retainer of the Nagato Han by Ki Yasukiyo, in 1848.

internal ties and lined with fabric so that only the lower one or two plates were flexible. To keep them in position, many have a loop of braid or cord fitted to the bottom of the stiffened portion that fastened to a small toggle on the kote, just above the elbow. A few samurai dispensed with sode altogether, considering them to be of doubtful value in action, but most surviving armours of the period are fitted with them – the wearer could leave them off if he chose to do so.

Only two substantially new forms of kote were added to the shino gote and tsutsu gote of the mid-Muromachi period, although many variations were made which differed in details. The first of these was the *kusari gote*,

Centre left: Maki e dangaye do gusoku, a modern armour with different styles of lacing in the upper and lower sections, decorated with a lacquered design. This suit was made for a boy of about seven years old.

Left: A pale blue laced nuinobe do fitted with o sode. Although anachronistic, these shoulder guards were still worn by people of rank. Momoyama period.

made entirely of mail except for the tekko and the kanmuri no ita. It was so sober that it never became popular, and lack of protection against the force of a blow mitigated against its effectiveness. The second variety was initially promoted by the Satake family of Hitachi and rapidly became popular everywhere. The book *Kosei Roku* is the first to refer to *oda gote*; the name is derived from the family of armourers who first made them. Oda gote are characterized by having *hyotan* or *fukube* (gourd-shaped plates) embedded in the mail over the forearm and upper arm. Some are smooth with perhaps an applied flower-shape decoration, but most are pleated (*shiwa fukube*) with rows of tiny lines at each end.

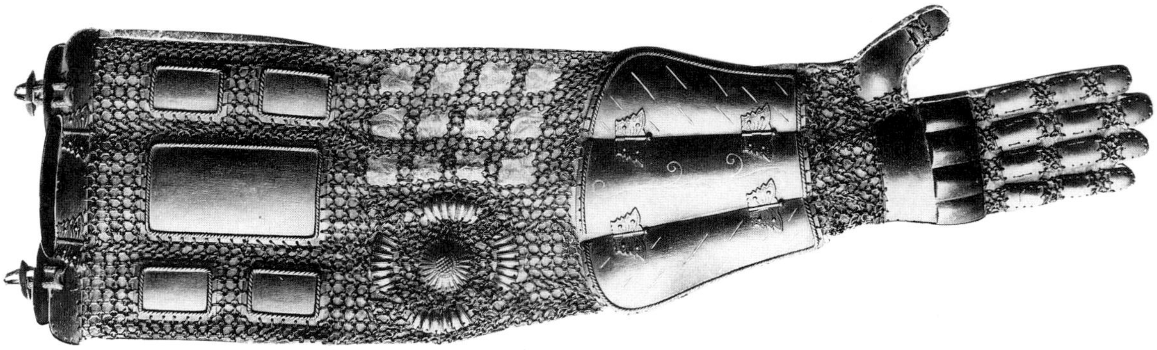

Right: Tsutsu gote, an armoured sleeve with the forearm plates hinged to each other, probably of Kaga manufacture. The plate over the back of the hand is extended by finger plates.

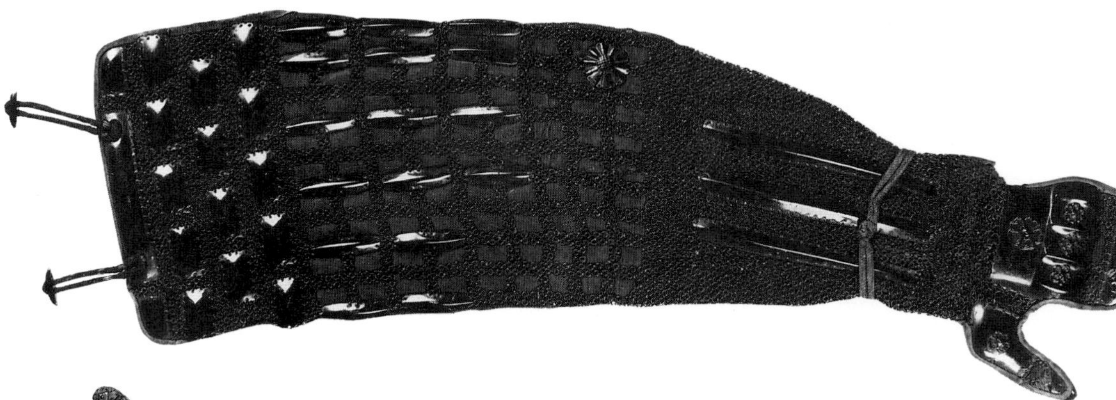

Right: Shino gote, an armoured sleeve with splints defending the forearm.

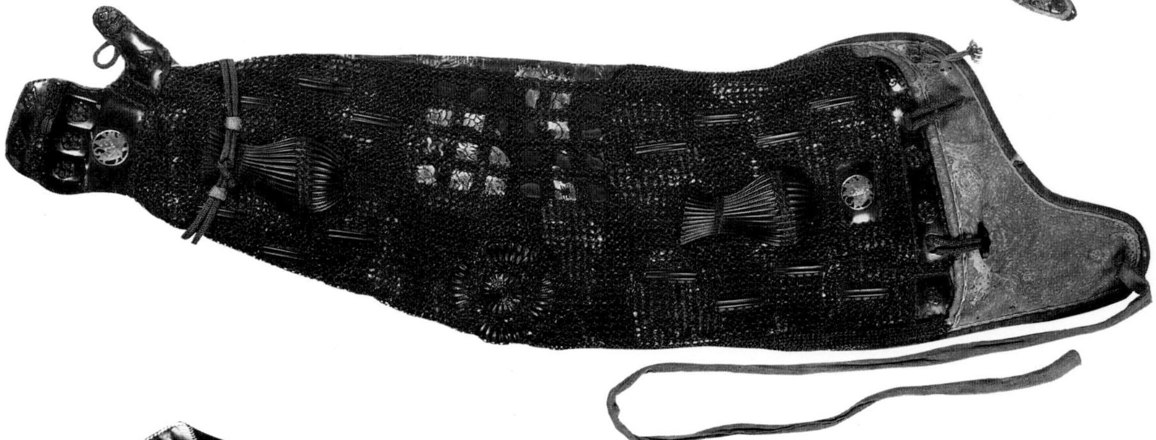

Right: Oda gote with the characteristic gourd-shaped plates applied over the forearm and upper arm. In this example the plates are closely pleated, with rows of tiny rivets at each end.

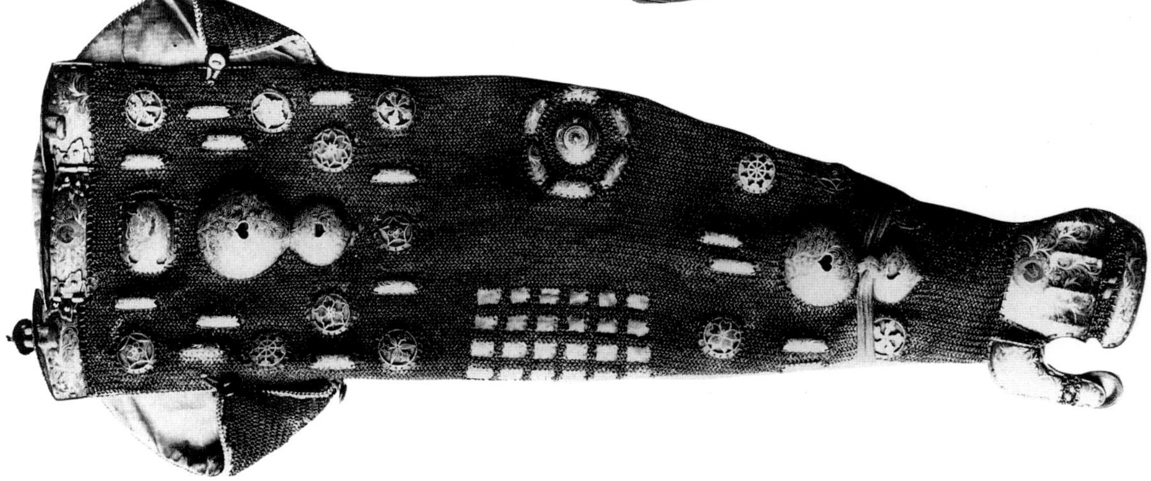

Right: Oda gote of Kaga manufacture. The plates are decorated with silver overlay and set in chirimen nanban Kusari, European-style mail with small, closely packed links.

They were generally supplemented by narrow, fluted plates, *ikada* (rafts), set into the mail at intervals on either side of the fukube. Around the hiji gane (elbow plate) were set four curved strips, similar to ikada but with radial flutes, called *matsuba wa* since they resembled conventionally drawn pine needles. Most oda gote are further decorated with a profusion of pierced flower-shaped plates, often of the greatest delicacy, applied to the tekko and kanmuri no ita. Their similarity suggests that the metalwork for these sleeves

Left: Ikada haidate, an apron-like defence for the thighs of mail and small plates sewn onto fabric of Indian origin.

Below: Kawara haidate, overlapping s-section scales, of lacquered leather on dark blue hemp cloth.

Below left: Etchu haidate; here the armoured section is reduced to a sparse grid of mail and splints.

Below right: Shino haidate has rows of elongated plates connected by mail.

was the speciality of a particular workshop, which supplied them to other armourers for mounting with their own work. Since similarities can also be detected between other components of armours, reputedly by different smiths, it seems probable that by this time raw plate and many standard components were being virtually mass produced and distributed within the trade.

Following the general trend towards sim-

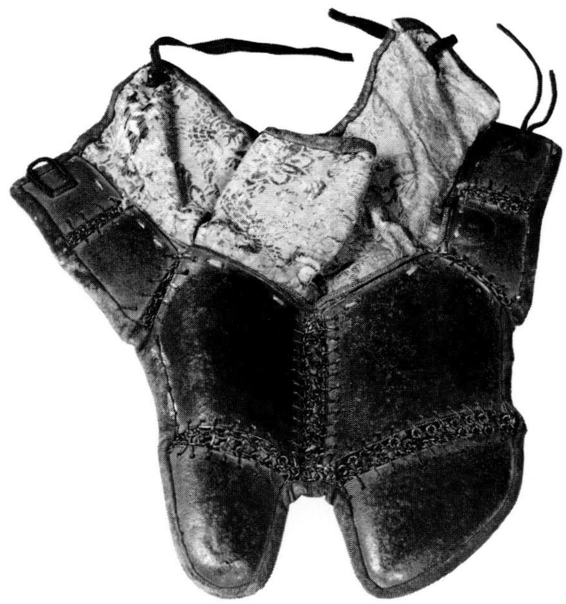

Right: Tsutsu suneate, plate shin guards.

Far right: Kogake of mail and plates. These armoured overshoes were held in place by the ties of the straw sandals.

plification, the haidate (knee and thigh armour) was made lighter by modifying the scale construction used in the Muromachi period or by replacing it with mail or plates. *Ita haidate* were made from flat scales arranged into four or five rows containing between seven and fifteen or more scales in each. Those made from the larger scales were lacquered after lacing to stiffen the rows so that they formed almost rigid plates and were frequently decorated with mon or other lacquered designs. An alternative form, called *kawara haidate*, was made from s-sectioned scales which overlapped like roof tiles and then laced together. When mail formed the sole defence, haidate were called *kusari haidate*, but most have some *ikada* (small rectangular plates) fitted into the mail to form *ikada haidate*. A similar type with ikada and plates over the knee, resembling the hiji gane and matsuba wa of the oda gote was called *oda haidate*. *Shino haidate* consisted of short shino assembled in rows joined by mail, being most abbreviated in the type called *etchu haidate* in which short narrow shino, virtually ikada, were connected in rows by narrow strips of mail to form only a grid of metal over the surface. Whatever the type, haidate could be sewn either onto a divided apron of fabric, matching the fabric of the kote, or to the front of a pair of baggy breeches, which occasionally were armoured with mail at the back. The apron type, except for the very stiff ita haidate, have tabs of fabric on either side that were tied or buttoned behind the leg to prevent the haidate being displaced and bumping against the leg while walking.

Little change was made to the armour for the lower leg, with tsutsu suneate and shino suneate continuing in production. The etchu armourers made one variant of the latter which dispensed with the fabric backing and the knee guard, which was especially favoured when fighting in wet conditions since there was nothing, other than the ties, to become soaked. Some kusari suneate (mail shinguards, sometimes with ikada) were made which suffered from the same defect as kusari gote – they provided no protection from a blow. They do not seem to have been too popular, judging by the dearth of surviving examples when compared to the numbers of surviving plate shinguards.

In addition to the armour itself, and sometimes provided with it, were a number of minor accessories. For the armpits,

Below: Wakibiki, an armpit guard, of mail. This was an accessory which could be worn with any armour.

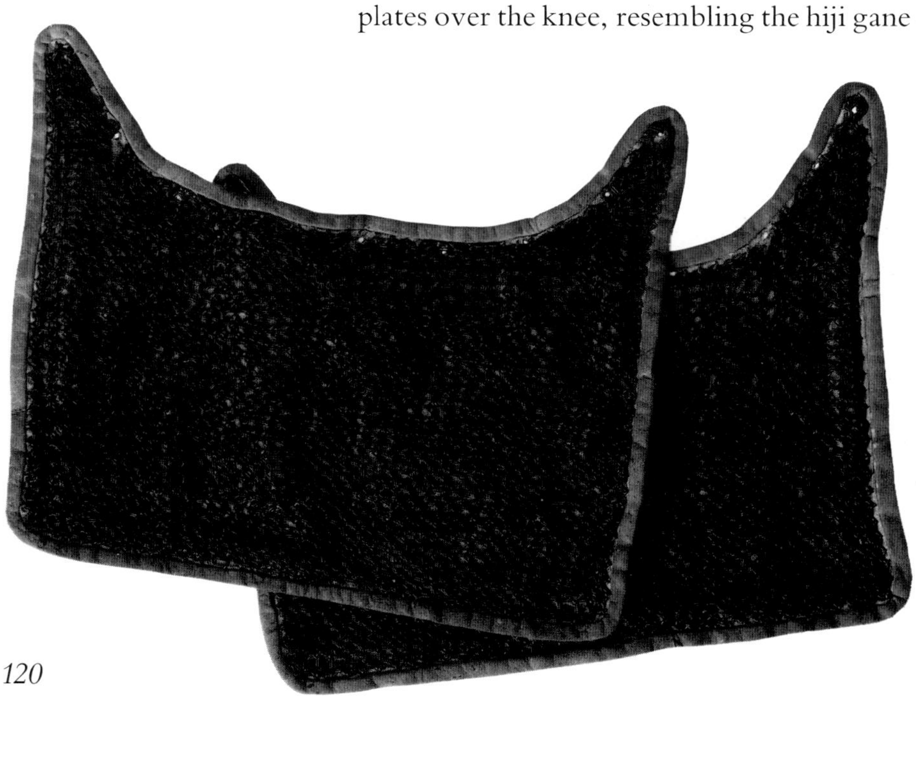

Above: A manju wa, a short armoured waistcoat worn beneath armour to protect the armpits and upper chest. It is of silver and blue brocade over brigandine of leather plates. Edo period.

U-shaped pieces of armour made of mail sewn onto a fabric backing (*wakibiki*) were made. They were either laced directly to the underside of the sleeve so that they hung against the sides of the body, or were made as separate pieces which were tied to the body before putting on the do. Other wakibiki were made of plate or scales, which, despite the incorporation of lacing and hinges, were far too stiff to be worn beneath the do. Some Japanese museums mount these hanging under the arm but outside the do, in such a way that they would move into position over the gap above the waki ita with the action of raising the arm, which is almost certainly the way they would have been worn. Neater, and probably far more comfortable, was the *manju wa*, a type of short sleeveless jacket made with flaps that passed under the arms and over the shoulders to tie on the chest. These were either of mail or kikko and were provided with an armoured collar, obviating the need for a separate armoured collar. Some examples are fitted with fastenings for the sleeves so that they could be put on as a single unit. Armour for the feet (*kogake*) was also available; it was an overshoe without a sole, made of iron or leather plates connected by mail or hinges. Kogake were fastened by ties behind the heel and the ankle and held in place on the foot by the ties of the sandal. Most samurai abandoned the yoroi hitatare for wear with tosei gusoku, preferring instead a narrow-sleeved shirt-like garment, derived from the dress of the lower classes, worn with short breeches and leggings.

Armours had been traditionally stored in lacquered chests which had short flaring legs

Above: Shitagi, a garment which was worn under armour, of hemp printed with a design of Chinese grass. Edo period.

Above right: Shitagi of hemp cloth having a brocade collar. Edo period.

fitted to the sides rather than the corners, and a lid which was fastened by heavy tasselled cords. With the introduction of tosei gusoku and the need for mobility during protracted campaigns, small portable armour boxes were introduced, occasionally made in pairs for more lavish armours. Most are straight sided, about two and a half feet (0.75m) high and rather less than two feet square, but other decorative shapes are common. They were, of necessity, light, and were made from thin wood, wickerwork or even papier mâché, which was lacquered or covered with leather and reinforced at the corners and edges with ironwork. Most have locks or hasps and staples and are fitted with looped hinged handles for carrying on a pole. A few, designed for light armours, had padded shoulder straps and were carried on the back of a single porter.

These improvements to armour, and the necessity for change which the samurai accepted, came at a momentous time. Europeans, exploring the East for trade, brought guns with them. These not only revolutionized the form of warfare the samurai had known, but brought about unity in Japan after centuries of internal strife.

Right: A box for storing and transporting armour with its leather storage cover. Momoyama period.

Far right: Armour being stored in a traditional chest.

水干無文
布直垂無文

CHAPTER SIX
The Arrival of the Southern Barbarians

Far right: Set of ornate large-bore guns displayed in a rack. This type of gun, kakae zutsu, was designed for attacking fortifications.

During the sixteenth century the sea powers of Europe, in a move to end the monopoly of merchants using the Silk Road across Asia, sent expeditions in search of a sea route to the sources of spice and silk. This long and dangerous voyage was undertaken by a small band of Portuguese adventurers who, in a second attempt to reach the trading centre of Peking, were washed ashore after a violent storm. They landed on the small island of Tanegashima, off the coast of Kyushu, in either 1542 or 1543.

As the first Europeans to set foot in Japan they caused no little sensation, but it was as nothing to the delight and excitement caused by the matchlock guns they carried. The Japanese immediately not only understood their mechanism, but also grasped their potential and, for an exorbitant sum, these primitive weapons passed into the possession of the local daimyo. It is just possible that the Japanese knew something of guns and gunpowder from the Chinese, but there is no evidence of this in the careful descriptions they have left of demonstration firings. The Lord of Tanegashima was delighted with his purchase and immediately set his swordsmith to work in making copies. Forging a barrel was a simple metalsmithing process, but when faced with cutting the thread of the breech plug the swordsmith was totally defeated; such technology was totally unknown in Japan. The problem was finally resolved, so legend has it, by exchanging his daughter for lessons with another Portuguese who arrived a short time after. To the man's credit, within

Below: Bronze cannon on a sliding mount to absorb the recoil. Cannon, generally rather small, were quickly adopted by the Japanese after the arrival of the Europeans in the 1540s.

six months he had produced a large number of copies (traditionally the figure is said to have been 600), which the Lord of Tanegashima traded, spreading knowledge of this new weapon throughout the country within a short time of its introduction. It is difficult to assess accurately the rate of spread, but by 1555 Takeda Shingen had bought at least 300, and 20 years later, Oda Nobunaga, then a relatively minor daimyo, had 3000 gunners in the army which defeated the forces of Takeda Katsuyori at the battle of Nagashino.

Military planners were quick to reach the same conclusions about the gun as the Europeans before them. It was relatively cheap to produce, effective under the right weather conditions and could, after the minimum of training, turn the rawest recruits into a valuable adjunct to other forces. Here at last was a weapon that could turn the ashigaru from a rabble into the equal of the finest samurai, without the long, arduous training that both archery and fencing demanded. The guns made were smooth-bore snapping

Right: Ashigaru (foot soldier) armed with a musket. The match is coiled around his wrist. Guns of this type made the ashigaru a formidable fighting force, threatening the supremacy of the samurai.

Below: Procession of spearmen and musketeers, their guns covered in striped fabric bags to protect them from the weather.

matchlocks which varied from long muskets for use on foot to short carbines and even pistols that could be handled on horseback, which is curious because such guns were rare in Europe. Guns with similar mechanisms had been in vogue during the 1520s, but in Germany, not in Portugal. In these matchlocks the powder was ignited by the smouldering end of a length of cord impregnated with saltpeter to make it burn evenly. To simplify handling, the cord was held in the jaws of a pivoted lever, the serpentine; when the trigger was pulled a spring propelled the serpentine into the priming powder. Most European guns were far less complex – the serpentine was connected directly to the trigger by a simple mechanical link so that they moved together. It was also the normal European practice to position the serpentine in front of the priming pan. The Japanese guns had it fitted behind, in such a way that it moved away from the user when it was fired.

Gun barrels were made from a U-shaped strip of iron which was welded into a tube around a steel bar or mandrel of slightly smaller diameter than finally needed, to allow for subsequent fine boring and polishing. At the breech end of the barrel, the bore was sealed by a screwed plug and a small pan for the priming powder was welded on the right-hand side. A standing guard of brass was attached where the pan joined the barrel which had the dual function of reducing corrosion from the burning powder and preventing water running down the barrel and seeping under the pivoted brass pan cover which protected the priming from damp and wind. On average, the barrels of existing muskets are about three feet (0.9m) long with a bore that can vary between 0.5 and 0.8 inches (1.27 and 2.03cm) in diameter. A few large-bore (2-3½ inches, 5.08-8.89cm) guns were made with barrels about two feet (0.6m) long that are aptly called *kakae zutsu* (hand cannon). Supported on a rest, these monsters were used to batter down gates or other light fortifications in a similar way to modern hand-held rocket launchers. Most

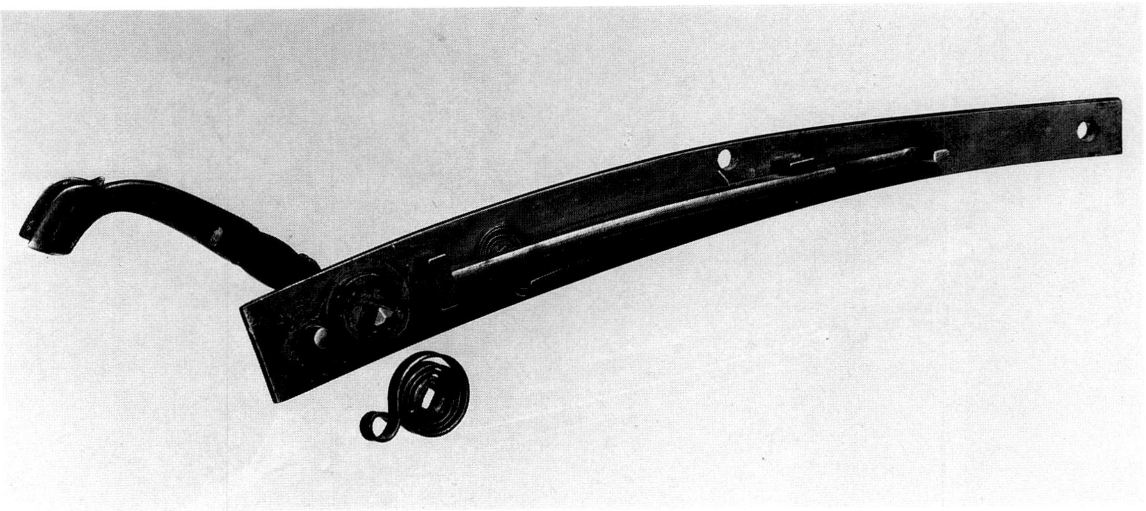

Right: Interior of gun lock by the Kunitomo group showing the tumbler and springs.

are highly decorated. Although called 'wall guns' in the West because of their similarity to the weapons used in European castles and forts, there is no evidence that they were ever used in that role. A further group of guns, called *hiya zutsu*, resemble small cannon. However, they were never used in war; their purpose was, as their name suggests, to shoot fire arrows and launch fireworks at festivals and other public occasions.

During the Edo period a few novelty guns were produced with multiple barrels which either radiated like the fingers of the hand from a common breech block and fired simultaneously, or were arranged with their bores parallel in such a way that they could be rotated to bring each barrel to the firing position in turn. None of these were ever actually used in anger; they were either experimental oddities or symbols of power to be carried in parades – quite a few of the revolving type still exist where it was not even considered necessary to drill touch holes between the pan and the barrels. Contrary to common belief, the gun makers of Japan were not wholely unaware of the developments in firearms that occurred in Europe during the seventeenth and eighteenth centuries. At least one snaphaunce pistol is known and a Japanese wheel lock is reported to exist in the reserve collection of a museum in England. Flintlock tinder lighters were common in the Edo period, and Hokusai depicts a double-barrelled flintlock pistol in his book *Manga*. These guns are rare, not because the gunsmiths could not make them, but because the government of the day actively discouraged any attempt to do so.

Japanese matchlocks often have their barrels decorated with lacquer or, more commonly, with overlay (*nunome*) in silver or gold. The more decorative were obviously intended for display rather than for use, being exhibited on racks or carried in front of personages of rank in processions. Themes for this decoration tend to be rather limited, with mon, the ever-popular dragon or the occasional inscription predominating. Some guns are signed by the maker underneath the barrel at the breech, but since many guns were turned out as part of a large contract, they were frequently left unsigned.

Irrespective of size, all guns, including cannon, were fitted with sights in the form of blocks, drilled, grooved and slotted in different ways. The standard arrangement was to fit a foresight just above the muzzle, and a backsight positioned about a third of the length down the barrel from the breech. Most backsights have slots or a combination of vertical and transverse holes, which suggests that they were once fitted with detachable leaf sights to allow for different ranges. To the authors' knowledge, no such additional sight blades have survived. The brass-lined cavities in the stock of some guns may have once held these, but in one specimen known to the authors, this held a supply of bamboo splints, intended for fastening the match into the serpentine. One gun in the author's possession which has every appearance of being of some age is fitted with a silver bead fitted into the rear face of the foresight, enabling it to be seen when sighting against a dark target; a feature having a considerable history that is still used to this day.

The stocks were of red oak, full-stocked to the muzzle, with the barrel held in place by a series of bamboo pins passing through the stock and into lugs dovetailed into the underside of the barrel. An exception to this is the kakae zutsu, some of which were fitted with reinforcing bands around the stock and barrel. All types were equipped with a simple wooden ramrod housed in the stock beneath the barrel. There was no tang attached to the breech plug as was common on European guns; instead the square end of the plug fitted into a recess in the stock, reinforced by a band of brass at this point to prevent splitting. Like the guns on which they were modelled, there is no shoulder stock. Instead they terminate in a form of curved pistol grip designed to be held against the cheek – the recoil being taken by the heavy barrel and by allowing the gun to move backwards and downwards on firing. What little stock furniture there was includes ornamental washers around holes and sometimes a trigger guard, invariably made of brass, both to prevent corrosion and because it could be cast in almost the final form, requiring only the minimum of finishing. A few of the more decorative guns have inlays of pierced and engraved brass let into their stocks.

Locks were of two basic types. The first had an external brass mainspring operating upwards on the tail of a serpentine which pivoted on a brass spindle passing through the lock plate and into the wood of the stock. This pivot was held in place by a bamboo pin fitted vertically just to the rear of the barrel. The serpentine was held in the cocked position by the nose of a long, horizontally operating sear, protruding through the lockplate above the tail, and pivoted against a light internal spring in such a way that it retracted into the plate when the trigger was pulled.

The second, more complicated mechanism, had the serpentine pivoting through the lock plate, and fitted with a tumbler and spiral brass mainspring on the inside. Operating in a notch cut into the tumbler and holding the lock cocked, was a sliding horizontal sear, pulled back by the trigger against the force of a smaller spiral spring. The gun in the author's possession mentioned above is of this type and the bearing surfaces of both the sear and tumbler are fitted with hardened steel inserts as a precaution against wear. In addition the tension of the sear spring can be varied, allowing the user to adjust the trigger pull to his liking.

In both types of lock, no screws were used, all supports were riveted to the lock plate and the various components fastened to them by pins of brass or bamboo. Even the locks themselves were held into the stocks by tapering pins of brass, fitted into tapering holes in the wood of the stock. The positions of these pins is revealed on the opposite side of the stock by inlet brass washers. Most gunsmiths provided an extra hole to allow a punch to be used to push the lock plate out of its recess when dismantling the gun.

The function of the springs operating the

Left: Matchlock musket by the Kunitomo group. Guns of this type were produced in their thousands within a few years of the introduction of firearms.

Far right: The Banrin kabuto (horse rushes helmet) of Toyotomi Hideyoshi with a crest in the form of a spray of leaves.

serpentine of Japanese guns has often been misunderstood, and the apparent inability of the Japanese to make them of steel has been noted. Steel would, in fact, have been inappropriate for the role these springs had to play. All guns of this type relied on the match, with its glowing coal, igniting the priming without itself being snuffed out on the base of the pan. Gunsmiths in Europe were well aware of this danger, even though the speed and pressure exerted by the serpentine was controlled entirely by the trigger pull. To prevent a misfire, the base of the pan of European guns was punched with a pattern of ribs and dots which ensured that at least parts of the glowing coal remained alight. The brass springs of the Japanese, while weak, moved the serpentine with sufficient rapidity, but with insufficient force to damage it when halted by contact with the pan surround, the glowing coal entering the pan to ignite the priming.

Three major groups of gunsmiths are known to have been working in the Momoyama and early Edo periods, but many more individuals worked as retainers for various daimyo. The first of these groups was based in Kyushu and continued to use the name of Tanegashima even though it had spread into the nearby provinces of Satsuma, Amakusa, Hizen and Higo. All its guns were fitted with distinctive blackened-wood stocks, occasionally further decorated with mon or stylized tendrils in gold lacquer. Most of the guns supplied to the armies during the Momoyama period were the product of the Kunitomo group founded in 1560 in the regions around Kyoto. It was from these makers that Oda Nobunaga obtained the guns which were used with such telling effect at Nagashino. Kunitomo weapons had pale-coloured stocks and generally simple but elegant octagonal barrels. A distinctive feature of the group's work is the practice of filing grooves across the width of the serpentine to resemble the nodes of bamboo. It also used cherry-blossom-shaped inserts around the holes for the lock pins. At best the group made superb guns, but much of its mass-produced work was so bad that it gained the nickname *udon ju* (noodle guns) because the barrels flexed and bent during firing. The third group was centred around the town of Sakai, near Osaka, where production started in 1554. Guns produced by the Sakai workers became renowned for the quality of their locks and ornamental brasswork, so much so that they were frequently commissioned by daimyo to mount barrels by other makers. Their own barrels were generally octagonal, decorated with applied silver designs, and terminating in bulbous fig-shaped muzzles.

Right: Ashigaru (foot soldier) putting on armour. Note in all the illustrations of these soldiers, the swords are shown as being put on before the armour.

Under ideal conditions, these matchlocks had a maximum range of about 300 yards, but were only capable of hitting a man-sized target consistently at 50 yards or so. While this effective range seems limited by modern standards, it was perfectly adequate when the target was a massed group of troops and somebody would be hit, even if it was not the person aimed at. After a few rounds the smoke would have prevented the two armies seeing each other anyway. Modern experimenters have found that reloading took about two minutes, but they were untrained and no doubt were far more careful than a soldier fighting for his life in the middle of a raging battle. During the Momoyama period, the gunners were provided with two flasks, a larger one for the ordinary powder and a smaller one for the finer priming powder. These were made of lacquered wood or paper with tubular nozzles fitted

Above and above right: Okashi gusoku, armour of munition quality comprising an okegawa do with rudimentary protection for the thighs together with a conical jingasa. Armours such as this were made in their thousands for issue to low-ranking soldiers.

with a stopper, which in the case of the larger flasks was itself a tube which acted as a measure for the powder charge. The more advanced commanders equipped their gunners with bandoliers, after the Western fashion, consisting of a series of paper tubes hung from a belt worn over the shoulder, each containing a pre-measured charge of powder. Attached to the belt was a box or pouch to carry the lead balls as well as a priming flask. Using these, the gunner could empty a charge down the barrel, drop in a ball and ram it home in a matter of seconds. What was time consuming was priming the pan and refitting the match without accidentally setting fire to loose powder. To speed up the rate of fire, gunners were arranged in ranks, the front row firing while those at the rear reloaded. By rotating the ranks, a withering and almost constant hail of fire could be maintained while supplies of powder lasted.

As was true of all early guns, the vagaries of the weather dictated their use. The pan cover was arranged to slide under the vertical flash shield and this did much to keep the priming dry, but only while the pan was kept shut. Many illustrations show short, pistol-like guns *bajo zutsu* being carried in lacquered cases, worn at the waist in a similar way to modern holsters; longer guns had cloth bags which offered some protection while in storage or when being transported. Other paintings depict a stiff-paper shield fitted above and around the lock to keep off the worst of the wind and rain, but this must have made repriming almost impossible. The fact remained that in a good downpour or a high wind guns were at best an unreliable weapon, and at worst were totally useless, other than as a club.

Tanegashima, hinawa ju or *teppo*, as guns were called, enabled the more imaginative commanders with only limited forces to embark on campaigns that would have been suicidal without them. Among the first was

Takeda Shingen, who ordered 300 guns in 1555 for trials. He became such an advocate of their use that in 1571 he issued an order to his generals to reduce the number of spearmen and replace them by gunners. Most of his battles, however, took place in and around his own province of Kai, and so had little impact on the political situation of the country as a whole, but the superb organization he employed to maintain his armies became the model for later commanders.

Following the Shingen's lead, large armies were formed and trained in the use of the new weapon, and drilled in tactics which exploited its potential. Those recruits capable of buying their own armour did so, but the poor samurai and the ashigaru had, as always, to be content with cheap munition armour supplied by their lord. The most rudimentary of these consisted of a simple plate do, sometimes of lacquered rawhide, or more usually an okegawa do of thin metal, painted with the commander's mon or with stripes of colour for identification, and fitted with simple plate gessan fastened to the do by sugake lacing. If they were lucky they were issued with a simple zunari helmet, but most were equipped with a conical iron or leather hat, *jingasa*, lacquered like the do, and worn with a cloth shikoro at the sides and back. In emergencies, these jingasa could, like the steel helmets of more modern wars, serve as a cooking pot or as a wash basin. These simple armours were originally provided with kote consisting of a few plates sparsely linked by mail, sewn onto a stout hemp backing. Only rarely were haidate or suneate provided, since the protection they afforded was not considered worth the extra expense and they also inhibited mobility. All ashigaru were issued with a sword, *okashi katana* (lent sword), and such other weapons or equipment as needed. When on the march, much of the equipment and stores needed by the army was carried on the backs of ashigaru since pack horses were scarce and wheeled transport was almost totally unused.

Born into this world of military aggression and intrigue were three men, two minor nobles and a peasant, who were destined to change the whole direction of Japan's history. None of them was different from or more noble than their contemporaries, except that they were more able than most, but they found themselves in the right places at the right times. Oda Nobunaga was born in 1534 into a household that had clawed itself to power in the province of Owari by 'gekokujo' during the 1530s. With a ruthlessness he was to display all his life, when only 17 years old he took control of the family fortunes, against fierce opposition from his relatives. Seven years later, a recruit by the name of Tokichi joined his army as an ashigaru, having stolen money from his previous master with which to buy an armour. He showed such exceptional ability and qualities of leadership that he rapidly rose to become one of Nobunaga's most able generals. This former peasant, later called Toyotomi Hideyoshi, was the second of these men of destiny.

The third member of the trio, Tokugawa Iyeyasu, met with the others in 1558 as an opponent in a tentative border attack on one

Below: Foot soldier armed with a spear. Note how the gessan is draped over the swords and how provisions were carried in a cloth, tied at intervals, and worn around the shoulders.

Right: Renjaku nuinobe do showing the cords passing over the shoulders to emerge at the waist in front.

Far right: Koshi tori hotoke ni mai do gusoku, a smooth-lacquered do with lacing at the bottom. Momoyama period.

Left: Ryo takahimo renjaku do gusoku, a 'modern' armour fastened by ties at each side. Foreign influence is evident in the medial ridge to the do and the use of Indian fabrics for the sleeves and haidate.

of Nobunaga's strongholds. Since Iyeyasu was only 17 at the time, he was a minor commander of Imagawa Yoshimoto, lord of Mikawa, Totomi and Suruga, the last of which adjoined Nobunaga's province of Owari. Yoshimoto had ambition, if little military skill, and in 1560 he had assembled an army of 25,000 to march on Kyoto to tackle the now-feeble Ashikaga. The only real barrier between him and the capital was Nobunaga and his small force of some 2000 or so men. To everyone's surprise, Nobunaga attacked the larger force and, partly by deception, succeeded in killing Yoshimoto. The following year, Iyeyasu, now no longer under obligation, joined Nobunaga as another of his generals.

Nobunaga was not the romantic that Yoshimoto had been, and realized that a direct assault on Kyoto with banners in the van was no longer the way to win wars. He first looked westwards, and gained control of the rich rice-producing province of Omi. He then either took, or stationed agents in, cities such as Otsu, Kusatsu, Kamigyo and, especially, Sakai. As a result of this policy he could provision and supply his ever-growing armies and draw on the services of craftsmen such as Imai Sokyu of Sakai, a supplier of guns. In a brilliant series of campaigns, Nobunaga wiped out the forces of the fifteenth Ashikaga Shogun and continued to conquer province after province, aided by his

generals Hideyoshi and Iyeyasu.

Like the European knight before him, the samurai found the gun a great leveller, showing respect to neither rank nor the quality of one's armour. Even daimyo appeared on the battlefield wearing sturdy tosei armours devoid of superfluous decoration. To alleviate the plainness, many of these armours were lacquered in bright colours, fitted with extravagant crests, or even wigs of hair. Vividly coloured *jinbaori* (surcoats) in expensive fabrics were worn over the armour, even in battle. Tokugawa Iyeyasu, renowned for his frugality, owned two armours of the simplest kind, distinguished only in that they are both lacquered in gold. He also owned another, made after Hideyoshi had jokingly referred to him as the 'Cow of the Kanto', completely covered in hide with the hair left on and with huge buffalo horns on the helmet. Following an engagement against Takeda Shingen, who had selected all those wearing red armour to position themselves in the front rank, Iyeyasu determined to imitate the idea and gave instructions to the Ii family to henceforth wear only red lacquered armour. As a result, any red lacquered armour became known as *hikone gusoku*, after the name of the Ii family's castle town.

A few of the more cautious had bullet-proof armours made, and marks of musket balls on some show that they had been subjected to a proof test by their makers. These *tameshi gusoku* were necessarily of great weight and most were provided with some form of solid plate do, and usually a zunari or other simple helmet; the thickness of the plates needed precluded a more complex type of design.

Sakakibara Kozan, although writing over 200 years later, makes reference to armour plate made with a hard-steel face, welded to a soft-steel back. Armourers appreciated that if the steel billet, after folding and welding, was flattened into a plate with the welds parallel to the surface, it was apt to flake when struck. If, on the other hand, it was beaten out with the weld planes at right angles to the plate surface, it split along the lines of the welds. To avoid these defects, a steel billet was formed in the latter way, then cut in two and the halves welded to each other with the direction of the grain crossed: a process called *jumonji kitae* (cross-pattern forging). When this was welded to the backing of softer iron, the face resisted penetration and splitting, and was supported by the malleable back. In an attempt to identify whether this process was actually used, the author carried out Rockwell hardness tests on two pieces of armour by Miochin smiths made about 300 years apart. In both cases there was considerable difference in hardness between the front and back surfaces of the plates that suggests that this method of making plates was, for some armour at least, actually employed.

To enable these and other heavy do to be worn for long periods of time, they were sometimes fitted with an internal system of suspensory cords called *renjaku*; an almost identical solution to the same problem was utilized by the armourers in the Royal

Above: Spears and heraldic banners were carried for identification. All weapons were provided with scabbards to protect them from the humid climate.

Far left: An armour presented by the governor of Edo to King James I of England.

Far left: Portrait of the Irish noble, Sir Neill O'Neill painted by J M Wright in 1680. The artist has introduced an imported Japanese armour – the style is typical of those produced by the Iwai for presentation and should be compared with those shown on pages 136 and 139. The servant carries the helmet bowl, the neck guard having been fitted around the waist in the manner of a European culet.

Armouries at Greenwich for a very heavy armour for Henry VIII of England. The cords were of braided silk or of cloth sewn into a roll, about an inch in diameter, anchored to the back plate at the level of the shoulder blades then passing over the shoulders to emerge through two holes in the front of the do just above the waist. One rare example that still retains its original renjaku is fitted with a single cord of braided silk, threaded through two holes in the backplate, at which point its weave changes from round to flat for that portion that sits on the shoulders, becoming round again about the level of the chest. The *renjaku do* was put on in the usual way, then hitched up until the weight was taken off the watagami and transferred to the renjaku, then the ends of the renjaku were tied together in front. A renjaku do in the author's collection has the watagami reduced to flat, unpadded strips of rawhide protected by small steel plates which are

Above left: The second of the two armours presented to King James I of England, recently repaired and relaced. These presentation armours were rather stereotyped and old-fashioned in style but were the normal wear of high-ranking samurai.

Above: Helmet and do inspired by European models. Momoyama period.

Right: A European cabasset modified for Japanese use by the addition of a plate around the lower edge to carry the neck guard. This is one of the very few examples in which the helmet has not been reversed by the Japanese.

inadequate to support the do, except just for the few minutes needed to put it on and adjust the cords. Just how this suspension made a difference is hard to imagine; the actual weight of the do is still taken by the shoulders. Presumably it was the elasticity of the cords that mattered, lessening the jolting of the armour while riding or walking.

Although renjaku were popular, the very heavy tameshi gusoku were never very common and by the mid-Edo period had all but ceased to be made. Most samurai considered the extra weight and the restriction it imposed on movement too high a price to pay for the dubious protection it provided.

Close on the heels of the Portuguese came the Spanish, to be followed in turn by the Dutch and English, all eager for trade and, in the case of the first two nations, keen to gain converts to the Catholic faith. Because these travellers had to overwinter in Goa or Macao before undertaking the last leg of their two-year journey, their ultimate landfall was usually Kyushu and, in particular, the southern port of Nagasaki. For this reason all Europeans were described by the Japanese as *nanban* (southern barbarians).

Right: Nanban kabuto, made from a cabasset decorated and mounted in Japan.

The goods they imported were as diverse and varied as the adventurers that brought them, but demand fluctuated as in any market. Will Adams, the English pilot of a Dutch expedition that sailed around Cape Horn before being driven by a storm to Japan, wrote several letters home during his long exile. In one, written to his 'good friend' Augustin Spalding in Bantam in 1613, he offers advice on the kind of goods in demand at the time:

> Now the commodities yt ye bring from Holland are these: cloth, leed [lead], still [steel], louking glasses, drinking glasses, dans-klass-glasses [telescopes], amber, dieeper and holland [fabrics], with other things of small importance.

One humorous note was included in a letter from a Dutch merchant to his suppliers requesting the usual imports of cloth, steel, telescopes and the like – his list finished with a plea for several more barrels of cough mixture. In exchange for these imports, the Europeans shipped home products from the exotic East. Adams' letter goes on to describe the current prices and mentions that the ship that came from Pattania carrying luxury fabrics from China, left Japan with exports of porcelain, lacquer wares and munitions among other things.

Among these munitions shipped to Europe were quantities of swords, spears and armours. Several well-known people of the time are known to have owned and prized Japanese swords – among them Sir Francis Drake and Rembrandt van Rijn. Presentation armours and weapons were sent to various European monarchs as diplomatic presents. James I of England received two armours made by Iwai Yozayemon from the Governor of Edo which are still preserved in the Tower of London together with a sword. Others must have been brought by merchants as items for trade since one appears, as an artist's prop, in a portrait of the Irish noble Sir Neill O'Neill. The young arms enthusiast Louis XIII of France collected all manner of weapons in his Cabinet D'Armes. Among the items listed in the inventory of 1729 are

Left: To gasa bachi, a style of helmet bowl inspired by the hats worn in China and Southeast Asia.

armours, swords and polearms that can be identified, despite the rather vague descriptions, as Japanese. Armours sent as diplomatic presents to France are now preserved in the Army Museum in Paris. All these presentation armours were rather old fashioned, being provided with akoda nari kabuto and o sode, but represent the style that nobles were expected to wear as an indication of their status. In the Historisches Museum in Dresden is a wheel-lock pistol whose stock, like its accompanying powder flask, is decorated with black lacquer, inlaid with chips of mother of pearl, in the characteristic style of Momoyama export lacquer. The gun itself, which is Flemish and dated around 1620, must have been shipped to Japan by a Dutch merchant in the unfinished state to be returned for sale after being decorated.

Oda Nobunaga took a very tolerant view of the Europeans, particularly the Jesuits, whom he regarded as a counter to the more militant of the Buddhists. Like many samurai, he admired the military organization and attitude of these 'Soldiers of Christ', while despising the political intrigues of some of the Buddhist sects. On one famous occasion, he surrounded Mount Hiei, to the north of Kyoto, and set fire to Enryakuji Temple, which had lent support to an opponent, killing everyone on the mountain and burning every building in the temple complex to the ground. Oda Nobunaga met his death in 1582, not in glorious battle, but while at his ablutions, betrayed by one of his own generals. Within a year, Nobunaga's death had been avenged by Hideyoshi, who assumed leadership of his forces and continued the process of unification. By the late 1580s the entire country, for the first time in hundreds of years, was virtually under the domination of one man – and that man a commoner.

Among the last to capitulate were the Daimyo of Kyushu, many of whom had been baptized as Christians. Some were undoubtedly true converts, but others regarded Christianity as little more than a new sect of Buddhism, and one that was very much worth encouraging for the trade which followed the priests. Even though wars were sweeping the country, the 'black ships' continued to arrive, bringing with them luxuries and novelties including armour and other weapons, for trade.

At least one sword blade which survives from this period originated in Solingen, Germany; it was reshaped and retempered by a Japanese swordsmith and mounted, as a dirk, in a scabbard covered with imported Dutch leather. In the nineteenth century Masahide wrote that he had examined many Dutch swords and recognized that they were not folded and forged like Japanese swords but were simply beaten out at one heating. Imported steel from Holland and India was especially prized by swordsmiths during the late sixteenth and early seventeenth centuries, no doubt for its sales appeal. Many blades from that time have inscriptions on their tangs attesting that they were made from 'southern barbarian iron'. Masahide, practical as ever, stated that although it looked different in the rough, it worked exactly the same and the swords were indistinguishable from those made of native steel.

Equally popular were sword mounts, particularly tsuba, in the foreign style. A few of the better ones were passable copies, in russet iron and gilding, of the pierced shell guards

Left: Tojin gasa kabuto, a type of nanban helmet inspired by the head gear of Chinese and Korean envoys.

Left: Kebiki odoshi go mai do gusoku, a close-laced five-plate do. This armour shows many small features of European influence including a ridge to the front plate, roped rims to the major plates and a pleated ruff around the collar.

of small-swords. As was often the case with fashionable styles, mindless duplication of the unfamiliar motifs resulted in tsuba consisting of little more than a plate pierced with hundreds of holes, amply justifying Western collectors' derogatory description of them as 'coffee strainers'.

Little now remains of the armour entering Japan from the West, and that which does survive consists mainly of breasts and backs, the occasional gorget and various open helmets of the morion or cabasset variety. Armour for the limbs, as well as the various types of close helmets being worn in Europe at the time, seem never to have been used; presumably because they were too different in character to those used by the Japanese.

Genuine nanban gusoku was a rarity that only the rich could afford to acquire and modify to their taste. Rather ordinary quality 'breasts and backs' of Italian or Flemish manufacture seem to have been the usual imports – modified into nanban do by fitting them with gessan and watagami before giving them a russet finish in place of their European polish. When the gorget was worn, it was outside the cuirass, forming what was called a manchira (in an attempt to imitate the Spanish word for cape – mantilla), contrary to the intention of the European armourers who made them.

Rather more common than nanban do are *nanban kabuto*, made from imported Spanish morions or cabassets. These helmets, most of which are raised from one piece of steel, have tall skulls shaped like half an almond that terminate in a small bent stalk at the apex. Some have a narrow brim turned down at the sides and rising to an upturned point at the front and back; others have a narrow flat brim all round. A tubular plume holder of brass or iron was fixed to the back of the skull just above the brim, continuing a row of ornate, brass-headed rivets that fastened the internal leather strap for the lining. Most are of very common quality, being turned out in their thousands for light munition armours in Italy and possibly Spain, although a few were made as alternative light helmets to accompany expensive armours.

In the hands of the Japanese these helmets were adapted to take a shikoro by being fitted with a koshimaki riveted to the inside of the lower edge of the skull, cut out in front over

Left: Momonari kabuto, a helmet inspired by the European morion.

Far left: A 62-plate ko boshi kabuto, by Miochin Nagamichi. It belongs to the armour opposite. Helmets of this type covered with over 1000 small rivets were supreme examples of the armourer's craft, but of doubtful value in battle.

Left: Me no shita ho (facemask) of russet iron in the Nara style belonging to the armour opposite.

Above: Red, white and blue laced ni mai do, an armour which joins by a hinge under the left arm. One of ten similar armours owned by Toyotomi Hideyoshi and thought to have been used by his guard or by his doubles (kagemusha).

the eyes. Strangely, the Japanese usually reversed them so that the stalk at the apex pointed forwards, to satisfy the samurai ethic of always advancing. Because the plume holder was then at the front, it was discarded and replaced by a tsunomoto to take a crest. Once again the surface would be russet and perhaps decorated with gold and silver overlay to conform to Japanese taste.

A famous armour of Tokugawa Iyeyasu is one of the few surviving examples that incorporates several pieces of European manufacture. The do was originally an Italian peascod cuirass of about 1580, with a pronounced medial ridge. On the backplate a pair of typical watagami have been attached by similar rivets to those at the waist, while the front has been pierced to take shoulder-strap fastenings. Attached to the lining strap are leather iyozane gessan in six sections, lacquered red and laced in dark blue silk. Over the do was worn the gorget, as a manchira, decorated en suite with the cuirass, with the outer edge and the small flange around the neck lacquered red. The helmet has been modified from a typical cabasset by fitting the usual koshimaki and red lacquered shikoro. The small brim has been cut away in front and replaced by a concave peak in the tosei style. All remaining components are of standard Japanese patterns and consist of a hanbo, oda gote, haidate and shino suneate.

For those unable to acquire the real thing, copies of nanban gusoku were made, varying from very accurate reproductions of the originals to strange creations that resemble little else on earth, but which could be passed off to those in the more remote parts of the country who had never actually come into contact with the 'foreign devils'. Attempts to copy nanban do were more or less confined to making them from single front and back plates and shaping the front to form a medial ridge. With helmets, the armourer's imagination ran riot. All sorts of wonderful shapes and styles were produced whose only commonality was that they were not recognizably Japanese. A considerable number had high, almost pointed crowns, overlaid with elaborately shaped iron plates covering the joints. Many are fitted with a horizontal brim that may well have been inspired by Korean or Chinese originals.

One style of helmet modelled on the cabasset that was to prove lasting was the *momonari kabuto* (peach-shaped helmet). The majority of these are similar in shape to the skull of a cabasset but with a flange running from front to back, cut with a step at the apex to represent the stalk. Very few are provided with a brim, being fitted instead with the brow-plate-peak combination of the zunari bachi. These helmets became and remained popular because weapons slid easily off their smoothly curved surfaces, and because they could be made cheaply and easily. This helmet represented one of the few unusual styles which even the poorer samurai could afford.

Those samurai too conservative to wear these obvious copies of foreign styles were nevertheless prepared to accept small but

Left: Jinbaori, a surcoat worn over armour, of a member of the Honda family.

fashionable European influences on their armours. Medial ridges on do were considered beneficial, stiffening the front plate and, on plate do, providing a glancing surface off which weapons would slide. Any do so shaped is described as *omodaka do* (water-plantain leaf) or *hatomune do* (pigeon breasted). Also popular was an imitation of the roping which decorated the rolled edges of most European armours from early in the sixteenth century. Since the edges of Japanese armour were not rolled, this decoration was simulated by shaping the applied soft metal edges of the plates into a rope-like form, to give what was called *nawame fukurin.* Japanese artists of the day loved to depict costumes of the Europeans, especially the long, padded pantaloons and the ruffs worn around the neck and wrists. These ruffs were imitated with small pleated frills of several layers of silk, which were sewn around the collars of better armours, to form what are called *kesho eri.* Occasionally these frills are found elsewhere on the armour, bordering sode or haidate and particularly around the cuffs of kote.

Along with these obvious imitations of European culture were other more subtle influences. New materials were brought into the country which were avidly taken up for their novelty value. Both the Dutch and English imported a closely woven woollen cloth, which became widely used for military equipment, but never, it seems, for civilian clothing. From the limited colours of the surviving examples, it would seem that it was imported pre-dyed in either bright red, black, brown, yellow or white. For some inexplicable reason, blues and greens are rarely, if at all, encountered. Almost immediately, this fabric became the favourite material for covering kikko work on collars and knee guards, and for making jinbaori and other military clothing. It was so widely used that supply could not keep up with demand, and a trade developed in Kyushu of producing a counterfeit from cotton and rabbit hair.

Since the traders had to stop en route in either India or China, the products of these and neighbouring countries were added to the bill of lading. Ivory, sometimes gathered from the remains of mammoth in the tundra of Siberia, was imported for carvings, the scraps being used for toggles on more expensive armours. From the same region came the

Below: Sheet of embossed, gilded and painted leather made in Holland during the late seventeenth or early eighteenth century as a wall covering. This type of leather was used by the Japanese to cover sword scabbards and so on.

Above: Front plate of a go mai do covered with imported Dutch leather of identical pattern to that shown on the previous page. Note the ties for attaching the gessan which were laced onto a leather belt, a not uncommon feature of tosei armour.

Right: Together with the gun, the yari was the main offensive weapon of the period.

skins of polar bears, which are seen glued to the lower edge of shikoro, sode and gessan, as an alternative to the black fur of the native Japanese bear. A whole range of exotic fabrics appeared, ranging from brocades, velvets and damasks to figured satins, and even the humble cotton and calico. An armour in the author's collection has the sleeves and haidate covered with a block printed Indian chintz, while another has the front of the do covered with a piece of leather that is Dutch in origin, embossed and gilded with rococo scrolls and painted with acanthus leaves in red and white. This leather, called 'gouldleer' by the Dutch, was originally made in sections measuring about three feet (0.9m) by two feet (0.6m), and dates from the beginning of the eighteenth century. In Holland it was generally used for wall hangings, but the Japanese adopted it for covering sword scabbards, saddles and the like.

One of the few imported ideas that proved to be something of a retrograde step, yet which was taken up quite avidly, was mail made in the European manner. In this construction, all links were circular and each was linked through four others. To the mail-maker it was a boon in that he had only one shape of link to make, but when incorporated with plates, as much Japanese mail was, the fact that none of the links lay parallel to the plane of the plates made connecting the two difficult. Despite this, *nanban kusari* became popular, especially for cheaper work, when it was made of thin wire with the joints merely butted together rather than riveted as was the practice in Europe. One variety of nanban kusari that was a distinct improvement, involved the use of very small links in relation to the diameter of the wire. The result, as its name of *chirimen nanban kusari* suggests, was a dense smooth structure whose surface resembled crêpe de chine.

Even before the whole of the country was under his domination, Hideyoshi was faced with half a million or so samurai, and an unknown number of the remainder of the population, bearing arms. With little to occupy their time as the fighting drew to a close, they were a potential danger to the unity he was so near to achieving. In 1588 he issued a proclamation that all weapons, other than those belonging to the samurai, were to be seized and used in the construction of a great Buddha. This 'Sword Hunt' more than any other factor, finally divided the population, creating an elite warrior class. The days of the samurai-farmer were now over, and many were faced with the agonizing decision of leaving their land for the service of a lord, or remaining on the land with the consequent loss of status. Those who chose the military life moved to the towns springing

Right: Nagamaki and its scabbard. These pole arms with their long, sword-like blades were popular for arming the front-rank troops of both Muromachi and Momoyama period armies.

Below: Foot soldiers armed with spears carrying a trophy head and looted swords.

up around the castles of the daimyo, becoming retainers whose lives and actions were controlled by obligation.

Having solved part of the dilemma, Hideyoshi then began to realize a long-cherished ambition that would solve another part – the conquest of China. Because of its vast size and ability to absorb invaders rather than confront them, China's government had grown complacent. Hideyoshi's scheme was to attack and conquer Korea, and use it as a base from which to launch an attack on the Chinese capital. By 1592 he had assembled a force of some 300,000 men, in seven divisions, mainly under the command of Christian daimyo, which was dispatched in a motley collection of boats and ships from Kyushu, Iki and Tsushima.

The muster for the fourth division, commanded by Hideyoshi's former enemy Shimazu Yoshihiro, has survived to give us some indication of the composition of these forces:

15,000 general troops under the command of Yoshihiro's son
300 banners with 5 hand spears
300 spears, of which 200 should be long and 200 (sic) should be hand-spears
Besides these, the men should provide hand spears according to their capacity. . .
1500 men with guns
1500 men with bows
600 men with sashimono; these should be armoured.

In addition there is the quaint instruction that shows the military mind has always been the same throughout history:

Only distinguished men should be mounted; however, all those who cannot go on foot should be mounted. Therefore, the number of mounted is indefinite. The mounted men might well bear helmet and armour.

The hand spears, *te yari*, referred to in the list were about seven feet (2.1m) in total length, for ease of handling at close quarters. They were fitted with heads about six inches (15cm) long, having a cross section that was either of an elongated-diamond shape, *ryo shinogi yari*, or in the form of a flattened triangle, *sankaku yari*. Both types had cutting edges along both sides. These short spears were carried by both foot soldiers and horsemen, and were handy enough to be swung about to take advantage of their cutting edges, as well as for thrusting. The longer spears were similar except in weight and length and generally had proportionately larger heads. Most were between 10 and 12 feet (3 and 3.7m) long, but Oda Nobunaga is reputed to have used one that was 18 feet in length. Being less easily handled for fighting at close quarters, they were mainly used, like the pikes of Europe, to protect other troops from cavalry. They were gripped near the butt by the right hand and thrust forward with a pumping action through the left hand; metal tubes fitted with a hand guard were sometimes employed to reduce the friction. Many spears were fitted with metal cross-bars, *hadome*, a foot or so below the head,

Right: The blade from a yari (top) and a jumonji yari (bottom). The latter is unusual in having its central blade shaped with a sword point.

which could be used to parry a sword or could be hooked behind the opponent's legs to knock him to the ground.

Other types of pole arms in use differed from the yari only in the shape of their heads. *Jumonji yari* consisted of a straight central blade with two others at right angles near the base (their name alludes to their cross shape when mounted). Being sharpened along all the edges, they could be used for striking or cutting in all directions in a similar way to the European halberd. The *katakama yari* (side sickle spear) was similar to the jumonji yari except that it only had one side blade, occasionally curved upwards slightly. Kato Kiyomasa, one of Hideyoshi's ablest generals, was famed for his skill with this weapon, and is supposed to have hunted tigers with it during the Korean campaign. Pole arms with other strangely shaped heads are not uncommon. Some had L- or T-shaped blades sharpened along all the edges and could only have been employed with a cutting action. Like all Japanese weapons, these strange and wonderful pole arms were all provided with scabbards when not in use, some of which must have tasked the ingenuity of their makers to the limit. One curious weapon that could not be fitted with a scabbard had a multi-pronged barbed head mounted on a shaft whose upper end is reinforced with spiked iron strips to prevent it being cut or grasped. These *yagara mogara* were designed to snag in the armour or clothing and were used for pulling down horsemen or trapping and holding men on foot. During the Edo period they became the favourite weapon of the police, being used for taking captives unhurt, as the law at the time required.

Both naginata and nagamaki continued in use, as apparently did the no dachi, the latter more for its psychological impact than for its effect on the outcome of a conflict. These weapons were used with considerable impact at least once during the Korean campaign, as a Korean writer records: 'All the Japanese soldiers carried on their shoulder enormous swords; and when their host was seen from the other side of the river the rays of the sun were reflected upon their blades like flashes of lightning.' However, the books *Cho Hitsu Roku* and *Date Narizane Ki* give the game away by explaining that these 'terror weapons' were nothing more than pieces of wood covered with a paint made from tin.

Almost all except the highest ranks now wore the uchi gatana, (generally abbreviated to *katana*), and the *wakizashi*, both with armour and civilian dress. Those who could afford to do so had pairs of swords, *daisho* (long and short), made with matching mounts and decoration. As it was a period of exuberant luxury despite the wars, daisho from this era tend to be lacquered in bright colours with extravagant gilded or painted decoration – the antithesis of later samurai taste.

The number of archers in the Shimazu muster reflects the importance still being placed on the bow. Its power had been increased yet again; its effective range was by this time almost as long as the gun and its rate of fire was better. The improvement in power and range was achieved by making the bow almost entirely from bamboo. In place of the wooden core used previously, three or four bamboo slats were now glued at right angles between the bamboo back and belly,

Left: A foot soldier with a bow and quiver mounted in a rack for carrying. The gun never entirely replaced the bow and arrow because the gun was useless in wet or windy conditions.

Left: The site of the Battle at Sekigahara, 1600, at which Tokugawa Iyeyasu gained control of the country.

Above: Armour and weapons presented to Mori Kobayakawa Takakage by Hideyoshi for his services at the Battle P'yok-je-yek, during the Korean campaign.

wood being used only as a filler at the sides. The bow also had one considerable advantage over the gun – it did not need expensive powder. Arrows were to some extent re-usable and in any case a Japanese product; good powder on the other hand was an expensive item of trade with the Europeans, particularly the English, as the homemade product was inferior.

Despite Hideyoshi's grand schemes, the Korean invasion, and a second attempt five years later involving 150,000 men, failed

Above and above right: Front and back of a jinbaori or surcoat of Kobayakawa Takakage. The mon was granted to Takagake by Hideyoshi and dates this garment to the period just before the owner's death in 1597.

because the lines of supply were inadequate, especially in the face of the efficient Korean navy. Those who survived and returned to Japan were rewarded and honoured in the traditional way, but in reality the whole affair was a disaster, whose only benefit had been temporarily to remove from the country a number of potentially disruptive commanders and their armies. Among those rewarded was Mori Kobayakawa Takakage, who had led the sixth division in the first invasion. On his return at the end of the first invasion attempt, the Emperor, acting on Hideyoshi's instructions, presented him not only with Hideyoshi's son, whom he adopted, but also with an armour and swords as a reward for his part in defeating the Chinese and Koreans at P'yok-je-yek in 1593. Since Takakage died in 1597, the date of manufacture of this armour, which survives in almost pristine condition, can be narrowed down to the period 1594 to 1597. The importance of this armour, closely examined by the authors, lies in its indisputable provenance, and in that it should represent a model of the type of armour to which a fighting samurai, albeit an elderly one, would have aspired.

The helmet is a 62-plate hoshi bachi, reputedly made by a member of the Saotome family, but more likely Haruta work in view of the concave tosei mabisashi. To enhance its appearance, the peak has been covered with printed leather. The helmet is fitted with a maedate in the form of the imperial chrysanthemum mon flanked by leaves, and waki date bearing the kiri mon used by Hideyoshi; this mon also occurs elsewhere on the armour, having been granted to Takakage for his use. The mask is a typical Nara me no shita ho, lacquered black with the hole under the chin furnished with an ornate gilt eyelet. Unusually, the nuinobe do is provided with renjaku, shoji ita and gyoyo, the latter permanently attached to the watagami. On the front of the do are two rings, the saihai no kan and the tenugui no kan, in copper gilt. This second ring is fitted to the left breast, which is normally regarded as an Edo period innovation. The o sode are also atypical in being lined inside with brocade, like a tosei sode – most o sode only having a narrow vertical strip of leather where they come in contact with the kote. Still accompanying the armour is a lacquered display stand, bags for the individual pieces and its two boxes, which retain their leather storage covers.

Hideyoshi died during the second abortive invasion of Korea, which, incidentally, was commanded by his son Hideaki, whom Kobayakawa Takakage had adopted. Hideyoshi's other son, Hideyori, was left in the protective care of regents, one of whom was Tokugawa Iyeyasu. True to form, the regents manoeuvred to take control, finally polarizing into two groups. One was led by Iyeyasu and the other by one of Hideyoshi's administrators, Ishida Mitsunari. The antagonists finally met at Sekigahara, in the province of Mino, in October 1600. In total, 154,000 troops were in the field, with rather more than 30,000 held in reserve. Guns had no effect on the outcome of the battle since the whole affair took place in pouring rain. It was the bow, sword and spear that won the day for Iyeyasu, but only because Hideaki changed sides at a crucial moment.

As victor, Iyeyasu was in control of a unified country and, being of noble birth, was entitled to become Shogun. Once again the military capital was moved, this time to Edo (now Tokyo), which rapidly grew to become the largest city in the world. For a while he was content to allow Hideyori to live, but by 1614 he felt his position threatened. He found a feeble excuse for an attack in an alternative reading of an inscription cast into a bell associated with Hideyoshi's great Buddha, which he interpreted as a slight. Hideyori sent out pleas for help, but only those whose land had been confiscated after the Battle of Sekigahara responded. Altogether some 90,000 packed into Osaka castle, the largest and strongest castle in Japan, and prepared for a siege. Some idea of the scale of the fortifications can be obtained from the fact that Hideyori had moats dug which were 240 feet (73m) wide, and that the perimeter of the outer works was nine miles (14.5km) long. Iyeyasu mustered 18,000 men and eventually, after heavy losses, captured the outworks. There followed a long period of attrition, during which both cannon and miners were used to good effect. The collapse came, however, when the defenders ventured out to fight on the surrounding plains, and were cut off, allowing the attackers to gain entry. Fire completed the task of destruction and Hideyori, trapped in the blazing main tower, committed suicide. Iyeyasu was now in complete control, without serious opposition, but he was now 74 years old. He died the following year, leaving behind a unique legacy to his son – a unified Japan. There was every chance that this situation would continue.

Left: Armour display stand for the armour of Kobayakawa Takakage.

Far left: Stirrups used by Takakage during the Korean campaign.

CHAPTER SEVEN
Japan in Isolation: the Edo Period

The Edo period officially begins with the establishment of the Tokugawa Shogunate at Edo, but it was not until Iyemitsu, Iyeyasu's grandson, came to power that the period took on its characteristic pace and lifestyle. Iyeyasu, on the whole, had been tolerant of the Christians, but his son and grandson were far less so. Iyemitsu's attitude hardened after a group of Christian farmers and samurai rebelled against the excesses of the local daimyo at Shimabara in 1637. Intolerant of the political ambitions being shown by the Jesuits and their converts, Iyemitsu inaugurated a programme of expulsions and repression, designed to remove all traces of the religion from Japanese soil. At

Below: Map of Edo and the defensive ring of provinces held by loyal daimyo.

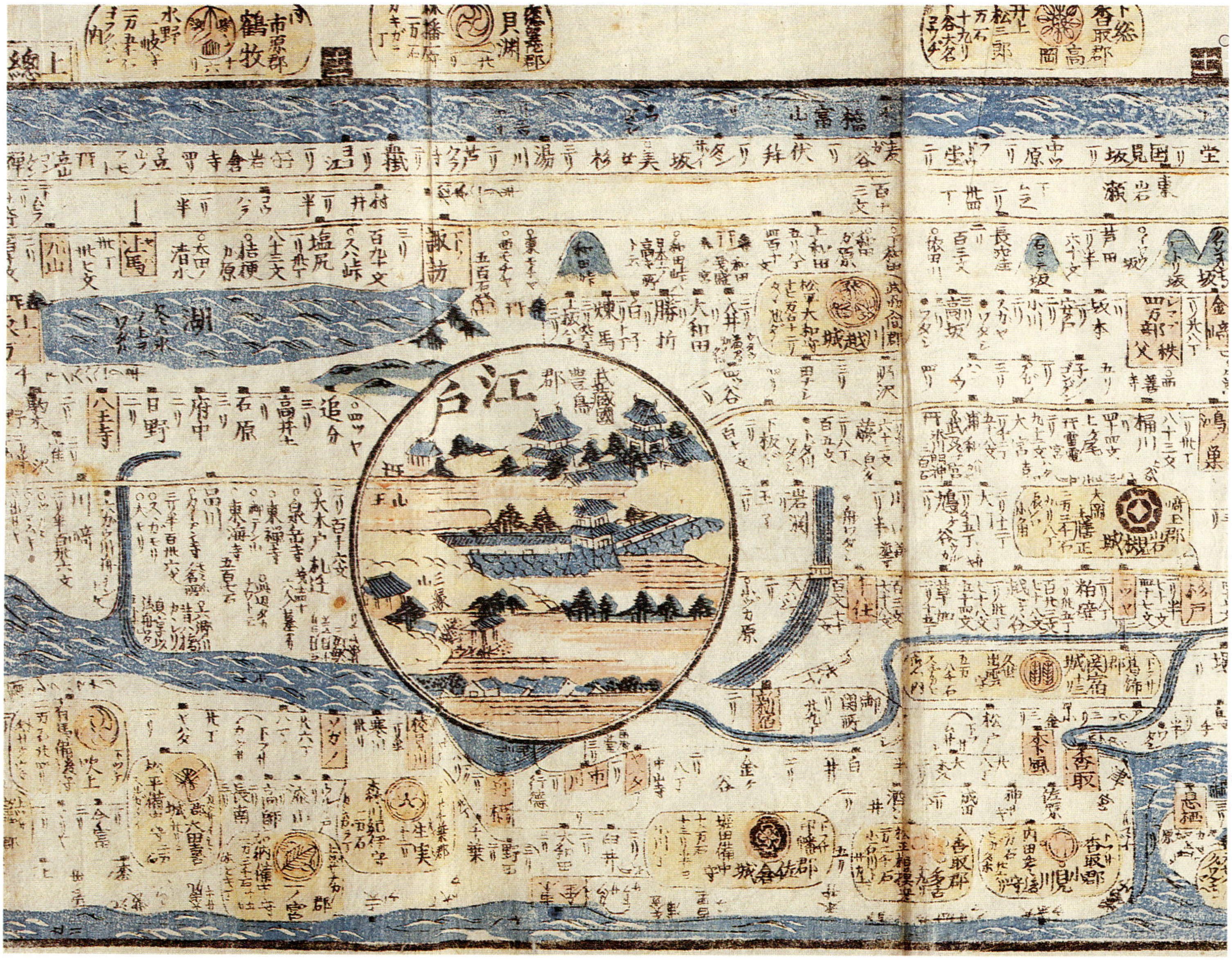

Left: Kami shimo of brown and white hemp cloth decorated with the owner's mon. This costume was worn on formal occasions by the samurai of the Edo period.

the same time a policy of seclusion was instigated, preventing all overseas travel and inhibiting contact with the rest of the world; the only exceptions being small isolated trading stations run by the Dutch and Chinese at Nagasaki.

Internally, legislation was enacted which profoundly affected the social structure and life of the country. Of the greatest importance to the arms student was the legislation which confirmed the rigid social structure initiated by Hideyoshi. Under the Tokugawas, society became even more stratified, with almost no opportunity of crossing the divisions between the classes. A constant stream of laws and edicts was issued, but never clearly set down, which attempted to regulate in the minutest detail the lifestyle, behaviour and attitudes of everyone.

At the pinnacle of this social order were, theoretically, the Emperor and the *kuge* (nobles), who made up the imperial court in Kyoto. In practice, the court continued in the almost totally emasculated role it had played for centuries; that of conducting ceremonials, devoid of purpose and designed to keep it occupied. The real apex of the structure was occupied by the samurai – themselves strictly stratified with the Shogun and his court officials at their head. Below him came the daimyo, previously a loose term applied to any great landowner, but now defined as one whose income was greater than 10,000 *koku* of rice per year (one koku was approximately the amount of rice needed to feed a person for a year). For reasons of security, the daimyo were carefully categorized on the basis of their allegiance to the Tokugawa at Sekigahara. *Han* (territorial holdings) were allotted to daimyo on the basis of their supposed loyalty and Edo was ringed by daimyo whose loyalty could be relied upon. Each daimyo supported and issued stipends to the other grades of samurai who made up his retinue and who in turn might support others of even lesser rank.

Many of the samurai retained by the shogun, and to a lesser extent those of the daimyo, continued in their role as members of

Below: Kusari katabira, a mail shirt, with detachable half sleeves (han gote) of European-style mail on brocade. This was an alternative, light defence to plate armour. Edo period.

various military units and armies, but armies whose roles were becoming increasingly legislative. Even before the end of the seventeenth century, laws had to be passed to ensure that samurai kept their weapons and armour in good order. By 1694, matters had grown worse – the government resorted to passing laws to enforce the practice of the martial arts. Year by year, more and more samurai, who were expected to be equipped and ready for war at all times, found themselves instead struggling with the mountains of paperwork required by the Tokugawa bureaucracy. In this and other ways the government discouraged the formation of power groups while simultaneously recognizing the need for a military class to maintain the social order. Confucian ideals of loyalty were advocated at every opportunity and an idealized version of Bushido, The Way of the Warrior, with its basis in the distant past, was codified. By emphasizing the sword as the 'soul of the samurai' and recounting stories of single-handed bravery and unthinking loyalty shown by the samurai of old to his lord (and by logical extension, through him, to the shogun), skills such as the maintenance of large armies and their tactical use in the field or the use of massed musketry, were gradually eroded.

Thus were the samurai of the period occupied. They bustled about the castle towns wearing their two swords and curious ceremonial dress (*kami shimo*) with its stiffened wings of hemp cloth, carrying out the business of their lord, or keeping the peace in their role as magistrates and police. In Edo, there were two permanent magistrates (*machi bugyo*) controlling 25 assistants (*yoriki*) and below them 120 police officers (*doshin*). These minor officials, the doshin, like their non-samurai attendants, carried as symbols of their office the *jitte* (a steel rod fitted with a side hook), which, together with yagara mogara which were positioned at the barriers and check points dividing the city into areas, were used to disarm and apprehend wrongdoers, without bloodshed. Should a situation arise in which a yoriki needed to be called, he would attend on horseback wearing a mail shirt, *kusari katabira*, fitted with detachable armoured sleeves, under his outer coat, and a lacquered or iron jingasa on his head. His task was to supervise the arrest, using his sword or spear only if all other attempts failed.

Another official duty undertaken by the samurai was the organization of fire fighting, a responsibility of the greatest importance in towns and cities built almost entirely of wood and paper. In 1657, a fire in Edo killed 108,000 people and another in 1772 destroyed half the city. By the end of the seventeenth century, the government had organized squads of trained men, supervised by samurai, who competed to be first to attend the blaze and plant their banner on an adjacent rooftop, thus claiming the right to deal with the outbreak and receive payment. So seriously was this duty taken that in the castle towns the daimyo themselves attended, wearing lacquered paper mâché fire helmets with long, hood-like cloaks attached to them which fastened over the face to give some protection from the heat and sparks.

Positioned in theory just below the samurai, but in practice almost at the bottom of the social scale were the prime producers of food – the farmers. These were organized on a village basis with a headman responsible to the daimyo for tax gathering and production targets. Individuals within the village were responsible to the headman, who in turn was responsible to higher authorities for the villagers. It was in the headman's interest to maintain civil obedience; if anything went wrong, both he and his family would be severely punished. This system of mutual responsibility, for both reward and punishment, was one of the main factors which held

Right: Jingasa of iron decorated with mon in silver overlay. These light open helmets were worn when riding or in camp and were frequently of lacquered leather for lightness. This diminutive example was made for a child during the Edo period.

the social structure together. Below the farmers were artists and craftsmen, many of whom in practice enjoyed a status far higher than their supposed station, by reason of their patronage and ability. A few were even granted samurai status because of the excellence of their work, or held positions of authority as advisers and craftsmen in various han. On rare occasions samurai moved socially in the opposite direction, mixing and working with artisans; for example, during the early Edo period Rurisai Genuemon was so obsessed by military strategy and technology that he not only influenced the design of armour but also probably made it himself.

Finally, at the bottom of the social ladder came the merchants and brokers, non-producers who in practice managed to live opulent lives despite the constant edicts from the government to encourage frugality. Many became so rich that they bought respectability, marrying their daughters into samurai families in exchange for the discharge of debts. It was this class of townsmen which was mainly responsible for the cannons of taste so familiar in the art of the Edo period. Outside the social hierarchy, and never satisfactorily categorized, were a few small groups like doctors and priests, as well as the *eta* or *hinin*, people who carried out tasks considered taboo.

Swords could be carried by several of these groups, but only the samurai would wear the pair of swords that were their badge of office. Those who could afford the considerable expense wore daisho, but many more wore whatever they could afford or had inherited. Since the blade of a sword could easily be removed from its mount, it was not uncommon to have different sets of mounts, *koshirae*, made for the same blade for use on different occasions. When a blade was not being used, it was kept in a scabbard and hilt of plain wood, *shirasaya*, and the mounts were assembled on a wooden replica of the blade, *tsunagi*. Swords were always stored in bags of rich brocade, and might then be placed into lacquered boxes, *katana zutsu*, made to house them. Racks, *katana kake*, were positioned by the door of every samurai household to receive the long swords of visitors.

Other classes, if permitted a sword at all, had to be content with a single short sword or one of the many varieties of dirk, generically termed *tanto*, but differentiated on the basis of the mount. Women of the samurai class carried a small dirk, *kaiken*, in the fold of their kimono, both as a weapon of defence and, in the last resort, as a means of committing suicide. Some townsmen, more brave or more contemptuous of officialdom than others, made the most of things and pushed the length of the blade to the legal limit of approximately 2 feet (0.6m) and wore it in a long scabbard, implying that they were entitled to wear a katana. Members of the merchant class, in particular, had their swords or dirks lavishly mounted, encouraging the production of highly decorative sword mounts, and breaking away from the austere styles that had become fashionable with the samurai.

Below: Fire helmet and cape of a member of the Mori family. The supervision of fire-fighting was one of the samurai's duties during the Edo period.

Above: A cap and cape worn by the women of a daimyo's household in the event of a fire. Fires were a great hazard in the newly built towns and cities springing up around the castles of the daimyo. Edo period.

Above right: Armoured jacket of mail and plates covered with patterned hemp. The absence of mon suggests that this was made for a non-samurai. Edo period.

Right: A highly decorated jingasa.

During the Momoyama period, most samurai had been content with sword fittings that were both functional and showed a restrained taste and a subtlety of design that is still admired today, although their sword scabbards were lacquered in bright colours and designs that appear almost vulgar by comparison with the blacks and sombre colours of the Edo period. Mostly these had been made in iron, patinated to rich shades of brown, and textured to give not only a visual but a tactile quality that cannot be appreciated unless they are handled. The long-established Goto school had produced soft-metal fittings according to their own strict cannons, but these were for wear in court and were never meant for the masses. Townsmen, anxious to display their wealth and intent on living life to the full, signalled the boom in fine metalwork used not only for sword fittings, but also for *netsuke*, pipes and pouch clasps. Their demands stimulated the artists and craftsmen into the production of metalwork that surpasses, both in quality and in design, almost any metalwork made before or since.

Above left: Hamidashi, a variety of dirk with a guard only slightly larger than the hilt.

Above right: A tanto (dirk) with a pommel in the form of an elephant's head. Elephants were known only by illustration in Japan.

The Japanese have always abhored raw metal, with the exception of gold, silver and the steel of blades, preferring to accelerate corrosion and produce a coloured surface patina. With this in mind, alloys had been devised, centuries before, solely for the colours they developed on their surfaces when chemically treated. Paramount among them was *shakudo*, an alloy of copper containing up to five per cent gold, which acquired a purplish-black patina of great richness. *Shibuichi* was an alloy of copper with about 25 per cent silver, which could exhibit various shades of silvery-grey and had a fine flecked effect if properly mixed. Added to these two principal alloys were *sentoku*, a type of brass which gave various yellow and brown colours, and various lead bronzes which provided the darker browns and greens. Using these alloys, together with gold, silver, copper and iron, the craftsmen produced coloured pictures of incredible complexity and, in many cases, an artistry that defies their medium.

The techniques these craftsmen employed were similar to those used by jewellers the world over, but developed to levels of technical complexity rarely seen elsewhere. Surfaces were textured using punches which, if rough faced and used in a random pattern,

1

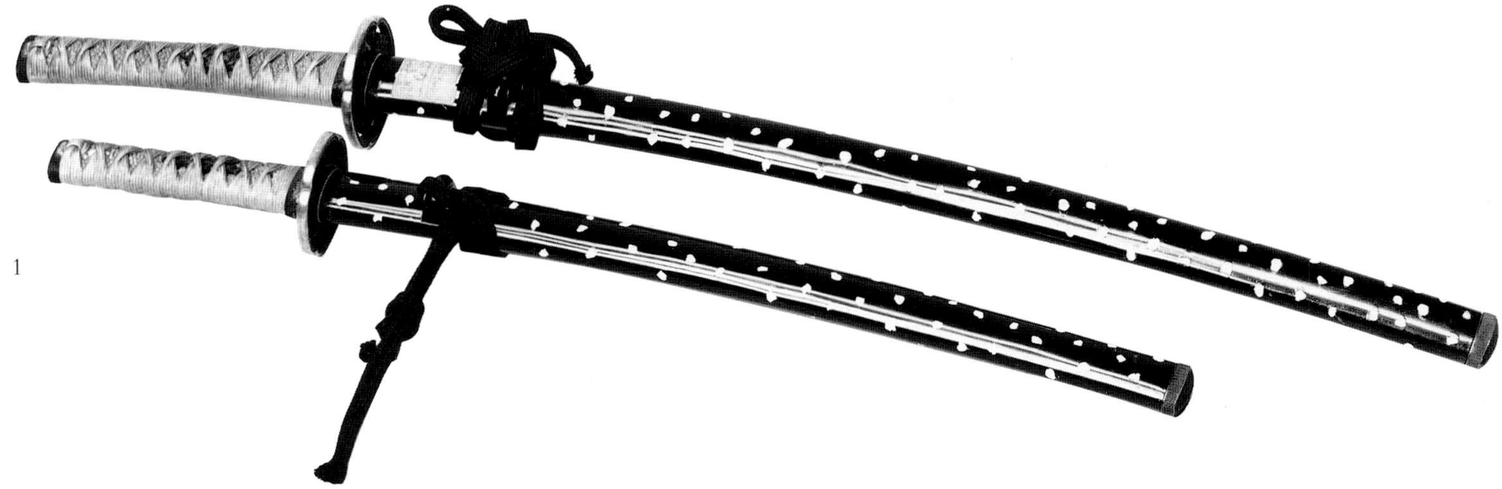

2

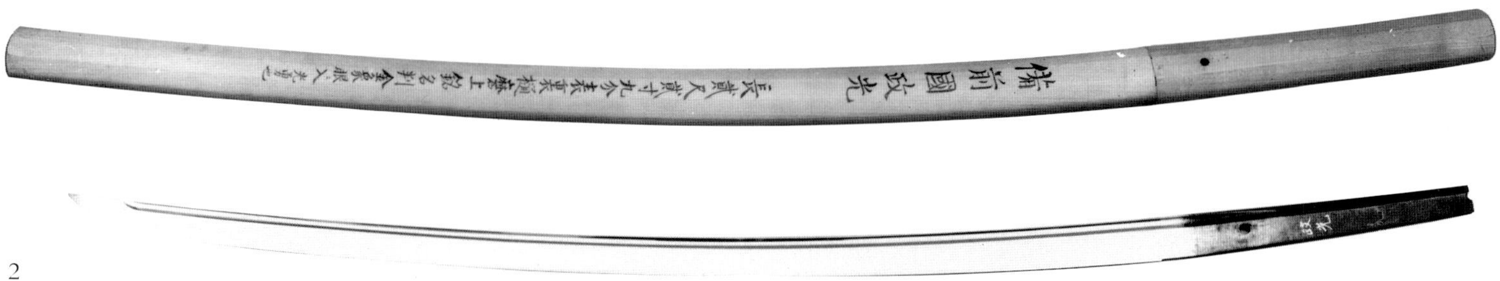

3

4

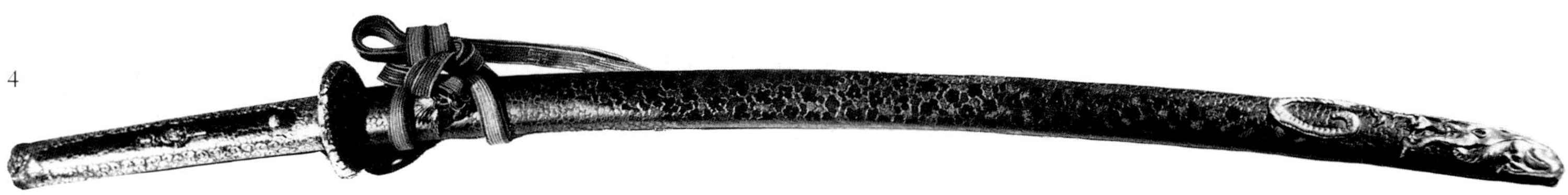

1. Daisho, the pair of swords which only the samurai were permitted to wear. The lacquer of the scabbards is inlaid with fragments of bone.

2. Blade by Bizen Masamitsu and its shirosaya inscribed with the name of the blade's maker. The shirosaya is a plain wooden scabbard used to store an unmounted blade.

3. Short sword in a superb mount typical of the type used by wealthy townsmen.

4. Sword richly mounted in silver as a birthday present.

imitated the surface of stone (*ishime*); while more regularity and a smoother punch gave a texture like wrinkled leather. The most Japanese of these surface treatments was obtained with a minute cup-punch which raised the ground into hemispheres, often so minute as to be all but invisible to the naked eye, but arranged in carefully spaced rows that generally follow the outline of the piece. Early *nanako* (fish-roe ground) was made with a punch having a group of three or more indentations, but later work is so careful and precise, with the hemispheres maintaining straight lines over complex three-dimensional curves, that a single punch must have been used.

Chasing, engraving and carving the metal were also employed to delineate the design. One special engraving technique was *katagiri*, in which one face of the cut was vertical, while the other formed a shallow angle with the surface – the depth of cut varying the width of the channel. When used on silver or shibuichi, the effect of the shadow cast by the vertical wall of the cut simulated an ink painting on paper. Metals were carved using tiny chisels, and, even more remarkably, finished and polished, apparently as effortlessly as wood or ivory. *Taka bori* involved carving the metal in relief, whereas *shishiai bori* had the design carved in sunk relief, below the level of the surrounding ground.

Right: Various dirks and short swords showing the inventive variety of decoration and mountings. During the Edo period swords became more ornamental but were seldom used for their real purpose.

Opposite: A selection of tsuba (sword guards) showing the wide variety of styles, shapes and subjects.

Far left: Tsuba of shakudo, an alloy of copper and gold, with inlay by Goto Mitsutada depicting the rival generals at the Battle of Uji river.

Left: Tsuba by Hitotsuyanagi Tomonaga showing Yuten Shonin exorcising a ghost.

Overlay, *nunome*, was a technique that could only be applied to an iron or steel base, and although not too durable, was capable of great richness and was widely used both for sword mounts and for decorating armour. In this process, the surface of the iron, sometimes already carved, was covered with a series of intersecting cuts made with a chisel or a knife held at an angle to the surface so as to throw up tiny pointed burrs. The overlay itself was limited to different colours of gold, silver or pure copper, other metals being too hard. The design was executed by applying the overlay in the form of wire or foil, tapped and burnished into place so that the teeth-like burrs were forced into the softer metal holding it in position.

Inlay, *hon zogan*, involved cutting a depression into the base, the exact size and shape of the piece to be inlaid, having slightly undercut edges and a raised burr around the outline. Into this was fitted the metal to be inlaid, cut with its sides sloping towards the top, then the burr was forced down onto the edges of the inlay to hold it in place. Sometimes the inlay was polished flush with the surface to give *hira zogan*, but in most cases it was left proud of the surface, *taka zogan*, and subsequently carved. On cheap work soldering was used to fix relief decoration in imitation of taka zogan.

Much fine work which appears to be inlay is in fact fire gilt. This is made by coating the metal where needed with a gold and mercury amalgam, then heating to drive off the mercury and leave the gold fused onto the surface. This same universal technique, often repeated several times to obtain a satisfactory coating, was used to produce the gilt copper so widely used on military equipment.

During the seventeenth and eighteenth centuries the makers of sword fittings gradually moved away from the simple styles in iron, producing more and more complex work. Numerous schools were founded,

Below: Tehen kanamono of a helmet by Saotome Ietada in shakudo decorated with nanako. The artist has lightened the effect of the black shakudo against the dark russet iron of the helmet by interposing a plate of gilded copper.

Above: Detail of a painted screen showing the interior of a workshop for the manufacture of sword fittings.

each developing and perfecting their own techniques but only a few can be mentioned here. Kaneiye and his followers carved away the background of the iron to produce designs in low relief, which might be enlivened by small touches of gold, inspired by the works of Chinese painters. Workers in the province of Nagato (Choshu) specialized in iron tsuba in which the subject matter was painstakingly depicted in the round by pierc-

ing and meticulous carving. The oft-copied school founded by Soten, working in Hikone, used a similar technique, but combined it with overlay in shades of gold and silver to depict minute and skilfully rendered figures in battle scenes and other stories from history and legend. Etchizen Kinai and his followers also worked in iron. Their speciality was dragons, with their characteristic long chins, which were carved with the utmost precision in the round. Later groups, among whom the Nara, Yokoya and Yanagawa were important innovators, extended their repertoires by using soft-metal alloys to produce fittings that were works of art, rather than practical, if decorated, utilities. Certain schools developed and perfected particular themes for which they became famous; the Konkan specialized in fish subjects and the Omori in curling waves, dotted with minute flecks of gold spray. As in so many spheres, fashion played its part and was responsible for the production of somewhat banal copies of popular subjects and styles; these were turned out in their thousands by back-street workshops.

Above: Tatehage okegawa go mai do, a five-piece do of vertical plates, decorated with Fudo riding a dragon. Signed by Miochin Muneo and dated 1858.

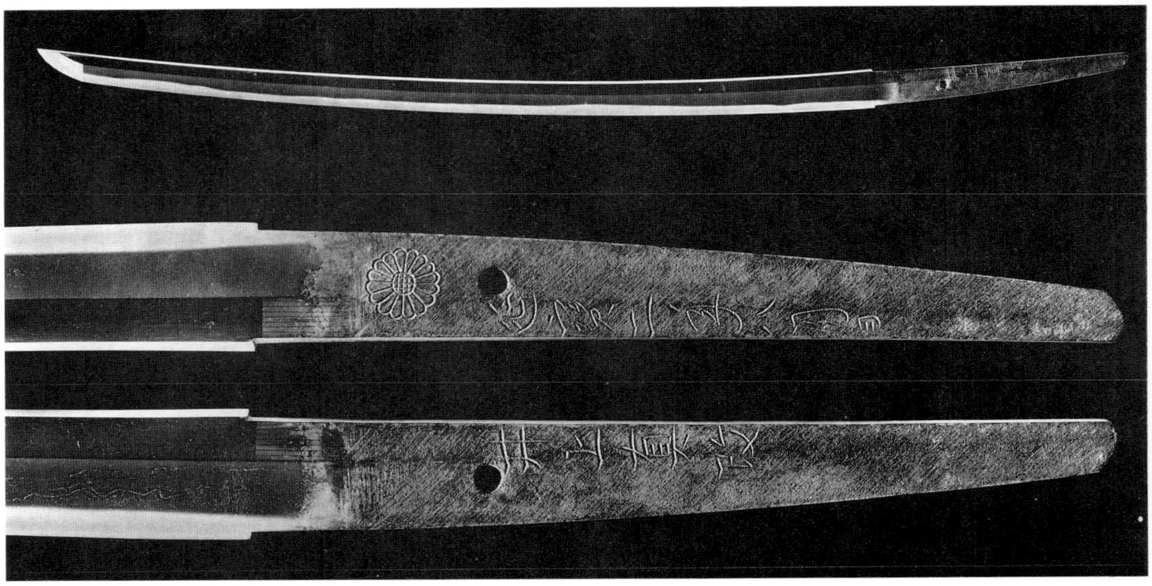

Right: Blade for a long sword by Inoue Shinkai, circa *1674. Despite the mediocrity of many Shinto swords, craftsmen such as Shinkai produced fine blades.*

During the Momoyama period swordsmiths had moved all over the country to meet the demands of the armies and as a result cross-fertilization of ideas took place. However, disastrous floods during the sixteenth century wiped out all but a few of the Osafune Bizen smiths, with the result that their influence was largely absent. What emerged during the seventeenth century were new styles that blurred the differences between the original traditions. This chronological boundary, coinciding with the rule of the Tokugawas, heralded the beginning of the shinto (New Sword) period. Initially there was an upsurge of brilliant work, led by craftsmen such as Umetada Myoju and Horikawa Kunihiro at Kyoto, and Noda Hankei in Edo. These in turn trained and encouraged others, such as Tadayoshi of Hizen, whose family turned out consistently good blades for generations. Rather predictably, many of the swords made during later years of this peaceful period were mediocre, being enlivened only occasionally by smiths such as Nagasone Okisato of Edo and Tsuta Sukehiro and Inouye Shinkai of Osaka. These latter smiths were among the many who catered not only for samurai but for wealthy townsmen, developing flamboyant styles of blades with decorative hamon and extensive horimono, which, while technically superb, were works of art rather than practical swords.

Swordsmanship was practised using wooden blades and, later, padded armour, but few Edo period samurai had experienced the reality of using cold steel against an opponent. Equally, many of the swords being produced were weapons whose real strength was never put to the test. A few samurai

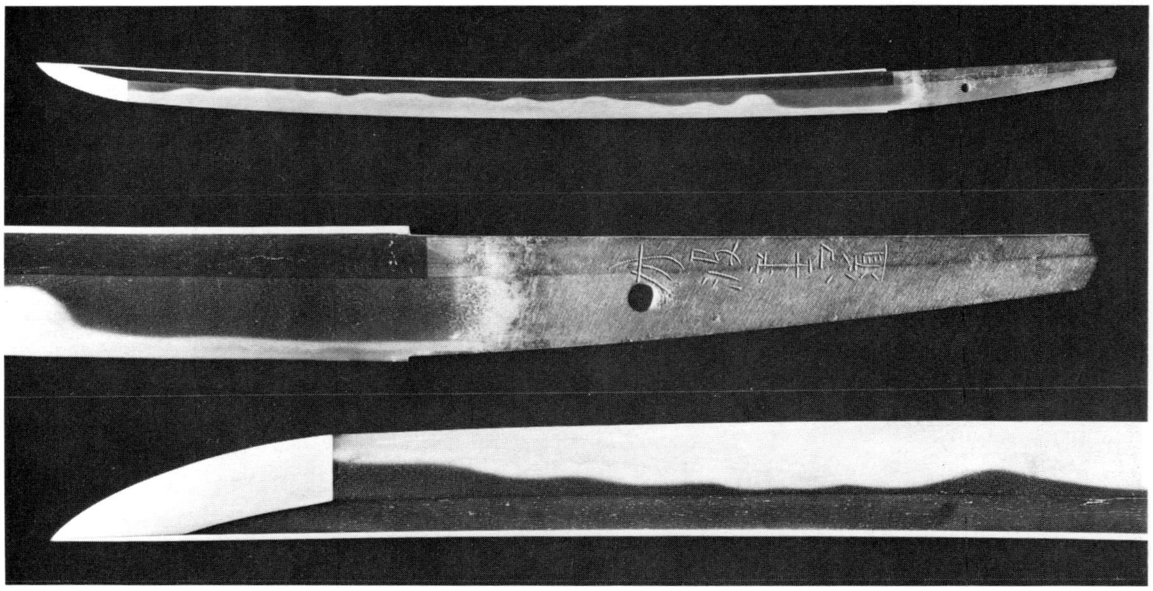

Right: Blade for a long sword by Tamba no kami Yoshimichi (1565 – 1635), a renowned swordsmith of the Shinto period.

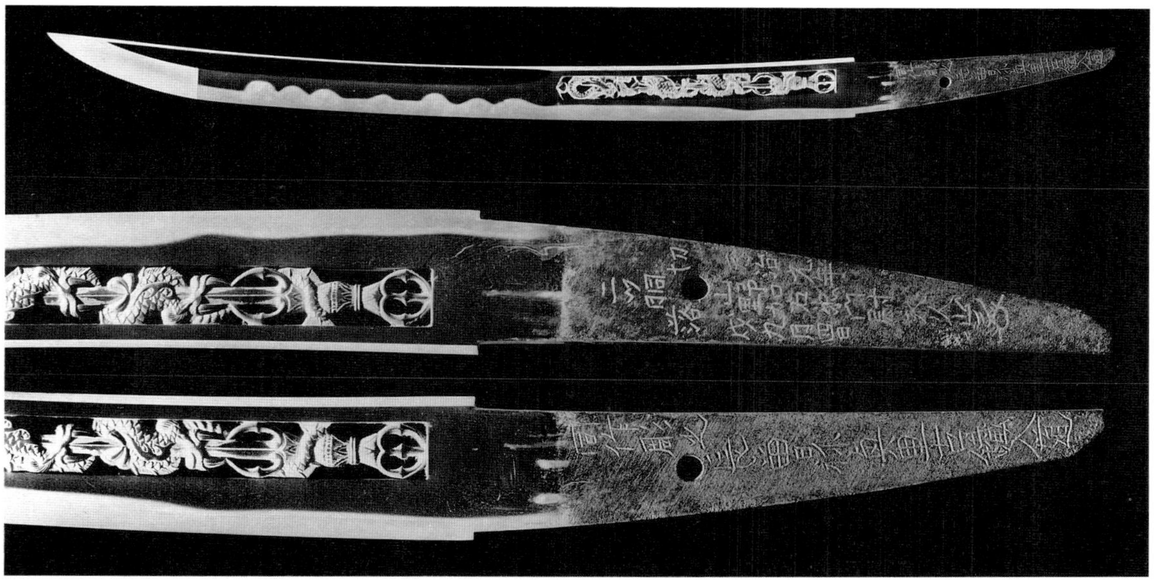

Left: Blade for a short sword by Nagasone Okisato Nyudo Kotetsu with the result of a test inlaid in gold recording that two bodies had been cut.

resorted to murdering commoners for some imagined slight as a means of trying out their swords; this was not in itself a crime but it was frowned upon. Others, more humanely, used bundles of wet straw tied around a bamboo pole as a substitute for a human body, or tested their swords on helmets and other pieces of armour.

According to Tokugawa law, the bodies of executed criminals became the property of the state and might be used to test swords, although bodies of murderers, tattooed people, priests and untouchables were taboo. A system of official testing, *tameshi giri*, was established using this raw material supplied by the execution yards. Although requiring official permission, swords could be submitted to one of the hereditary officials drawn from either the Yamada, Chokushi or Nakagawa familes for testing.

For the test itself, the body was arranged on a mound of sand, and tied to bamboo stakes to hold it in position. The tester, wearing kami shimo and carrying a blade fitted into a special iron-bound hilt, then studied the corpse and decided which of his repertoire of cuts was appropriate. Severing the arm at the wrist was considered the easiest, while a cut across the hips, *ryo kuruma*, or a diagonal cut through the shoulder girdle, *o kessa*, the most difficult. After making the cut, first the body was carefully examined, then the blade for damage and for signs of adhering fat. If satisfied, further, more difficult, cuts might be made, and the final result was sometimes inlaid in gold on the tang of the blade. Masahide comments that blades by differing smiths were divided into five categories of sharpness according to the results of such tests, and that experience showed that

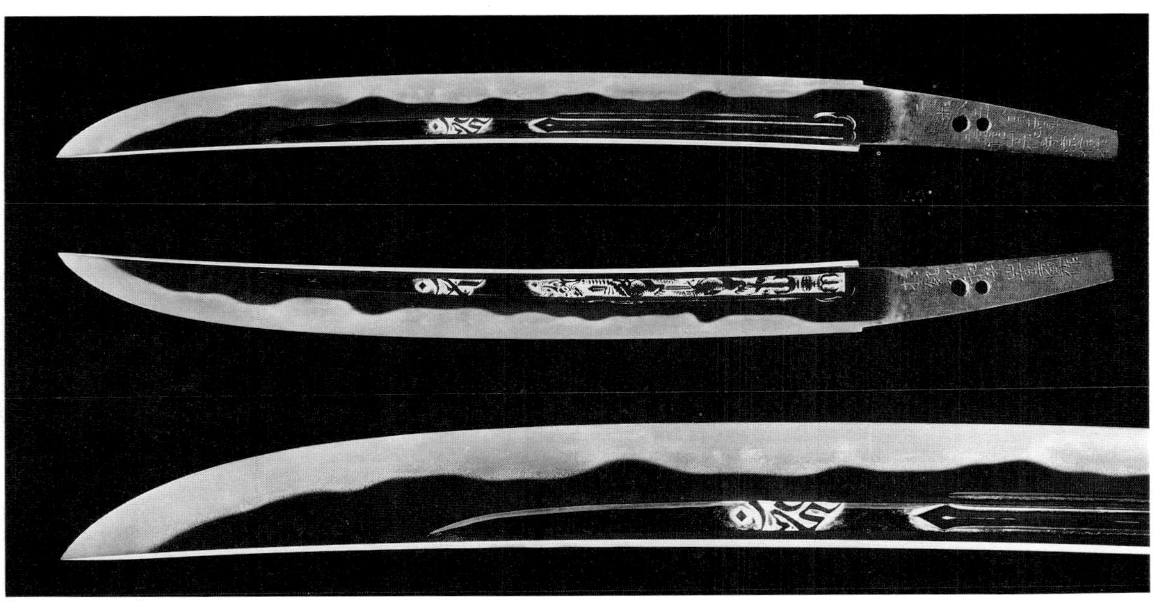

Left: Short sword by Oite Kishu Wakayama Shigekuni dated 1622, an excellent smith of the Yamato Tegai school.

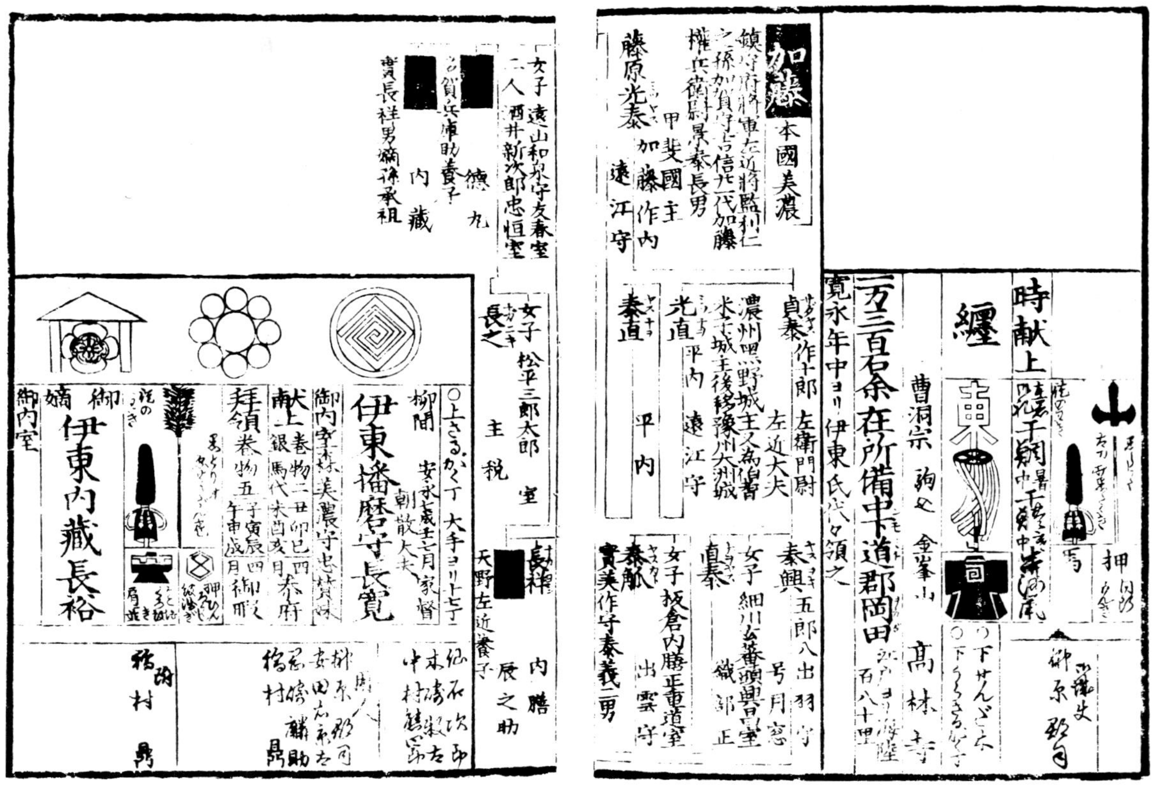

Right (both): Page from a heraldic handbook showing the mon and heraldic equipment of Ito Harima no Kami Nagahiro.

the most efficient length lay between one foot four inches and two feet four inches (40-71cm). Longer swords were too difficult for the average man to use effectively. It was also found that the cross section given to the blade by the polisher had a significant effect on its cutting ability; a slight convexity to the surfaces improved its ability to cut flesh while a flat surface was most suitable for the straw bundles.

One of the ways in which the Tokugawa curbed the powers of the daimyo was to enforce a biannual attendance at court, *sankin kotai*, modified for those whose province was a considerable distance from the capital. These peregrinations or *daimyo gyoretsu* kept them shuffling between their home provinces and Edo with huge retinues of samurai and servants, whose numbers were specified according to income, stretching their resources to the limit and preventing any idea of insurrection. The roads connecting the capital with the remainder of the country became of great importance, and were provided with inns and waystations to accommodate the members of the processions. There was not, however, free passage; barriers and checkpoints were manned by Tokugawa officials who made reports on traffic to and from the capital and apprehended those

Right: Spears and their heraldic scabbards were carried in processions to identify the travellers.

without proper authorization – particularly the wives and families of the daimyo who were confined in their mansions in Edo as hostages during the absence of the daimyo. As symbols of the daimyo's status, these processions were headed by retainers carrying tall yari with ornamental scabbards whose shape and decoration had heraldic significance. They were followed by others carrying guns, tachi, bows and quivers in special racks and other symbols of rank. The daimyo and his senior staff rode in palanquins, sometimes carrying a small bow for protection, *kago hankyu* (also called *riman kyu* after Riman Hayashi of Kii province who invented the device); these weapons were made as sets comprising a short whalebone bow and diminutive arrows held in a lacquered leather case – the samurai equivalent of the 'derringer'.

The Maeda family of Kaga, considered a potential threat by the Tokugawa, far from being impoverished by this system had the largest income of any – just over one million koku. Like many in their position, they were 'invited' by the shogun to undertake ruinous public works that threatened their financial stability. Determined to avoid the debts that so many in a similar position had been forced into, the Maeda instigated two schemes to bring money into the provinces. They traded with the Dutch and Chinese at Nagasaki, and put the lower ranking soldiers to work making armour. No doubt professional armourers supervised the operation and did the more difficult parts of the work (some Miochin and Haruta smiths are known to have moved to Kaga), but the products they turned out were distinctive. Output began in earnest during the middle of the seventeenth century under the fifth daimyo, and continued until the time of the thirteenth daimyo in 1725. During that time they were responsible for manufacturing a considerable quantity of sturdy and practical armour, as befits that produced by the samurai class. For helmets they had a penchant for kawari bachi or hoshi bachi with zaboshi, to which were applied cut-out iron decorations, sometimes splashed with a silvery alloy, *sawari*, partially fused onto the russet surface to represent dew or rain. One invariable feature of Kaga helmets is that they were never fitted with cords made from the rope-like 'drum cord' as was used elsewhere, preferring instead to use rolled cloth – initially hemp, but later crêpe

Left: Kago hankyu of whalebone with its quiver of arrows. These diminutive weapons were designed for use from within the cramped confines of the palanquins in which the nobles travelled.

de chine rolled and sewn around a core of soft threads.

Kaga do were of many types, but with the emphasis on those built up from a few relatively large plates, frequently laced in white silk with the edges to the plates finished to one of the standard outlines. When not given a russet finish, many do were covered in

Left: Suji kabuto by the Unkai group of Kaga. The applied iron decoration on the peak, the iron tehen kanamono and the grouped lacing are typical of the work of these armourers. The austerity of the helmet bowl has been relieved by applying boyo (stick-like) shinodare to the plates.

Opposite left: A 120-plate suji bachi decorated with a theme involving a dragon, embossed on the peak, chasing a sacred jewel, mounted in the tehen. A straight-bladed Buddhist sword has been applied as decoration to the front plate while the neck guard has a mon incorporated in the lacing.

Opposite right: Mune tori okegawa do gusoku by Miochin Munesada circa *1653. The helmet and do are engraved with debased Sanskrit characters.*

Right: A typical armour made by the Kaga clan in russet iron with white lacing.

wrinkled 'Chinese leather' or were decorated with gold and black lacquer which had a 'hammered' texture. The fronts of many kaga do were decorated with a circular design, generally of a dragon in either applied metalwork or in raised lacquer, a style called *maki e do*.

Particularly characteristic are the watagami, which were hinged to the boko no ita so that they could be removed or swung back when putting on the do. The edges were turned up to form a shallow channel section, which added considerably to their stiffness. On some do, this flange was enlarged around the neck opening at the back, to form a low-standing metal collar. Kohaze were of a distinctive four-lobed shape while the seme kohaze was waisted and grooved around its edge – both parts were frequently made of ivory. Huge numbers of kote were turned out which had the kanmuri ita in three pieces, each with a standing flange on the upper edge, joined by butterfly-shaped hinges. Many were oda gote with the plates damascened in silver and, reputedly, with special types of mail which was sometimes said to be of brass to avoid corrosion. Many of these features were often displayed in the work of the Unkai, a group of Miochin armourers who moved to Kaga, working from the mid-seventeenth to the mid-eighteenth centuries. This group specialized in the highest grade work, producing armours for the wealthy decorated with applied iron work, splashed with sawari, that often draws its themes from Buddhism. Much of their work incorporates exotic materials such as velvet and ivory and often shows foreign influences, no doubt because of the province's connections with the Dutch and Chinese at Nagasaki.

By and large, most samurai during the greater part of the seventeenth century continued to wear the practical armours of the Momoyama period, brightening them somewhat by the addition of more elaborate gilded metal decorations and printed leathers but without detracting from their essential utility. The Neo group of Nara, founded towards the end of the Momoyama period, continued to produce work of outstanding quality – Neo Masanobu, in particular, continued the traditions of Nobuiye and Yoshimichi by producing superb high-sided suji bachi and hoshi bachi, generally of 62 plates. Occasionally they made helmets of 120 or even 140 plates, but these necessitated plates

that were so narrow that the interior edges had to be cut in a waved pattern, to create space for the staggered rows of rivets – this was a wonderful tour de force, but the helmets were weakened by the numerous perforations and were very heavy. As in all periods, leather armour continued to be made, particularly by the Iwai armourers. It was often of considerable thickness and almost as practical as metal and was particularly favoured by elderly men because of its light weight. The basic forms were obtained by shaping the wet rawhide in wooden moulds; these were then modelled with kokuso before lacquering. Both hoshi bachi and suji bachi were produced and, with metal details applied to the basic leather shell, they are virtually indistinguishable from helmets made from steel.

For the first time in their history, the Japanese armourers turned their attention to the protection of the horse. Complete armours, *uma yoroi*, were produced from small embossed scales of leather, generally gilded, sewn onto fabric. Most of these armours consist of a large rectangular section for the crupper, with a small extension along one long edge covering the tail, two triangular sections laced together along the mane forming a crinet for the neck and perhaps an additional panel over the chest resembling a peytral. More elaborate versions incorporated metal plates and mail along the crest of the neck, and had flanchards linking the peytral with the crupper at the sides. The head of the horse was covered by a chanfron, which was often simply of lacquered papier mâché but was occasionally steel, in the form of a dragon's

head or a caricature of a horse. The whole assembly was held in position by ties to the saddle and to other parts of the normal harness, with additional ties or toggles between the adjoining sections of the armour.

As the prospect of war gradually faded, the emphasis on practicability waned in favour of further decoration. The Miochin, in particular, demonstrated their skill by producing embossed or *uchidashi do* which, although often superbly executed, thinned the metal and produced a surface that would trap the point of a weapon. Although not the first to produce such work, Miochin Munesuke (1642-1735) became renowned for it. He specialized in yukinoshita do with superbly embossed front plates. These designs took all manner of forms, but characters, Chinese lions and Buddhist divinities were particularly favoured – the latter were sometimes so deeply embossed that the figure is almost in the round. Munesuke, together with his grandfather Kunimichi, concocted the impressive genealogy of the Miochin family, listing an unbroken lineage from the earliest times and claiming for himself the title Premier Armour Expert of Japan. Adopting the strategy of the Honnami family, who acted as appraisers of swords, Munesuke began to issue certificates of authenticity, giving the provenance and a value to pieces of unsigned and often ancient armour. He invariably attributed authorship to one or other of his fictitious ancestors listed in his genealogy. By the beginning of the eighteenth century the fashion for embossed armour was at its height, with embossed plates forming the main elements of do, sode and haidate. Even complete helmet bowls were hammered from one or more sheets of iron. Miochin Ryoei, whose exact working dates are unknown, excelled in producing

Far left: Red, white and blue laced ni mai do gusoku, having the yurugi ito replaced by mail. Edo period.

Left: Helmet belonging to the armour opposite by Neo Masanobu of Nara.

Top right: Goshozan suji bachi of rawhide lacquered to resemble russet iron.

Right: Interior of the helmet bowl above showing the fastenings of the applied metal suji (flanges).

Above: Horse armour of lacquered leather scales sewn to fabric. Armour for horses was only made in the Edo period and was never proved in battle. Edo period.

Above right: Chanfron for a horse armour in the form of a caricature of a horse. Chanfrons were often of papier mâchè and had little defensive value. Edo period.

helmets modelled to represent sea shells or plant subjects, beaten from a single sheet. Although much of this work was of the finest quality, and showed immense mastery of a stubborn medium, as armour it was all but useless – of necessity it was made of soft iron and was sometimes so thin that it could be bent in the hands. Not all embossed work, however, was totally impractical. A few armourers applied the decoration over robust armours, with the joint so carefully fitted as to be imperceptible. Rather strangely, having gone to all this trouble, the solid plate behind the embossing was sometimes cut away.

Right: Horse harness. The large flanchards were to protect the horse from the heavy iron stirrups.

Below: Uchidashi gusoku by Miochin Ki Munesuke. Embossed armour such as this became popular during the peaceful Edo period as the reality of warfare receded. Mid-Edo period.

Right: Black and blue laced maru do. Edo period.

Left: A fantastic armour of loosely tied plates. It resembles a Karasu tengu, *a mythical bird-like creature.*

Above: Front plate of an uchidashi ni mai do embossed with an eagle. Edo period.

Below: Uchidashi hoate, a face with embossed cheeks by a Miochin armourer. Edo period.

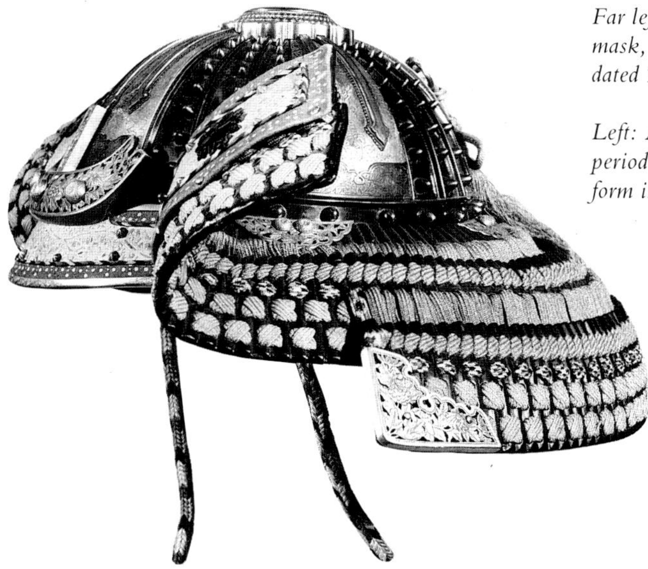

Far left: Me no shita ho, a half mask, by Miochin Matsutaka dated 1806.

Left: A richly decorated Edo period helmet of hemispherical form imitating earlier styles.

During the first decades of the eighteenth century the attitude towards decoration rose to further heights as the emphasis being placed on the legends and heroic epics by the Tokugawa took effect. Samurai yearned for the splendour of the past, encouraged by such books as *Honcho Gunkiko*, a 12-volume work written by Arai Hakuseki, which contained a documentary history of arms and armour illustrated by examples preserved in shrines and temples. In works such as this and *Gun Yo Ki*, published in 1734 by Ise Sadatake, o yoroi, do maru and haramaki were described in detail, together with the swords, costumes and accessories worn with them. The spirit of the antiquarian was in the air and the mood was one of nostalgia.

Catering for this longing, the armourers, and the Miochin in particular, revived the maru bachi, making it either with or without rivets as the customer required. Some were deliberately given a heavy coating of rust to give them an apearance of great antiquity, becoming *sabi mono* (rusty things), designed to evoke an emotion of nostalgic melancholia. Old styles of printed leather were reproduced and o sode were fitted to all types of armours with little thought as to how they should be mounted. Quite correctly, shoji no ita and gumiwa were fitted to the watagami, which incongruously often retained kohire. Being unsure about the various cords and ties, those at the ends of the kanmuri no ita were tied to the front and back gumi, the leather tie being knotted around the watagami – the shoji no ita and the kohire had to be pierced to accommodate it. Fittings for the sashimono were rendered almost unusable because of the bow fitted to the back of the armour, and were further impeded by large, spreading shikoro. Nodawa were provided with these armours, clashing incongruously

Below left: An uchidashi bachi, an embossed helmet bowl in the shape of an egg-plant. Attributed to Ohara Katsunari.

Below: An Edo reproduction of an o boshi maru bachi, a round helmet bowl with large rivets, inaccurate in that the rivets are positioned on the centre line of each plate rather than along the rear edge.

Right: Iro iro odoshi ni mai do gusoku, a multi-coloured two piece armour, showing early features incorporated into a typical Edo armour. The style of this armour is loosely based on a do maru of the Muromachi period.

Far right: Omodaka odoshi do maru, a do maru laced with a pattern resembling a water-plantain leaf, a superb Edo period reproduction of the earlier style.

with the various types of men gu. Being unsure about its position, some tried to wear this neck armour inside the do, no doubt painfully, others just tied it loosely and let it hang on the chest.

Before long copies were being made of the old armours. At first these were ludicrous pastiches incorporating features from different ages, but gradually they became more accurate, culminating in almost perfect copies of o yoroi, haramaki and do maru. Those with money went one better and bought old armours from temples, or searched family store houses, and refurbished them for use. In a plea for sanity, Sakakibara Kozan wrote his book *Chuko-katchu Seisakuben*, urging samurai to abandon these revival armours and return to using the more practical styles of the Momoyama period. A few heeded his plea, and had superb armours in the Momoyama styles made by such smiths as Miochin Muneyasu, but even he continued to make do maru or haramaki for those who wanted them.

Swordsmiths too, began to look back to the past for their models. Masahide and his followers at the beginning of the nineteenth century initiated a revival of the styles and techniques from the Shinshito period of the Nambokucho period, in particular. Following this lead others, such as Hosokawa Masayoshi, Naotane and his son Naokatsu, reproduced the elegant blades of the Koto period, working in whichever of the five traditions the customer demanded. Much of their work approached the quality of the blades created by the great masters of the swordsmiths' craft but this rebirth was to be shortlived; the outside world was beginning to take an interest in Japan.

During the 1840s the United States of America and the manufacturing powers in Europe were expanding and competing for trade with China. Russian outposts were established bordering the Pacific, and Britain, after an initial probe at Japan's

Far left: Armour in do maru style made for a daimyo of the Doi family. Late Edo period.

Left: Tatewaku odoshi ni mai do gusoku, a two-section armour, laced with vertical bars of colour to represent rising steam. A late Edo armour influenced by earlier do maru.

defences, gained Hong Kong and Shanghai. America, in particular, needed a refuelling post between San Francisco and Shanghai if the newly formed Pacific Mail Steamship Company was to have any chance of success, and Japan was the only suitable site. The United States Government realized that pressure would have to be exerted if successful negotiations were to be concluded. In 1853 four warships sailed into Uraga Bay near Edo carrying Commodore Matthew Calbraith Perry to inform the Japanese of the Americans' intentions. Thousands of samurai assembled, impotent against the guns of the warships, as preliminary negotiations were carried out. In the following year a treaty was signed and within a year, long before the treaty conditions could be met, the first visitors arrived. Within a few years, this trickle of foreigners had become a stream as other countries negotiated for the right to trade and more and more visitors flocked to see the country for themselves.

The attitude of the Japanese towards the arrival of the foreigners was divided. One faction wanted to expel the barbarians and re-

Below: A late Edo period version of a nodawa (defence for throat and neck) known as a guruwa.

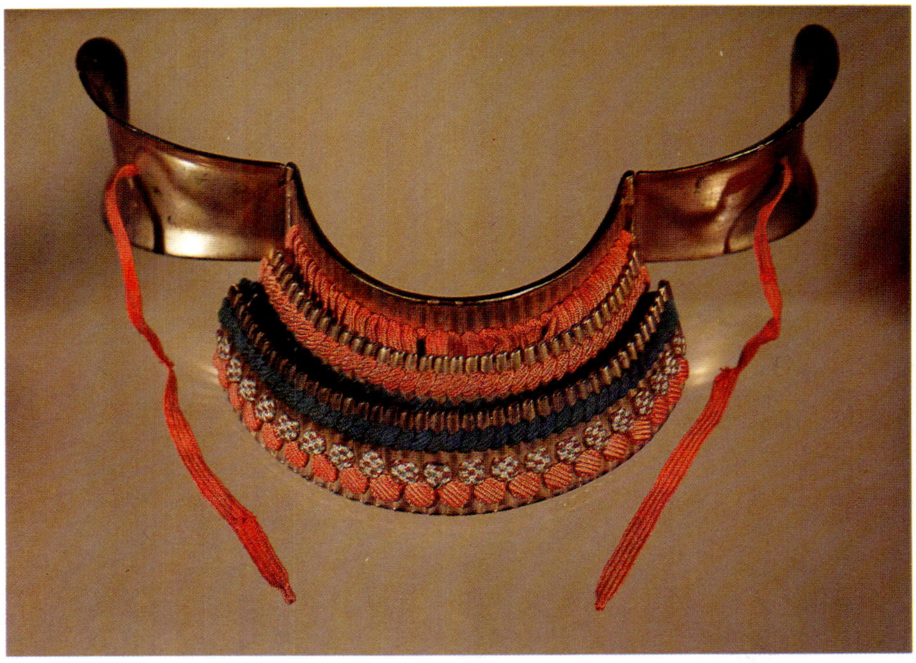

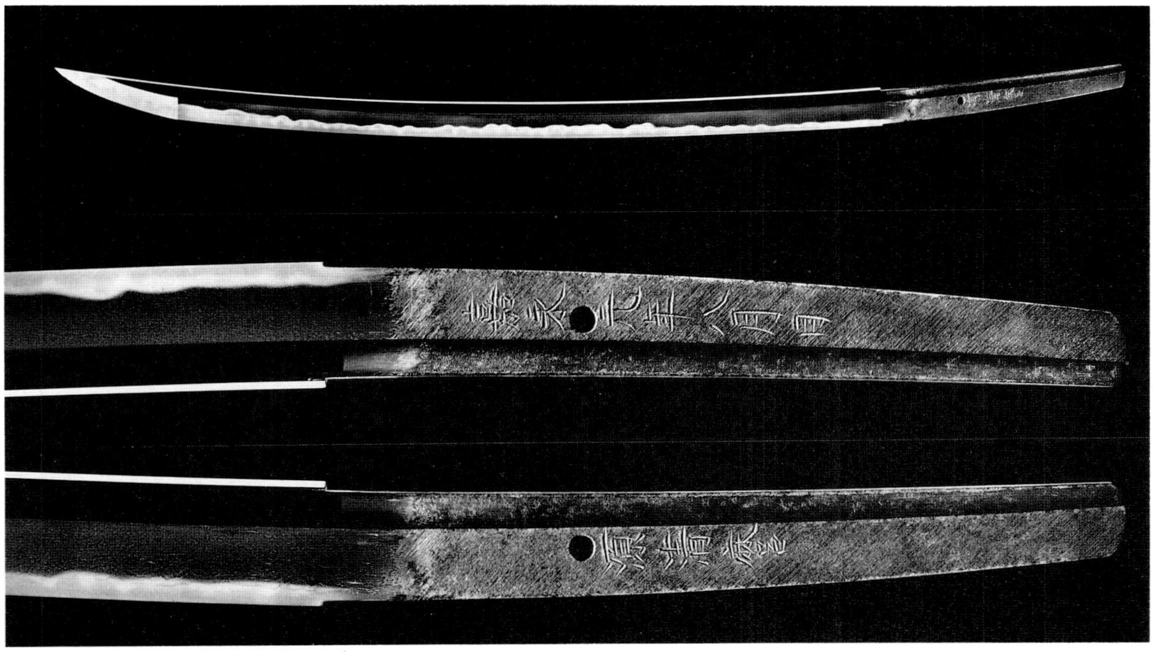

Opposite left: The jumonji yari on the left is a fairly common type, the sickle yari on the right is extremely rare.

Opposite right: A very late 'foreign' armour incorporating a French cuirassier's helmet and cuirass from the Napoleonic period.

establish the Emperor as the true ruler of the country but the remainder sensed the inevitability of a change in the social order. A few took matters into their own hands, reacting with violence not only against foreigners, but also against the more-progressive ministers of state. By 1868 the shogun had abdicated in favour of the Emperor and his last entry into Osaka castle was watched and described by Algernon Mitford, later Lord Redesdale:

. . . warriors dressed in the old armour of the country, carrying spears, bows and arrows, falchions curiously shaped, with sword and dirk, who looked as if they had stepped out of some old pictures of the Gempei Wars in the Middle Ages. Their jinbaori, not unlike herald's tabards, were as many-coloured as Joseph's coat. Hideous masks of lacquer and iron, fringed with portentous whiskers and mustachios, crested helmets with wigs from which long streamers of horsehair floated to their waists, might strike terror into any enemy. They looked like the hobgoblins of a nightmare.

In November 1868, the Emperor took on the mantle of power his ancestors had lost almost 900 years before, setting up his new palace in Edo Castle and renaming the city Tokyo. For a while the samurai continued to wear their swords, often incongruously matched with

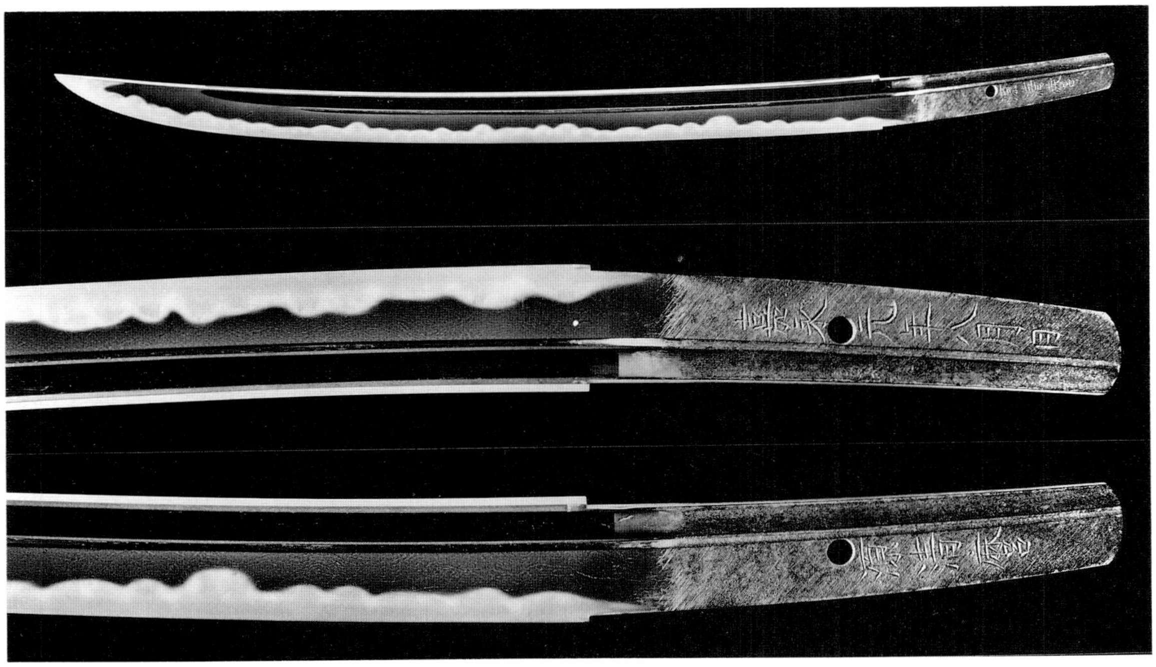

Left: Shinshinto wakizashi blade (nineteenth century short sword) by Minamoto Kiyomaro and dated 1848.

Top left: Blade for a long sword by Kiyomaro forming a pair with the blade above.

Left: An Edo period armour fitted with a leather cover for the front of the armour in the style of an o yoroi.

Right: A samurai poses before the camera of a 'barbarian'. The era of the samurai drew to a close with the arrival of Westerners during the 1860s.

European-style frock coats and top hats, but their protected status and the practice of wearing swords was abolished by an edict of 1876. Faced with the problem of making a living, many samurai joined the newly formed armed forces, but others, often too proud to earn a living, were obliged to sell their once-treasured swords and armour to pawnbrokers and curio shops, to be bought by the ever-growing numbers of tourists as souvenirs of a vanished society. In his book *Rambles in Japan*, published in 1895, H B Tristam, the Canon of Durham, writes about this phenomenon:

> The collections of old armour and swords in these shops were to me as fascinating as a display of the fashions in Regent Street to an English belle, while the prices, as far as I am able to judge, were extremely moderate. I made many purchases at a price really less than the value of the material. . . . In fact, ancient armour was a drug on the market, many of the poorer Samurai being compelled to part with their treasured accoutrements for rice.

In a fervent spirit of modernization and enthusiasm for all things Western, the Japanese discarded without hesitation many of their ancient treasures. A thousand years of accumulated artistry and meticulous craftsmanship in lacquer, silk and metal was abandoned in the space of a few years. Not all craftsmen, however, neglected their traditional skills; a few passed the principles of their trades to their descendants, and their grandchildren are only now beginning to reap the benefits as modern Japanese look back into their history from the technological society they have built. Once again, swordsmiths and armourers are producing heirlooms for future generations so that they might be reminded of their country's past.

Right: An articulated iron snake produced as a novelty by a redundant armour maker.

Glossary

Abumi A stirrup.
Abumi zuri no kawa Leather patch on the inside of tosei shin guards to prevent chafing of the stirrup leathers.
Ai Indigo colour.
Aibiki Shoulder strap fastenings of a tosei do.
Aizuchi Swordsmith's assistants.
Agemaki Bow of silk cord tied in a special knot hung from rings on armour – an especially large one was hung on the back as part of the shoulder-guard attachments.
Agemaki no kan Ring on back of do from which a large agemaki is hung.
Ago no o benri Protruding studs on chin of mask to prevent the helmet cords from slipping forwards.
Aka Crimson colour.
Akabe yoroi Neck armour – particularly that worn with tanko during the Yamato period.
Akoda nari bachi Style of helmet that developed during the Muromachi period which is distinctly swollen at the back and normally without prominent rivets.
Akome Iron ore.
Aoiba za Decorative iron plate surrounding the tehen of a Heian period helmet bowl.
Arare boshi bachi Term used to describe a helmet bowl made or decorated with large, exaggerated rivets.
Asa no ha gusari Mail in which each round link is connected to each of three others.
Asagi Pale blue colour.
Ase nagashi no ana Hole or tube under the chin of a mask to drain away perspiration.
Ashi Rings around a tachi scabbard to which the hangers are attached.
Ato me ate Backsight of a gun or cannon.
Ayasugi hada Regular wavy grain on surface of a sword.
Bajo zutzu A small pistol-like gun.
Birodo Velvet.
Bishamon gote Armoured sleeves having an integral small sode covering the upper arm.
Boko no ita Top plate at the back of a tosei do to which the watagami are riveted.
Byakudan nuri Transparent lacquer of a golden yellow colour.
Byo kakari do *see* byo toji yokohagi okegawa do
Byo toji yokohagi okegawa do Tosei do of horizontal plates fastened by prominent, often decorated, rivets.
Bu tachi A military sword as opposed to those worn at court or with civilian dress.
Chiisa gatana *see* wakizashi
Chirimen namban kusari European-type mail made with small, densely packed links.
Chochin bachi Helmet bowl that collapses flat for storage.
Daienzan bachi Helmet bowl having a more or less hemispherical shape.
Daimyo Term applied to holders of a considerable area of land – formalized in the Edo period to those with incomes above 10,000 koku per year.
Daisho A pair of swords having matching mounts, normally a katana and wakizashi combination.
Dangaye do Tosei do in which different styles of lacing are used in the upper and lower sections.
Do Armour for the body.
Do dan Mound of sand used to support the corpse in sword testing.
Do gane Ornamental metal band around the central part of a sword or dirk hilt.
Do maki Intermediate strip of iron forming the framework of a shoshaku tsuki kabuto.
Do maru Scale armour wrapping around the body and fastening under the right arm (*see haramaki*).
Donsu Damask.
Ebira Open quiver used in the Heian and Kamakura periods.
Ebizaya maki Dirk mounted in a scabbard and hilt carved with gadroons to resemble a shrimp's carapace.
Eboshi Tall cap of variable shape – often curving rearwards at the top.
Eboshi nari kabuto Helmet shaped to resemble an eboshi.
E gawa Leather decorated with a pictorial design.
Etchu haidate Haidate covered with only a sparse grid of mail and splints.
Etchu jikoro Tosei neck guard falling in a concave curve and terminating in a bottom plate which has a straight lower edge.
Etchu suneate Splint shin guards without a fabric backing.
Etchu zunari bachi Helmet bowl of simple construction having the longitudinal top plate overlapping the brow plate.
Fuchi Reinforcing band around the base of a hilt.
Fukigaeshi The turnback at the front edge of the upper row or rows of a neck guard.
Fukigaeshi no suemon Chrysanthemum-shaped ornaments applied to fukigaeshi of Heian period helmets.
Fujiwara iro A pale lilac colour.
Fukube Gourd-shaped plate applied to armoured sleeves.
Fukurin Applied metal rim.
Fuse ita Plate forming the top of a mabisashi tsuki kabuto.
Fusube gawa Smoked leather having a yellow or brown colour.
Gattari Attachment for a sashimono fastened to back of do at the level of the shoulder blades.
Gessan Pendant armoured sections attached to the lower edge of a tosei do.
Gessan jikoro Tosei shikoro having all but the uppermost plate divided into sections.
Goishi gashira Iyozane scales with heads of rounded shape.
Go kaden The five traditions of sword making during the Koto period.
Gose gawa Red leather decorated with groups of white spots.
Goshozan High-sided helmet having the back higher than the front.
Gumbai uchiwa A non-folding variety of war fan.
Gumi wa Leather loop fitted with an elongated metal bead on the shoulder strap of an armour to which the shoulder guards are tied.
Gunsen Folding war fan.
Gusoku A set of something – a complete armour.
Gusoku bitsu Box for the storage and transport of an armour.
Gyoyo Leaf-shaped plate used as a shoulder protector or to guard the fastenings of the shoulder straps.
Ha Cutting edge of a sword.
Habaki Collar of soft metal around the base of a blade.
Hachi The bowl of a helmet.
Hachiman kuro A very dark blue-black colour used for armour lacing during the Edo period.
Hachi tsuke no ita The uppermost plate or row of scales in a neck guard.
Hachiwara A parrying weapon consisting of a curved tapering square sectioned bar with a hook-like projection at the base.
Hada Forged pattern on the surface of a blade.
Hadome Parrying bar attached to the shaft of a spear.
Haidate Defence for the thighs shaped like a divided apron.
Hakushi Pale purple.
Hamon Outline shape of tempered edge of a blade.
Hanagami bukuro Pouch attached to the front of a do or behind one of the gessan.
Hana gata shobu gawa Blue leather with naturalistically depicted iris flowers and leaves.
Hana ni cho gawa Leather decorated with flowers and butterflies.
Hanbo An abbreviated face mask covering only the chin and lower cheeks.
Haniwa Fired clay figure or model set around the mound of a burial mound.
Happuri Plate defence for the forehead and cheeks.
Hara ate Abbreviated armour covering the front and sides of the body only.
Haraidate Tubular crest holder attached centrally to the peak of a helmet.
Haramaki Armour worn during the Heian and Kamakura periods which wrapped around the body and fastened under the right arm. From the Muromachi period, the term refers to an armour opening down the centre line of the back.
Harikake bachi A helmet bowl decorated and embellished by a light decorative superstructure of wood, paper, leather and lacquer.
Hasso byo A soft-metal rivet with an ornamented head.
Hatomune do Do having a medial ridge.
Hata Long banner hung by a cross bar from a pole.
Hayago Powder flask.
Hei A castle wall.
Heichozan High-sided helmet shape which is flat on top.

Hi A groove in a blade. Alternatively, the term refers to the colour vermilion.
Hibiki no ana Holes in a helmet bowl originally for attaching a helmet cord but later decorative.
Hibuta The pan cover of a matchlock.
Hiji gane Elbow plate of an armoured sleeve.
Hikone gusoku Red lacquered armour.
Hinawa ju Matchlock gun.
Hineno jikoro Close-fitting neck guard having a lower edge which is shaped to the shoulders.
Hineno zunari bachi Helmet bowl of simplified construction having a central longitudinal plate which is overlaid by a brow plate/peak combination.
Hira ne Flat arrowhead of the broadhead type.
Hira zogan Inlay finished flush with the surrounding surface.
Hirumaki no tachi Tachi having the scabbard and hilt spirally bound with a strip of leather under the lacquer.
Hiro sode Shoulder guard which widens and flattens towards the bottom.
Hishinui A cross-knot on the lowest row of scales of a piece of armour.
Hishinui no ita The lowest row of scales of a piece of armour.
Hishi toji A cross-knot other than on the hishinui no ita.
Hishi toji do A variety of yokohagi okegawa do in which the plates are connected by cross-knots.
Hishi toji hotoke do A smooth-faced do decorated by cross-knots.
Hitai ate Late form of happuri worn in place of a helmet.
Hiya zutsu Small cannon for launching fireworks.
Hizara The flashpan of a matchlock gun.
Hiza yoroi Old term for armour covering the thigh and knee.
Hoate A mask covering the chin and cheeks only.
Hodo haidate Haidate having the lower part of the armoured portion divided into pendant sections.
Hon kozane True scales.
Hon zogane Inlay.
Hori A moat.
Horimono Carved decoration on a blade.
Horo Cape-like cloth attached to the back of an armour which inflated with air when riding.
Hoshi A rivet.
Hoshi bachi A helmet bowl with prominent rivets.
Hotoke do A smooth faced do.
Hyo Dark green.
Hyotan Gourd-shaped plate forming part of an armoured sleeve.
Ichi mai fuse bachi Heian period helmet bowl beaten from a single plate.
Ichimai maze Alternation of iron and leather scales along a row.
Ichimanju jikoro Neck guard having only the top plate curved.
Igaki Ornamental plates around the base of a helmet bowl.
Ikada Small rectangular plates set in mail.
Ikada haidate Mail haidate with scattered ikada.
Iro Colour.
Iro gawa Self-coloured leather.
Iro iro odoshi Multi-coloured lacing.
Ishime Irregular rough texture like the surface of stone.
Ishizuke The chape of a tachi scabbard.
Ita haidate Scale haidate.
Ite jikoro Tosei shikoro in which the right fukigaeshi can be removed or folded back for archery.
Ito maki no tachi A tachi in which the hilt and upper part of the scabbard are bound with silk braid in a cross-cross fashion.
Iyozane Type of scale assembled with almost no overlap.
Iyozane do Tosei do of iyozane wrapping around the body and fastening under the right arm.
Ji ita Ornament of a gilt or silvered plate overlaid by shinodare applied to a helmet bowl.
Jinbaori Surcoat worn over armour.
Jingasa Conical open hat of iron or lacquered leather worn as a light defence.
Jitte A parrying bar carried by police during the Edo period.
Ji zamurai Land-owning samurai.
Jumonji kitae Method of forging armour plate with a crossed grain.
Jumonji yari Type of spear head having a central blade with side blades at the base.
Kabuto A helmet.
Kabuto gane The pommel of a tachi.
Kabuto no o The tying cord of a helmet.
Kago hankyu A miniature bow carried in a palanquin.
Kaihan Leggings.
Kaihan suneate Suneate without knee guards.
Kakae zutsu Large-bore gun.
Kake kusari An oval link connecting the circular links of mail.
Kake o The front tying cord of a sode.
Kama A sickle-like weapon.
Kami shimo Ceremonial dress of stiffened hemp worn by samurai during the Edo period.
Kanabo Long club of metal or wood.
Kane maze Technique of concentrating iron scales at vulnerable points of an armour.
Kanmuri no ita Cap plate of a sode or kote.
Kara boshi Large rivet having a hollow head.
Kara bitsu Chest used for storing armour.
Kara kozane Scales embossed from the back.
Karimata Forked arrow head.
Karuta gane do Folding armour of rectangular plates.
Kasa jikoro Wide spreading neck guard, often almost flat.
Kasa jirushi no kan Ring at the back of a helmet designed to carry a small identification flag, but on later helmets usually provided with an agemaki bow.
Kasari suneate Mail shin guards.
Kashira The pommel of a sword.
Kashira date Crest mounted on the top of a helmet.
Katagiri Engraving technique in which one side of the cut is vertical.
Katahada nugi do Type of *Nio do*.
Kata jiro Gilt or silvered plate applied between the suji of a helmet bowl as decoration.
Katakama yari Spear having only one side blade.
Katana Dirk worn in the belt during the Heian period. Alternatively, the characteristic long sword worn in the belt during the Momoyama and Edo periods.
Katana kake Sword stand.
Katana toji Sword polisher.
Katana zutsu Tubular lacquered case for a sword.
Kata yoroi Shoulder armour worn with the tanko during the Yamato period.
Katchu shi Armourer.
Kawari bachi Helmet of other than the conventional multi-plate construction.
Kawara haidate Haidate of S-sectioned scales overlapped like roof tiles.
Kawashiki Leather thong incorporated in the lacing holding scales into a row.
Kazuchi no tsurugi Early straight sword having a bulbous pommel.
Kawa tsutsu maki no tachi Leather wrapped tachi.
Kawa zutsumi do Do covered with a sheet of leather.
Kebiki Close lacing.
Kedate no ana Lacing holding the rows of scales together.
Keiko Early scale armour.
Kesho eri Collar decorated with a silk frill in imitation of a European ruff.
Kesho no ita Leather covered wood strip covering the heads of the scales where they afix to a metal plate.
Kikko A type of brigandine made of small hexagonal plates quilted between layers of fabric.
Kikko gane do A folding do made from hexagonal plates.
Kikuchi yari Early variety of spear with a straight, single-edged blade.
Kikujin Yellowish-green colour.
Kinran Gold brocade.
Kiritsuke iyozane Iyozane simulated by lacquer applied to a solid plate.
Kiritsuke kozane Kozane simulated by lacquer applied to a solid plate.
Kissaki Point section of a sword.
Kiwame fuda Certificate attributing the authorship of armour to a particular maker.
Ko Yellow.
Kobai Dark red.
Kobakama Abbreviated trousers worn under tosei armour.
Kobakama jitate Thigh armour sewn onto a pair of trousers.
Ko boshi bachi Helmet bowl with small standing rivets.
Kobushi kitae Sword construction in which a soft core was wrapped in hard steel.
Kodzuka Handle of a small utility knife carried in a pocket on the rear face of a sword or dirk scabbard.
Kogai Skewer-like implement carried in a pocket on the front face of a sword or dirk scabbard.
Kogai kanamono Decorative plate and ring combination attached to the rear edge of a shoulder guard to which the rearmost tying cord was fastened.

Kogake Armour for the feet.
Kohaze Toggle.
Kojiri Protective metal cap for the end of a scabbard.
Ko manju jikoro Small rounded neck guard.
Koma no tsurugi Early ring pommelled sword originally from Korea.
Komori zuke Intermediate band of leather connecting a row of scales or a plate to some other part of an armour.
Kon Dark blue.
Kosakura gawa Dark blue or green printed leather with an all-over pattern of small flowers.
Koseizan High-sided helmet, usually flat topped, which is taller than a hemisphere.
Koshi ate Sword carrier worn tied around the waist to enable a sword without ashi to be slung edge downwards like a tachi.
Koshi gatana Variety of short sword.
Koshi gusari Variety of mail having rectangular spaces to increase the flexibility.
Koshimaki Strip of metal forming the lower edge of a helmet bowl.
Kote Armoured sleeve.
Kozane A small scale as opposed to those used during the Heian period.
Kozane gashira Top edge of an iyozane cut to resemble two kozane.
Kuchi ba Dull brown colour.
Kuchi gane Metal band around the base of a hilt.
Kumade Rake-like pole arm.
Kura Saddle.
Kuro Black.
Kuro zukuri no tachi Black lacquered tachi.
Kusari Mail.
Kusari do maru Mail and plate version of a do maru.
Kusari gote Armoured sleeve of mail.
Kusari haidate Thigh armour of mail.
Kusari haramaki Mail and plate version of a haramaki.
Kusazuri Pendant sections of scales attached to the lower edge of the do to cover the thighs.
Kusugai do Yokohagi okegawa do in which the plates are joined by a variety of staples.
Kusureru Steel spoiled by over-forging.
Kutsu Stiff boots or shoes of fur.
Kuwagata Flat, stylized horns worn as a crest.
Kyubi no ita Defence for the left armpit, worn with o yoroi.
Mabizashi Peak of a helmet.
Mabizashi tsuki kabuto Ancient style of helmet having a horizontal fretted peak.
Machi uke Socket at the waist on the back of a do into which the sashimono assembly is fitted.
Maedate Crest attached to the front of a helmet.
Maki e do A do decorated with a lacquered design or picture.
Manchira European gorget which was adapted by the Japanese.
Manju wa Short armoured waistcoat worn beneath an armour to protect the armpits and upper chest.
Maru bachi *see daienzan bachi.*
Maro do A tosei version of the do maru, differing from the original versions of the armour in having an extra row of scales in the nakagawa.
Maru do yoroi Hybrid armour between an o yoroi and a do maru.
Masakari An axe.
Masa kogane Iron ore.
Matsuba wa Curved plates arranged in a ring around the elbow plate of an armoured sleeve.
Mei Signature.
Mei no ana A slit in the lining of a helmet through which the signature can be read.
Mekugi Peg holding a blade into its mounts.
Mekugi no ana Hole in the tang of a blade for a mekugi.
Men gu Face armour.
Me no shita ho Face mask covering the face and nose below the level of the eyes.
Menuki Ornaments attached to the hilt of a sword or trapped under its bindings which helped to improve the grip.
Mimi ito Braid around the edges of a piece of armour.
Mitsu kuwagata dai Kuwagata dai with an additional central socket to carry a crest.
Mitsu suji gaki Variant of sugake lacing involving three braids.
Mizu hiki Twin pipings of red and white twill set below the lower edge of a kesho no ita.
Mizu nomi no o Cord attached to the rear edge of a sode.
Moegi Leaf green.
Mogami do Do of horizontal plates, each of which is articulated by separate hinges.
Momen Cotton cloth.
Momonari bachi Pointed helmet inspired by the European morion.
Mon Heraldic symbol.
Moriage kozane Scales having the outer visible surface built up with lacquer.
Muku boshi Rivets with narrow pointed heads.
Muna ita Uppermost plate on the front of a do.
Muna tori hotoke do Smooth-faced do with a top section laced.
Mune machi Shoulder on the back edge of a blade at its junction with the tang.
Murasaki Purple.
Nagamaki Pole arm with a long sword-like blade fitted to a short shaft.
Naginata Pole arm having a curved, single-edged blade.
Nakagawa The part of a do which encircles the trunk.
Nakago Tang of a blade.
Naka kusari The circular links in Japanese mail which lie horizontal to its surface.
Namazu o kabuto Tall, laterally flattened helmet of rounded profile said to resemble the tail of a catfish.
Nanako Surface texture given to ornamental metalwork in which the ground is raised into a series of hemispheres.
Nanban Foreigners, particularly European foreigners.
Nanban gusari International style mail in which each link is meshed with four others.
Nawame fukurin Applied metal edging shaped to resemble a rope.
Neji Breech plug of a gun.
Neri gawa Rawhide.
Nibe Animal glue.
Ni mai do Do in two parts joined by a hinge under the left arm.
Nio do Do modelled to represent the human torso.
Nioi Lacing pattern in shades of one colour fading to white at the bottom.
Nishiki Brocade.
No dachi Simple tachi for retainer's use. Alternatively a very large sword carried rather than worn.
Nodawa Bib-like defence for the throat and upper chest consisting of a U-shaped plate with two or three curved rows of scales attached to it.

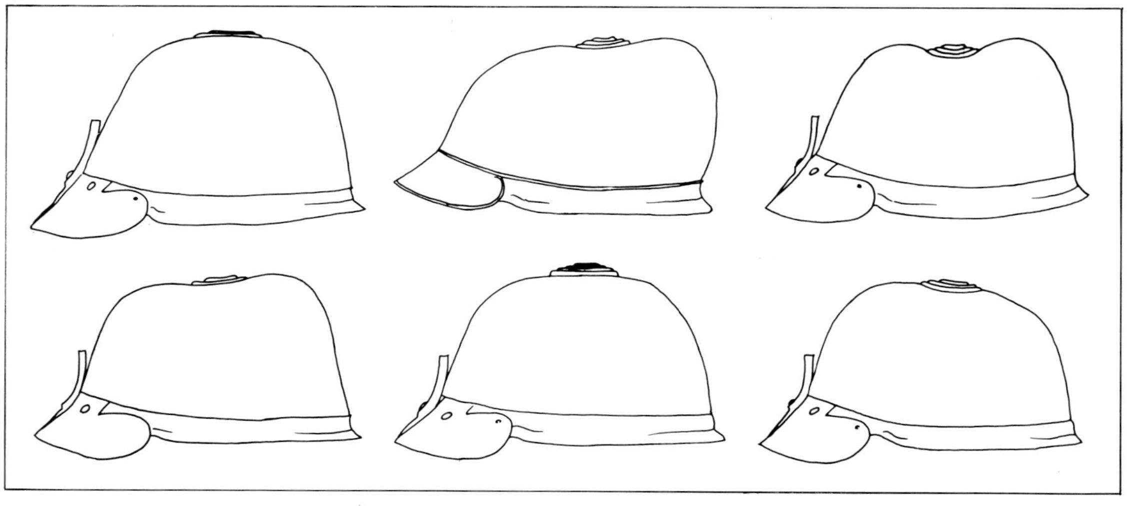

Top row, left to right: Koseizan bachi, reiseizen bachi (akoda nari bachi), tenkokuzan bachi. Bottom row, left to right: goshozan bachi, heichozan bachi, zenshozan bachi.

Nuinobe do *Sugake* laced *ni mai do* made of *iyozane*.
Nunome Overlay of gold, silver or copper on iron.
Obi Belt or sash.
O boshi Rivet having a large head.
Oda gote Kote having gourd-shaped plates applied over the forearm and upper arm.
Oda haidate Haidate of mail with ikada and knee plates resembling those at the elbow of oda gote.
Odoshi ge Lacing material.
Okashi gatana Sword issued to a low-ranking soldier.
Okashi gusoku Armour issued to a low-ranking soldier.
Okke mei A signature applied by another as a mark of respect.
O kessa In *tameshi giri*, a diagonal cut through the shoulder girdle.
Oki tenugui bachi A helmet bowl with almost vertical sides and top plates which are extended rearwards beyond the back of the bowl.
O manju jikoro A neck guard of large, rounded section.
Omodaka do A do having a medial ridge.
Omote kaku kuri Rivets closed on the outside, leaving them only slightly proud of the surface.
Oni damari The uppermost plate of the front of a tosei do.
Ori kugi A hook on the cheek of a mask around which the helmet cord is fastened.
Oshitsuke ita The uppermost plate at the back of a scale armour to which the shoulder straps are attached.
O sode Large rectangular sode.
O tateage suneate Shin guards having large standing plate defences for the knees.
O yoroi Armour having a separate defence for the right side of the body – the classic armour of the Heian period.
Rasha Woollen cloth.
Reiseizan *see akoda nari bachi*.
Renjaku do A tosei do fitted with internal suspensory cords.
Riman kyu *see kago hankyu*.
Rinzu Satin.
Roku mai do A tosei do having five hinges that is divisible into six sections.
Ryo kuruma In tameshi giri, a cut through the pelvic girdle.
Ryo shinogi yari Spear head of diamond section.
Ryo takahimo do A tosei do in either two or six sections with ties at each side of the body.
Sabi nuri A lacquered surface imitating rusty iron.
Sage o A cord or braid attached to the scabbard of a sword for securing it to the belt.
Sai hai A commander's baton hung with a tassel of hair or paper.
Sai hai no kan A ring on the right breast of a tosei do.
Saika bachi A type of multiplate helmet made in Saika.
Saka ita Plate at the back of an o yoroi laced in reverse to allow the shoulder straps to be swung backwards.
Saki me ate Fore sight of a gun or cannon.
Sakura iro Pink.
Same Ray skin used for covering sword hilts.
Samurai Member of the warrior class.
Sane A scale.
Sankaku yari Spear head of triangular section.
Sanko no byo Domed-headed rivets attaching the peak to the bowl of a helmet.
San mai zukuri Sword-blade construction having different grades of steel for the edge, core, back and faces of the blade.
Sarasa Calico.
Sasaheri Leather or braid edging around a fabric portion of an armour.
Sasa no ha Arrow head in the shape of a bamboo-grass leaf.
Sashinuki gote A pair of kote forming part of a short jacket.
Sashimono A flag or other device worn attached to the back of an armour.
Sawari Hard silvery alloy used as decoration on russet iron in the form of partially fused droplets.
Saya Scabbard.
Sei ita Narrow plate worn over the opening of a haramaki.
Seiro gusari A variety of mail in which the oval links are of two or three turns of wire.
Seme gane Decorative reinforcing ring around the scabbard of a tachi.
Seme kohaze A double-holed bead sliding on a loop of cord to close it over a toggle.
Sendai do Alternative name for a yukinoshita do.
Sendan no ita Guard for the right armpit, worn with an o yoroi.
Sentoku A variety of brass.
Seppa Ornamental washers placed on either side of a sword guard.
Shakudo Alloy of copper and gold, patinating to a purple-black colour.
Shi Purple.
Shibuichi An alloy of copper and silver, patinating to a grey colour.
Shiho jiro Helmet decorated with four groups of shinodare.
Shikigane A strip of iron laced behind a leather plate to maintain its shape.
Shikime zane Scale having three columns of holes.
Shikoro Neck guard of a helmet.
Shino A splint.
Shinodare An ornamental strip emerging from the tehen kanamono and extending down the front, sides or back of a helmet bowl.
Shinogi Ridge on a blade.
Shino gote Kote having splints as a defence for the forearm.
Shino haidate Haidate armoured with splints connected by mail.
Shino suneate Shin guards of splints connected by mail.
Shinshinto Swords made in the nineteenth century before the restoration of the Emperor.
Shinto Swords made between 1596 and the end of the eighteenth century.
Shira White.
Shirasaya Scabbard and hilt of plain wood used for storing an unmounted blade.
Shirisaya Leather or fur cover worn over the scabbard of a tachi.
Shishiai bori Sunk relief carving.
Shishi ko sakura gawa Printed leather decorated with Chinese lions and foliage.
Shitagi Shirt-like garment worn under armour.
Shita haramaki *see hara ate*.
Shita jikoro Auxilliary neck guard fitted below the regular one.
Shita toji Leather lacing fastening the scales into a row.
Shita toji no ana Lower group of eight holes in a scale.
Shiten no byo Vestigial rivets applied as decoration to helmet bowls.
Shito A form of dirk.
Shiwa fukube Pleated, gourd-shaped plate used for oda gote.
Shizuka no o Leather tie used to attach an o sode to the rear loop on the watagami.
Shobu gawa Dark blue leather decorated with irises and leaves.
Shohei gawa Variety of shishi ko sakura gawa incorporating the date 1352.
Shoji no ita A standing plate of rounded outline fastened to the upper surface of a watagami.
Shokaku bo Plate forming the top and front of a shoshaku tsuki kabuto.
Shoshaku tei ita Triangular plate under the beaked front of a shoshaku tsuki kabuto.
Shoshaku tsuki kabuto Ancient helmet having a prominent beaked front.
Sode Shoulder guard.
Sode tsuke no o Fastening cord of a shoulder guard.
So gusari Mail in which each circular link is connected to four others – the normal Japanese construction.
So men Mask covering the whole face.
Sori Curvature of a sword.
Sugake Lacing technique in which pairs of laces are threaded vertically up the row of scales to lighten the armour.
Sugi shobu gawa Debased variety of shobu gawa.
Suji Rib or flange.
Suji bachi Multi-plate helmet in which the rivets are countersunk leaving the flanged edges of the plates prominent.
Sumi yagura Subsidiary tower of a castle.
Suneate Shin guard.
Susogoi Shaded colour lacing growing lighter towards the top.
Tabi Sock.
Tachi Slung sword.
Tachi do A do sufficiently long in the body to rest on the hips.
Taka bori Relief carving.
Takahimo The fastenings of the shoulder straps of a scale armour. Alternatively, the fastening of the opening of a tosei do.
Takanoha uchi Braid patterned with chevrons.
Taka zogan Raised inlay.
Takuboku uchi Multi-coloured braid of white, green, purple and dark blue.
Tameshi giri Sword testing.
Tameshi gusoku Armour showing the marks of bullets used to test its defensive quality.
Tanko Early plate armour of the Yamato period.
Tanto Dirk.
Tasuki ni shishi no maru e gawa Printed leather with a design of Chinese lions in a diagonal lattice of foliage.
Tatami do Folding do.
Tatara Furnace.

Mabizashi tsuki kabuto with a fragmentary shikoro. Yamato period.

Tate Free-standing wooden shield.
Tateage The standing parts of a do covering the chest and back.
Tate eri Armoured collar.
Tate hagi okegawa do Tosei do made of vertical plates.
Tate mono Crest.
Te boko Short hand spear.
Tehen The hole in the crown of a helmet bowl.
Tehen kanamono Ornamental metal surround to the tehen.
Tekko A plate forming part of a kote which covers the back of the hand.
Tenkokuzan High-sided helmet whose top dips in the region of the tehen.
Tenshukaku Main tower of a castle.
Tenugui no kan Ring on the left breast of tosei do.
Teppo Gun.
Togari ya An acutely pointed arrow head.
Tominaga sashinuki gote Kote attached to a short jacket having an armoured collar.
Tonbo gawa Printed leather decorated with dragonflies.
Tosei do A 'modern' do, that is those evolved during the sixteenth century.
Tosei gusoku 'Modern' armour.
Tosei sode Small sode hanging from the fastenings of the kote.
Tsuba Sword guard.
Tsubo ita Plate forming the upper part of a waidate.
Tsubo sode A sode curved to the arm and narrowing towards the bottom.
Tsuka Hilt of a sword or dirk.
Tsume gata gawa Dark blue leather decorated with white truncated triangular shapes.
Tsunagi A wooden replica of a blade on which the mounts of a sword are assembled when in storage.
Tsunomoto Hook or spiked form of crest attachment.
Tsuru Bow string.
Tsurubashiri gawa Leather sheet covering the front of an o yoroi which prevented the bow string snagging on the heads of the scales.
Tsurumaki Bow string reel.
Tsutsu Gun barrel.
Tsutsu gote A kote having the plates over the fore arm hinged or sewn to each other.
Tsutsu suneate Shin guards of three or more plates hinged or sewn together.
Uchidashi do Tosei do decorated by embossing.
Uchi gatana Sword worn edge upwards through the belt during the Muromachi period.
Uchi ne Short throwing arrow or dart.
Ukebari Helmet lining.
Uke zutsu Wooden socket into which the sashimono pole was fitted.
Uma jirushi Large heraldic emblem or ensign.
Uma yoroi Horse armour.
Uname toji Lacing in which a length of braid is threaded in and out of a straight row of holes.
Uname toji do Tosei do in which the plates are fastened together by uname toji.
Urushi Lacquer.
Ushiro date Crest fitted to the back of a helmet.
Utsubo Enclosed quiver.
Uwa obi Outer sash or belt.
Uzura gawa Brown leather decorated with white and black spots.
Waidate Piece of armour forming part of an o yoroi which guarded the right side of the body.
Waka ita Plates attached to the upper edge of the nakagawa under the arms.
Wakibiki Arm pit guard.
Waki date Crests fitted to the sides of a helmet.
Wakizashi Short sword having a blade between one and two feet (0.3 and 0.6m) long and mounted with a tsuba – like a katana.
Waraji Straw sandals.
Wari ha kitae Sword construction in which the steel edge is inserted in a slit cut into the body of the blade.
Wari kogai A kogai which divides along the centre line into two parts.
Watagami Shoulder straps of an armour.
Ya Arrow.
Yadome Standing flanges on the cheeks of a mask.
Yagara mogara Pole arm having a multi-pronged barbed head used to entangle an opponent.
Ya hazu gashira Type of iyozane having the upper edge notched.
Yakiba Hardened edge of a blade.
Yamabuki Golden yellow.
Yanagi An arrow head in the shape of a willow leaf.
Ya no ne An arrow head.
Yari Spear.
Yodare kake Throat defence attached to the lower edge of a mask.
Yokohagi okegawa do Tosei do made from horizontal plates.
Yoroi Armour.
Yoroi hitatare Costume of brocade worn under armour.
Yoshino urushi Glossy finishing lacquer.
Yugake Archer's glove.
Yugote Loose sleeve worn on the left arm when practicing archery.
Yukinoshita do A variety of plate go mai do with external hinges.
Yumi Bow.
Yurugi ito Lacing attaching the kusazuri or gessan to the do.
Za boshi Prominent rivet head fitted with a washer cut with radiating lines.
Zenshozan High-sided helmet higher in the front than the back.
Zukin nari kabuto A variety of oki tenugui helmet.
Zunari bachi Helmet construction devised in Tosa which had a longitudinal plate over the centre of the head.

Bibliography

Books dealing entirely or in part with arms and armour.

Katchu no Token *Gen Shoku Nihon no Bijutsu* – Vol XXI, Tokyo

Katchu *Nihon no Bijutsu* – Vol XXIV, Tokyo 1968

Taiho Magazine: Spring 1973, Autumn 1974, Spring 1978, Tokyo

Anderson, L J *Japanese Armour. An illustrated guide to the work of the Myochin and Saotome families from the fifteenth to the twentieth century*, London 1968

Feddersen, M *Japanese Decorative Art*, London 1961

Handa, J and Sasama, Dr Y *Nihin Katchu neihin Shu*, Tokyo 1969

Hawley, W M *Japanese Swordsmiths*, Hollywood 1966

Hickman, B (Editor) *Japanese Crafts: Materials and their Applications. Selected early papers from the Japan Society of London*, London 1978

Honami, K, Sasama, Y Dr and Sone, M *Ko Buki no Shokukin*, Tokyo

Inada, H and Joly, H *The Sword and Same* (Translation of the Sword Books in Honcho Gunkiko together with a treatise on Same), London 1975

Kaneda Chappelear, K *Japanese Armour Makers for The Samurai*, Tokyo 1987

Knutsen, R M *Japanese Polearms*, London 1963

Newman, A R and Ryerson, E *Japanese Art*, London 1964

Robinson, B W *The Arts of the Japanese Sword*, London 1961

Robinson, H R *Japanese Armour (The Concise Encyclopaedia of Antiques: Vol V)*, London 1961

The Manufacture of Armour and Helmets in Sixteenth-Century Japan, (Translation of Chukokatchu Seisakuben by Sakakibara Kozan), London 1962

The Armour Book in Honcho Gunkiko, London 1964

A Short History of Japanese Armour, HMSO London 1965

Oriental Armour, London 1967

Japanese Arms and Armour, London 1969

Sasama, Dr Y *Shumi no Katchu*, Tokyo 1962

Nihon Katchu Zukan (3 vols), Tokyo 1965

Nihon no Meito (3 vols), Tokyo 1973

Zukai Nihon Katchu Jiten, Tokyo 1974

Katchushi Meikan, Tokyo 1976

Nihon Katchu Bugu Jiten, Tokyo 1981

Stone, G C *A Glossary Of The Construction, Decoration And Use Of Arms And Armour In All Countries And In All Times*, New York 1984

Yamagami, H *Japan's Ancient Armour*, Japanese Government Railways 1941

Nihon Katchu Hyaku Sen, Tokyo 1975

Books on related topics

Barr, P *The Coming of the Barbarians*, London 1967

Dunn, C J *Everyday Life in Traditional Japan*, London 1969

Hawley, W M and Kaneda Cheppelar, K *Mon: The Japanese Family Crest*, Hollywood 1976

Kato, H and Yoishimoto, S *Nihon no Kaemon*, Tokyo 1959

Turnbull, S *The Samurai: A Military History*, London 1977

Samurai Armies, London 1979

Warlords of Japan, London 1979

The Books of the Samurai,. London 1982

Samurai Warriors, London 1987

Battles of the Samurai, London 1987

Varley, H P *The Onin War*, Columbia University 1967

Books of value to enthusiasts

Koop, A J and Inada H *Japanese Names And How To Read Them*, London 1960

Rose-Innes, A *Beginner's Dictionary of Chinese – Japanese Characters*, Tokyo 1975

Index

ACKNOWLEDGMENTS

The authors would like to express their special gratitude to Dr Yoshihiko Sasama who, over the last twelve years has, in the best traditions of scholarship, freely shared his extensive knowledge and continued to show enthusiasm while patiently answering our many queries. Thanks must also be expressed to Barry Charlesworth, David Drury, Deryk Ingham, Tony O'Neill, Shigeki Oyama, Stephen Turnbull and the late Dr K Yoshida for their assistance and co-operation during the preparation of this work. Finally the authors would like to express their gratitude to Jane Laslett, the editor, who suffered much at our hands and bore it with fortitude, and to Melanie Earnshaw who performed miracles in finding suitable photographs with which to illustrate this book.

The publisher would like to thank Martin Bristow, the designer, Ron Watson for compiling the index, and the following agencies and individuals for providing the illustrations: B = below, L = left, R = right, T = top, BT = bottom, C = centre, A = above.

BBC Hulton Picture Library: page 73(below). Bodleian Library, Oxford: pp 43[MS JAP d.53(2)(R) first scene], 50[MS JAP d.40 fol. 15R), 62(MS JAP d.55(R)], 63T, [MS JAP d.55 (R)], 126-127 [MS JAP e 2(R) last scene]. Boston, Museum of Fine Arts: pp 4-5, 22, 24, 40T. Collection Ian Bottomley/Photo David Drury: pp 12T, 16, 17, 25R, 28R, 32, 48 both, 51T, 56, 59B, 64T, 72, 74TR, 75B, 80B, 88 both T, 89 both, 99, 100 both T, 101 both T, 102T, 103T, 104T, 105T TL and BR, 107T and BR, 108L, 110, 111R, 113 both, 116L, 118 middle 2, 119T and BL, 120, 121, 128, 129, 134, 143 all 3, 146T, 154, 155 both, 158T2, 163B, 165, 168T, 177BR. Bradford Art Galleries and Museums: pp 40C, 59T, 69T, 77T, 80T, 160T and 2B, 161, 172 both, 177 T2, 179B. Bramante Editrice/Museo Orientale: pp 84, 85, 91, 103BL, 104B, 118T and BT, 169B, 170, 171L. Trustee of the British Museum: pp 42, 70. Durham Oriental Museum: 66T, 83B, 119BR, 156, 159 both, 173, 176R, 183B. Werner Forman Archive: pp 15T, 26R, 27B, 47, 95, 102, 116R, 131, 140B, 164, 176BR. Geneva, Musée d'Ethnographie: p 180L. Archiv Gerstenberg: p 67. Honda Museum/ Courtesy ISEI, Tokyo: pp 11L, 27T, 45b, 101B, 108R, 109L, 135R, 145T, 168B, 174R. Anthony Hopson: p 132 both. Kyoto Arashiyama Museum: pp 10B, 11R, 34B, 78T, 82 both, 83 both T, 107BL, 114, 115, 124, 125, 139R, 147R, 162, 174L, 175R, 176L, 182. The Metropolitan Museum of Art, New York, pp 9, 88, 90, 175L. Mori Collection: pp 25L. 26L, 33, 37 both, 38B, 66BR, 81T, 109R, 117, 122, 135L, 151 all 3, 153, 157, 158 both B, 169T. National Film Archive: pp 96, 97. The National Trust: pp 2-3. Peter Newark's Historical Pictures: pp 144, 183T. Tony O'Neill: pp 26B, 31, 66BL, 73T, 74B, 86, 105 TR, 106 both, 111L, 126, 130, 133, 146B, 147L, 149, 179TR. Oyamazumi Jinja: pp 23, 34T, 35, 38A, 44L, 51B, 53, 54, 55, 58, 63B, 64B, 68, 75 both T, 87B. Pitt Rivers Museum, Oxford: p 6. Rijksmuseum, Amsterdam: p 145. Board of Trustees of the Royal Armouries, H M Tower of London: pp 1, 36 both, 39, 79L, 88B, 92, 93, 98 both, 100B, 103BR, 123, 136, 139L, 140T, 141T, 160C, 171R, 174B, 177BL, 180R. The Tate Gallery, London: p 138. Tokyo National Museum/ Courtesy ISEI, Tokyo: pp 8 both, 12B, 13, 14, 18-19. Tokyo Sword Museum/Courtesy ISEI, Tokyo: 41, 60, 61, 65, 69R, 81B, 166, 167, 181. Stephen Turnbull: pp 10T, 94 both, 150. Victoria and Albert Museum, London: pp 44-45, 46, 48, 71, 74TL, 77B, 78B, 81TL, 141B, 163T 2, 179TL.